A THEORY OF THE TRIAL

A THEORY OF THE TRIAL

Robert P. Burns

PRINCETON UNIVERSITY PRESS   PRINCETON, NEW JERSEY

Copyright © 1999 by Princeton University Press
Published by Princeton University Press, 41 William Street,
Princeton, New Jersey 08540
In the United Kingdom: Princeton University Press,
Chichester, West Sussex
All Rights Reserved

Library of Congress Cataloging-in-Publication Data

Burns, Robert P., 1947–
A theory of the trial / Robert P. Burns.
p. cm.
Includes bibliographical references and index.
ISBN 0-691-00727-6 (cloth : alk. paper)
1. Trials—United States. 2. Judicial process—United States.
3. Justice, Administration of—United States. I. Title.
KF8910 .B87 1999
347.73'7—dc21
98-54175
CIP

This book has been composed in Sabon

The paper used in this publication meets the minimum
requirements of ANSI/NISO Z39.48-1992 (R1997)
(*Permanence of Paper*)

http://pup.princeton.edu

Printed in the United States of America

10 9 8 7 6 5 4 3 2 1

For Mary, Matthew, and Betsy

Contents

Acknowledgments

I AM GRATEFUL to Mary Burns and Cynthia Bowman, both of whom edited the entire manuscript with insight and care. Steven Lubet, Beth Mertz, and Annelise Riles made extremely helpful suggestions on earlier drafts. Princeton's readers provided comments that have greatly improved the book. Britt Miller and Chris Brest helped with the graphics. Mary Tait did a fine job with the index. Princeton's Lauren Lepow performed an outstanding final edit. I am grateful to the Northwestern University Law School for supporting the research. I have been blessed with superb colleagues at the school with whom I have taught, developed educational programs, discussed and tried cases, and argued about the American legal order. This book has emerged from all of those activities.

Earlier versions of sections of the book have appeared in the *Georgia Law Review*, the *Journal of Criminal Law and Criminology*, and the *Ohio State Journal of Dispute Resolution*.

A THEORY OF THE TRIAL

Introduction _____

THIS BOOK grew out of a long attempt to understand an epiphany, one I have experienced and that seems often to occur in American trial courts. In the course of trial there emerges an understanding of the people and events being tried that has a kind of austere clarity and power. This experience surprises and "elevates" the participants, including the jury. The grasp of what has occurred and what should be done seems to have a kind of comprehensiveness, almost self-evidence, of which it is extremely difficult to give an account. It involves factual and normative determinations of very different kinds. The evidence and legal doctrine do not together *determine* the result in any logical sense, there is considerable freedom at play, yet the best course is apparent. The certainty that emerges is often less about the accurate representation of a past event—what I will call a "screenplay"—than it is a kind of knowledge of what to do. Judgment as it occurs at trial is a kind of skillful performance of a particularly complex kind. And those in a position to know seem almost universally to agree that the level of performance, day in and day out, is very skillful indeed.

The key to understanding this high level of achievement is the trial itself, a "consciously structured hybrid of languages" and performances, to which relatively little attention has been paid. This study is that *fides quaerens intellectum*, an account of the felt certainty that emerges in the course of the trial. Along the way, I rely on many different sources, but primary among them is a careful and detailed examination of the linguistic practices and performances that the trial comprises. My aim is to see how they come together to achieve the minor miracle of a convergence on and display of the practical truth of a human situation. Along the way, too, I summarize the evidence that it does indeed happen.

This is something quite different from an empirical study of jury "behavior," important as such studies have been. As I explain in chapter 5, jury studies are of very different sorts. Some involve the search for independent variables extrinsic to the trial itself—race or class, for example—that explain and predict jury determinations, through the mediation of empirical generalizations or "covering laws." Others, usually in the cognitivist tradition, focus on factors intrinsic to the trial, concluding that "the evidence" is the most important determinant of jury behavior, but inevitably describe that "behavior" as the "response" to the trial as the "stimulus event." Both sorts of studies seek to achieve causal explanation, or at least correlations with some predictive power. Though the empirical investigators themselves almost always conclude that juries are "remarkably competent," their methods cannot allow them to go very far in explaining the basis for this obviously normative judgment.

What is necessary is not causal explanation but what Richard Bernstein has called a "rational reconstruction," an attempt to show how the languages and practices of the trial actually achieve their human purposes. In this effort, we conceive of the trial not as a set of objectively considered stimuli or even bits of information, seen through the appropriately objectivizing eye of the social scientist, but as itself a mode of intelligent inquiry and responsible practice. Its purposes are quite different from those of most social scientific investigation, but they are equally an expression of human intelligence, one that puts the jury in touch with both cognitive and moral sources.

My goal here is close to what Hannah Arendt called "thinking what we do," that is, to raise to a higher level of self-consciousness the normatively based practices in which we are actually engaged. This goal is consistent with that most traditional, and paradoxical, of philosophical goals—to think the concrete. One important approach to this task has been, again to use Arendt's language, a "linguistic phenomenology," a careful, attentive description, ideally without presuppositions, of what we actually do, not in the style of a suspicious unmasking, but in order to identify the distinct principles and "spirit" that inform each important realm of human practice. This is a real task, because, as I show at length below, our inherited concepts almost always distort, and usually impoverish, such practices.

My enterprise is, then, an interpretation of the trial. Because it is an interpretation, I cannot compel the reader to accept my conclusions:

> There are strict dialectics whose starting point is or can reasonably claim to be undeniable. And, then there are interpretive or hermeneutical dialectics, which convince us by the overall plausibility of the interpretation they give.[1]

Thus my view of the trial will be justified only "by the mutual support of many considerations, of everything fitting together into one coherent view."[2] Such an interpretation requires me to consider the trial from a broad range of perspectives, to walk around it and look at it from every side—doctrinal, social scientific, tactical, ethical, epistemological, institutional, and purely descriptive. Though I draw on a wide range of humanistic, social scientific, and strictly legal sources and try to be respectful of the integrity of those approaches, I also try to keep my inquiry disciplined

---

[1] Charles Taylor, *Hegel* (Cambridge: Cambridge University Press, 1975), 218.
[2] John Rawls, *A Theory of Justice* (Cambridge: Harvard University Press, 1971), 579.

by a consistent attention to the thing itself: the actual practices of the trial. So description is central, and interpretation closely tied to it. I ask the indulgence of the practitioners of these important disciplines for my employing them as handmaidens to the central inquiry.

Thus the inquiry is not driven by the scientific ideals of "reductionism, causal explanation, and prediction."[3] I follow the advice here of a distinguished social psychologist, Jerome Bruner, that these ideals "need not be treated like the Trinity" and that "plausible interpretations [are] preferable to causal explanations, particularly when the achievement of a causal explanation forces us to artificialize what we are studying to a point almost beyond recognition as representative of human life."[4] I argue instead that a well-tried case produces a form of concrete universal where an event and its meaning are transparent to each other. It is precisely in giving an account of the forms of human meaning that the scientific paradigm is at its weakest.[5] What Arendt said of political understanding generally is also true of the trial. To understand the trial is to deploy "a style of 'attentiveness to reality' that is more the mark of the political actor than a scholar," because "political understanding relates more closely to political action than to political science. . . ."[6] My goal is to have the reader come away from this study with something akin to the kind of knowledge that an experienced trial lawyer or judge has in his or her reflective moments: not scientific knowledge, but "finding a footing" or "finding one's way around."[7]

My sources for what follows are varied. The first is over twenty years' experience in the trial and appellate courts, state and federal, litigating civil, criminal, and administrative cases, both individual and class actions. In particular, after deciding to pursue this study, I focused in a more intense way on four fairly complex cases in which I served as trial counsel: one civil and three criminal, two bench trials and two jury, three state and one federal. Most of the examples and much of the interpretation of the meaning of the trial's structure throughout this book come originally from those cases. Here I relied on my own judgments of the meaning of

[3] Jerome Bruner, *Acts of Meaning* (Cambridge: Harvard University Press, 1990), xiii.

[4] Ibid., xiii. On the inevitable limitations of the experimental method in the study of the trial, see Norman Finkel, *Commonsense Justice: Jurors' Notions of the Law* (Cambridge: Harvard University Press, 1995), 58–62. On the relative failure of the standard forms of causal explanation of jury verdicts, see Jeffrey Abramson, *We, the Jury: The Jury System and the Ideal of Democracy* (New York: Basic Books, 1994), 143–76.

[5] Bruner, *Acts of Meaning*, 2–11.

[6] David Luban, *Legal Modernism* (Ann Arbor: University of Michigan Press, 1994), 206.

[7] Herbert Dreyfus, "Holism and Hermeneutics," *Review of Metaphysics* 34 (1980): 12. The first phrase is Heidegger's, the second Wittgenstein's.

events as they occurred, followed by a careful study of the transcripts to test those interpretations. I have reviewed much of the vast social science literature on the trial; however, for reasons I explain below, I limit my review to those conclusions that seem the most reliable and important. The procedural, evidentiary, and ethical rules, and the judicial interpretation of those rules, are obviously important sources, and I have drawn on many years' study of those subjects in different ways throughout the book. Another important source has been my long involvement as a teacher with the National Institute for Trial Advocacy, the premier organization for the continuing legal education of trial lawyers. Here I have had the inestimable advantage of watching some of the most decent and skilled trial lawyers in the country demonstrate and explain their craft and of sharing conversations in which they answered questions and offered their perceptions. Those demonstrations and conversations have sharpened my understanding of what excellent trial lawyers do and why. They are important sources for my frequent references to "a well-tried case" and for my statements that "A lawyer will. . . ." For I am convinced, again for reasons I will describe at greater length, that to understand an institutionalized practice like the trial requires that we understand a set of contextualized ideals.

To an unusual degree, this study employs both what Clifford Geertz has called "experience near" and "experience distant" concepts. As Geertz maintained, it is by cycling between the most detailed descriptions of institutionalized practices and the broadest generalizations that we are likely to achieve real insight into both those details and our theoretical self-understandings. A particular reader may be far more interested in one end of this spectrum than the other. For example, given both the frequency and the superficiality of press coverage of major trials, a simple, careful description of the practices in which lawyers engage and the rules under which they perform can enrich the understanding of anyone interested in public affairs. If that is the motive for which a reader picks up this book, the earlier chapters are likely to be of more interest than the later. On the other hand, if the reader's interests are primarily theoretical, the earlier chapters will serve primarily to situate the issues that emerge later.

I anticipate multiple audiences and so have written to address the somewhat different concerns of those audiences. The trial is an extremely important American institution by any number of measures. Trials often figure near the center of stories that have very broad significance of various sorts. Think of the O. J. Simpson trial, the trial of Rodney King's attackers, or the trials in the tobacco litigation. Even the best media reports of those cases fail to provide the educated reader with sufficient context to understand the dynamics of the proceedings. Ubiquitous trial scenes on television dramas are more likely to mislead than to enlighten. Undergraduate and graduate education in American institutions, whether in history or political science departments, has not given students anything approaching the understanding of the trial necessary for critical judgment concerning many important issues of the day. I hope this sort of book may make a contribution to that understanding.

I hope as well that this book will provide a broader context for empirical investigators of the trial and for consumers of their work, including intelligent laymen, for lawyers litigating cases where that social scientific work about trials is at issue, and for judges. All rigorous scientific inquiry requires abstraction and simplification. When that work is done, there always remains the further question of its significance for trials as they are conducted in their full concreteness. In order to answer that question, we must understand what the scientific enterprise has abstracted *from*— what has been systematically ignored for legitimate methodological reasons. Otherwise we commit Whitehead's fallacy of misplaced concreteness, mistaking our simplifying abstractions for the real.

This book should also be of interest to serious students of the law in law schools and elsewhere. Theoretically, the trial in general, the jury trial in particular, is a central institution in our legal order.[8] An appreciation of its distinctive languages and performances cannot but enrich, and often quite radically changes, standard understandings of "what law is." An adequate philosophy of law must take account of those languages and practices. The trial makes law in the overwhelming majority of tried cases; law is what emerges from those languages and practices as a matter of constitutional right. The legal realists understood that the trial did not fit easily into inherited formalist conceptions of law, but were too much the creatures of the philosophical positivism of their age to give any constructive normative account of the institution. I attempt to remedy that shortcoming, at least in part.

Chapter 1 provides an account of a powerful normative understanding of the trial, one that explains many of its most striking internal features, which I call the "Received View." I then argue that the Received View grasps only a partial truth, something of which there is evidence even in the trial's own legal structure. In chapter 2, I offer a primarily descriptive account of the distinctive linguistic practices internal to the trial, that is, what trial lawyers *do* to prepare for and conduct trials. Chapter 3 provides what is also a primarily descriptive account of the most important rules—procedural, evidentiary, and ethical—under which trial lawyers practice, rules which often decisively structure the kind of truth that is

---

[8] Its importance suggests the poverty of our more usual expression, the "legal system."

allowed to appear in the courtroom. Chapter 4 is an example of an opening statement in a murder case, heavily glossed with my interpretation of
the usually implicit significance of the narratives presented by the prosecution and defense; it illustrates important aspects of the theory of the
trial emerging from the descriptive materials in the earlier chapters. Chapter 5 contains (1) a phenomenology and interpretation of aspects of the
trial so basic that their institutional and philosophical significance can
easily be missed, and (2) my account of the most important and reliable
conclusions about the trial that have emerged from the social science literature. Chapter 6 marks the transition to a much more theoretical idiom:
here I present an interpretation of the *significance* or *meaning* of the doctrinal, descriptive, and social scientific material that has gone before.
Chapter 7 provides accounts of what I term the "objective" and the "subjective" sides of the trial event. The former consists of an explanation of
a model, much more complex and interesting than that of the Received
View, of the issues that the trial's "consciously structured hybrid of languages" presents for the jury's decisions. The second portion of chapter
7 offers an account of the kinds of intellectual operations that the jury
has to perform in order to resolve those issues, and discusses some evidence that we actually can and do perform those operations. Chapter 8
is the most theoretical of the book; it attempts to identify the conditions
of the possibility that the operations which take place at trial converge
on the truth of a human situation. It then provides a compressed account
of the historical and institutional significance of the modes of decision
making that occur at trial within the structure of American institutions.

Two final notes. I refer to the decision-maker at trial as "the jury." This
is for ease of reference. Almost all of what I have to say applies with equal
force to bench and to jury trials. As I explain below, the social science
literature suggests strongly that in the great majority of cases it does not
matter whether the case is tried to a judge or a jury. The trial's the thing.
It is far more significant that a case is or is not allowed to go to trial,
rather than being decided on a motion to dismiss or summary judgment,
than whether a judge or a jury decides the case.

Finally, it is clear that the trial, the jury trial in particular, is under attack
at this point in our history. This attack expresses itself in "tort reform"
schemes, limitations on the jury's ability to assess compensatory or punitive damages, mandatory arbitration, systems of administrative adjudication where judges are subject to bureaucratic controls, and journalistic
discussions in the wake of recent highly publicized trials. The reasons for
this are complex. Most basically, the trial provides for a kind of highly
contextual moral and political decision making which is in deep tension
with the instrumental rationality of tightly organized bureaucratic organi-
zations, public and private, that otherwise dominate American public life.

This is an enduring tension. By contrast, it is no accident that the level of hostility to the trial has risen during a period (roughly the last thirty years) when Congress and the Supreme Court have quietly democratized the jury, bringing perspectives to this important institution that had long been unrepresented. In the longer run, this is a promising development, likely to enrich further what I believe to be one of the greatest achievements of our public culture.

I

The Received View of the Trial

[E]ven when philosophy seemed to turn to an
examination of politics, it embraced a conceptualism
which disdained any serious phenomenological
examination of political experience itself. The
themes of this political thought were the abstract
concepts of liberty, the state, right, sovereignty, and
so forth. . . . It was not surprising that political
thought became an academic exercise, shedding
no light on the political realities of actual life;
philosophers set the direction for political thought
and not thinkers writing out of their involvement
in politics. Finally, the impoverished realm which
philosophers understood as political led them to
concentrate their attention on the formal structure
of the state and the issue of ruling. Their questions
were asked from the perspective of the government
and not from that of the citizen.

    (James Bernauer on Hannah Arendt)[1]

WHAT IS a trial? The simplicity of the question is deceptive. Since Socrates
began posing such "What is . . ." questions about human practices,
we have learned that these apparently straightforward factual questions quickly open out into an ideal realm whose limits are always indeterminate. We do not really *understand* what a trial is unless we understand the interrelation between what we may only provisionally call
"what a trial is" and "what a trial can aspire to be." For us, "factual"
questions become practical questions, such as, "How should we shape
our public life?"

---

[1] James Bernauer, "On Reading and Misreading Hannah Arendt," *Philosophy and Social Criticism* 11 (1985): 11 (summarizing Arendt's view of much of traditional political philoso-phy). What Arendt thought true of the political realm is at least as true of the legal, or so I will argue throughout.

I begin by describing, in good Aristotelian fashion,[2] the dominant normative understanding of what a trial is. This understanding has considerable power and seems to explain a good number of the trial's most distinctive features. It is assumed to be true by the most prominent empirical investigators.[3] It is consistent with the dominant Anglo-American scholarly tradition in the law of evidence.[4] I will eventually argue that this understanding, which I call the "Received View," captures an important part of the truth but is so partial as to be a serious distortion of what the trial has become.

The Rule of Law

The Received View understands the trial as a necessary institutional device for actualizing the Rule of Law in situations where there are disputes of fact. The trial allows punishments to be imposed or civil wrongs to be righted only after a careful factual analysis of what actually occurred, *specifically structured for the application of an established legal rule to the exclusion of other possible norms.* Simply put, the trial is designed, so this understanding goes, to guarantee that the trier of fact will "follow the law." Defenders of the Rule of Law argue its importance from four somewhat independent bases. The first basis is one of substantive legitimacy. In natural law theories, the law embodies the principles of natural justice in a manner both deeper and more refined than the probable intuitions of any specific judge or jury.[5] In theories that trace

---

[2] Aristotle, *Metaphysics*, trans. Hippocrates G. Apostle (Grinnell, Iowa: Peripatetic Press, 1979), 19–34 (beginning the inquiry with a "dialectical" consideration of important current views on the subject).

[3] See, e.g., Reid Hastie, Steven D. Penrod, and Nancy Pennington, *Inside the Jury* (Cambridge: Harvard University Press, 1983), 18–23.

[4] William Twining, *Rethinking Evidence: Exploratory Essays* (Oxford: Basil Blackwell, 1990), 71–76 (describing the "rationalist tradition" in evidence scholarship).

[5] See, e.g., Edward Corwin, "The 'Higher Law' Background of American Constitutional Law," *Harvard Law Review* 42 (1928). In a late dialogue, Plato's Socrates argues that the Rule of Law is inevitably a second-best regime compared to one ruled by the man of wisdom. Because legal rules are abstract and so inevitably overgeneralized, even the best legal regime will fall away from the ideal justice that the philosopher's power to grasp the concrete could confer. Plato, *Statesman* 293d–311c, trans. J. B. Skemp, in *The Collected Dialogues of Plato*, ed. Edith Hamilton and Huntington Cairns, (New York: Pantheon, 1961). Of course, outside the *Republic*, which can be only a "city in words," the Rule of Law seems inevitable. Plato's view of the "second-best" status of the Rule of Law rests on epistemological grounds (the superiority of intellectual intuition over merely discursive reason, the usual human need to multiply abstract predicates in order to approximate any concrete situation) and on political grounds (the need to constrain by legal rules the disordered desires of any ruler other than the philosopher). Ibid., at 294b–c, 300c. This understanding of what we

the legitimacy of law to a version of popular sovereignty, including most positivist theories, the Rule of Law ensures that democratic judgment, constitutionally structured[6] and channeled, will be brought to bear on individual cases.

The second basis for the Rule of Law focuses more on the dangers of the abuse of power by individual government actors. Law's inevitable generality and relatively fixed meanings limit what a "magistrate" may do and prevent him from inflicting "arbitrary" injuries. The Rule of Law requires that "[n]o organ of the State may render an individual decision which would not conform to a general rule previously stated."[7] It "means that government in all its action is bound by rules fixed and announced beforehand—rules which make it possible to foresee with fair certainty how the authority will use its coercive powers in given circumstances and to plan one's individual affairs on the basis of this knowledge."[8]

A corollary to the law as limitation on the power of officialdom is its role in protecting the liberty of the citizen, the third basis for the Rule of Law. The Rule of Law is "closely related to liberty"[9] in that it allows the citizen, through his voluntary choices, to control the time and place the coercive engines of government may be brought to bear on him.[10]

---

might call the normative limitations of any general rules survived in a more practical idiom in Aristotle's argument for the necessity for *epieikeia*, or equity, in the *Nicomachean Ethics*, and thence flowed into the Western legal tradition, including arguments supporting the jury's "equitable" authority to do individual justice in the teeth of the law's general rules. Aristotle, *Nicomachean Ethics* 1137b–1138a, trans. Terrence Irwin (Indianapolis: Hackett Publishing Co., 1985), 144–45.

[6] Gordon Wood has argued that the real theoretical innovation of the Federalists was to trace even constitutional norms to the will of the people. Gordon Wood, *The Creation of the American Republic, 1776–1789* (Chapel Hill: University of North Carolina Press, 1970). Of course, throughout much of American constitutional history, courts and commentators identified constitutional law with a natural law above and impervious to popular will. See Corwin, "The 'Higher Law' Background."

[7] Leon Duguit, *Traité de droit constitutionnel*, 2d ed. (Paris: Fontemoing & Cie, 1923), 681.

[8] Friedrich A. Hayek, *The Road to Serfdom* (Chicago: University of Chicago Press, 1944), 72. And so, of course, it is important to defenders of the Rule of Law that the meaning of legal texts not be radically indeterminate. The indeterminacy of legal texts has been the major arguing point of the two major attacks on the Rule of Law in twentieth-century American jurisprudence, the realist and critical legal studies movements. See, e.g., Edward L. Rubin, "The New Legal Process, the Synthesis of Discourse and the Microanalysis of Institutions," *Harvard Law Review* 109 (1996): 1393, 1398–1402 (discussing critiques of legal process by both law and economics and critical legal studies and the need for a careful and detailed analysis of specific institutions before the next important steps in legal theory can be taken).

[9] Rawls, *A Theory of Justice*, 235.

[10] H.L.A. Hart, *Punishment and Responsibility* (Oxford: Clarendon Press, 1968).

Finally, the Rule of Law "implies the precept that similar cases be treated similarly."[11] Consistency itself will prevent a willful official from injuring Citizen A, whom he dislikes, if the rule he thereby establishes will injure Citizen B, whom he favors. Consistency, or the "principle of regularity," however, is not merely a policing device to constrain government action. It rests on substantive grounds as well—the principle of equal respect for persons, a basic norm of morality as well as of legality.[12]

The Trial in Service to the Rule of Law

The Rule of Law requires a process for making factual determinations. As Rawls puts it:

> If laws are directives addressed to rational persons for their guidance, courts must be concerned to apply and to enforce these rules in an appropriate way. A conscientious effort must be made to determine whether an infraction has taken place and to impose the correct penalty. Thus a legal system must make provisions for conducting orderly trials and hearings; it must contain rules of evidence that guarantee rational procedures of inquiry. While there are variations in these procedures, the Rule of Law requires some form of due process: that is, a process reasonably designed to ascertain the truth, in ways consistent with the other ends of the legal system, as to whether a violation has taken place and under what circumstances.[13]

Factual accuracy is clearly important to those who defend the Rule of Law on substantive grounds. The higher or more refined notions of justice embedded in the law[14] all, as applied, take the form of hypothetical imperatives.[15] For example, *if* the buyer has made an offer for real estate accompanied by a valuable consideration that has been accepted and is not against public policy, *then* the sale shall be specifically enforced. The condition to be fulfilled for the application of the law is factual, and substantive justice will be achieved if the facts are found accurately. Indeed, espe-

---

[11] Rawls, *A Theory of Justice*, 237.

[12] Alan Donagan, *The Theory of Morality* (Chicago: University of Chicago Press, 1977), 65–74 (a Kantian account of common morality as based on principles of mutual respect for the humanity in each person).

[13] Rawls, *A Theory of Justice*, 238–39.

[14] Higher law notions usually surround constitutional and common law, but there are understandings of legislation that rely on the likelihood of substantive justice's emerging in the forms of statutes. Indeed the understanding of parliament as a legislature and not a court is relatively recent. See Robert P. Burns, "Blackstone's Theory of the 'Absolute' Rights of Property," *Cincinnati Law Review* 54 (1985): 67.

[15] Jerome Frank, *Courts on Trial: Myth and Reality in American Justice* (Princeton: Princeton University Press, 1949), 14–16.

cially in systems of common law adjudication, the authoritative norms exist as a never completely determined tension among announced facts, results, and rationales.[16] When the "next case" arises, it is a matter of argument as to which facts were crucial to the result in the earlier case, and the first court's own recital of its rationale may prove to be only "dictum" and not itself authoritative. Facts are more closely drawn up into the rule than are the court's explanations of its decisions. For the individual case to be justly decided, facts must be accurately determined and available in a form that will allow the preferred norms to be "applied."[17]

For those who understand the Rule of Law as a limitation on arbitrary government action, accuracy in fact-finding is also important: officials who can manipulate the facts to bring them under any rule that allows them to pursue their plans will be wholly unconstrained by legal norms. Nor will citizens who wish to enjoy their liberty without coercive interfer-

[16] This is a point of divergence from Continental systems:

Decisions of high courts [of Continental systems], whether binding or not, were not treated as exemplars of how a life situation had been resolved in the past so that the case sub judice could be matched with these examples of earlier decision making. Rather, what the judge was looking for in the "precedent" was a rulelike pronouncement of higher authority, the facts of the case stripped to their shadows. Thus what conventional common-law doctrine would devalue as mere dictum was welcome precisely because it stood independent of the concrete constellation of facts in the case.

Mirjan R. Damaska, *The Faces of Justice and State Authority: A Comparative Approach to the Legal Process* (New Haven: Yale University Press, 1986), 32–33.

[17] The importance of accuracy in moral and legal theories where the fairness of distribution is intimately linked to the first principles, such as retributive theories in criminal law, is obvious. Accuracy has a more derivative status under utilitarian theories, whether followed because utilitarianism is a correct moral-legal theory (a modern "natural law" view) or because the democratic legislature has chosen to enact laws it judged to achieve the greatest good for the greatest number (a legal positivist view). For example, criminal laws may be understood as promoting and as justified by general deterrence. The importance of factual accuracy for utilitarian or other consequentialist law will involve all manner of counterintuitive twists and turns whereby a consistent utilitarianism dies a death by a thousand qualifications. Alternatively, utilitarians must employ factual hypotheses in which we have less confidence than we do in the moral intuition they seek to "justify" on utilitarian grounds. If the distributional principle for the imposition of punishment, as well as the general justifying aim of the criminal law, is solely utilitarian, it would seem that punishment should be inflicted only on those generally *believed* to be guilty rather than those who actually are, and then only if the resulting pain, perhaps experienced with special anguish, inflicted on the innocent person is outweighed by the pain to be endured by potential victims of crimes successfully deterred. And the question of whether a judicial system should convict persons in fact innocent to maintain a public perception that crime does not pay involves a "prudential" judgment weighing the increase in general deterrent effect against popular resentment, anxiety, and possible social unrest. For an argument that the criminal law is utilitarian in general justifying goal, but *not* in distribution, see Hart, *Punishment and Responsibility*, 9. See generally David Lyons, *Forms and Limits of Utilitarianism* (Oxford: Clarendon Press, 1965).

ence be safe if officials are simply *unable* to determine reliably whether a citizen has stayed within the lines protected by the law. Finally, factual accuracy is crucial if similar cases are to be treated similarly. Without it, legal results will be distributed randomly and without regard to similarities and differences among real-world situations.

Without the right kinds of procedural devices to determine particular cases, the notion that the Rule of Law actually prevails must become illusory or ideological.[18] Lawyers in the English-speaking world have been too practical, and too committed to the Rule of Law, to allow that to happen, at least without a fight. Of course, one need only glance at human history to understand that "a government of laws, not of men" is an utopian ideal. Yet much of the genius of the Anglo-American tradition has been poured into the construction of institutions that actually attempt the incarnation of utopian ideals.[19] What follows is a description of how American procedures, including the trial, seek the ideal, the concrete establishment of the Rule of Law.

Litigation and Trial under the Received View

Pretrial Practice

An aggrieved party or the state initiates a civil or criminal case by filing a complaint that either explicitly or implicitly invokes valid law. In the civil context,[20] the judge first decides, assuming the facts stated in the

---

[18] The Rule of Law can be "ideological" under either a particular or a general conception of ideology. "The particular conception of ideology is implied when the term denotes that we are skeptical of the ideas and representations advanced by our opponent. They are regarded as more or less conscious disguises of the real nature of a situation, the true recognition of which would not be in accord with his interests. These distortions range all the way from conscious lies to half-conscious and unwitting disguises; from calculated attempts to dupe others to self deception. This conception of ideology, which has only gradually become differentiated from the common-sense notion of the lie, is particular in several senses. Its particularity becomes evident when it is contrasted with the more inclusive total conception of ideology. Here we refer to the ideology of an age or of a concrete historico-social group, e.g. of a class, when we are concerned with the characteristics and composition of the total structure of the mind of this epoch or of this group." Karl Mannheim, *Ideology and Utopia: An Introduction to the Sociology of Knowledge*, trans. Louis Wirth and Edward Shils (New York: Harcourt Brace Jovanovich, 1985), 55–56.

[19] On the utopian character of market institutions and their legal substructure, see Karl Polanyi, *The Great Transformation: The Political and Economic Origins of Our Time* (Boston: Beacon Hill Press, 1944).

[20] In the criminal context, (1) the availability of the general denial, which a lawyer may present ethically *regardless* of the truth of the allegations in the indictment, (2) the privilege against self-incrimination and the subsequent unavailability of the defendant as an adverse witness, and (3) the absence of a summary judgment procedure all suggest that the Received View of the trial is especially inapposite in criminal cases. I focus mainly on civil trials in

complaint are true (or, under more liberal regimes, assuming some set of facts which reasonably might be true), whether the complaining party is entitled to any relief. This requires a determination as to whether the complaining party has, to use a deliberately vague term, invoked valid law that the alleged action of the defendant has violated.

The judge's second task is to decide whether there exists "an issue of fact." If the defendant admits the allegations that the complainant alleges, there will be no issue of fact, and if the complainant has invoked valid law, he will be entitled to "judgment on the pleadings." Even if the defendant denies the allegations in the complaint, the court may decide, based on affidavits and depositions, that there exist no "substantial issues of material fact," that is, no real disputes of fact which matter under the applicable law. The court will then grant "summary judgment." Only if there exists a substantial issue of material fact will a trial be necessary.[21] The purpose of the trial is to resolve those issues of fact and *only* those issues of fact which the law makes significant.

The Jury's Tasks within the Received View

Within the Received View, there is no reason to hold a trial unless there exists a real dispute concerning material facts, facts that the law makes significant. The trial will, accordingly, require the jury to perform a num-

---

the text since those *seem* to be more consistent with the Received View. See *American Bar Association Model Rules of Professional Conduct*, Rule 3.1. (Despite the requirement that a lawyer may not controvert an issue unless there is a basis for doing so that is not frivolous, she may "nevertheless" defend a criminal case so as to require proof of every element.)

[21] Controversy surrounds the circumstances under which summary judgment should be granted, controversy that has a strong political edge to it. See Jeffrey W. Stempel, "A Distorted Mirror: The Supreme Court's Shimmering View of Summary Judgment, Directed Verdict, and the Adjudication Process," *Ohio State Law Journal* 49 (1988): 95. Some have complained that federal courts hostile to civil rights legislation have abused summary judgment in order to deprive plaintiffs of access to juries and so to "fair" fact-finding. Defenders of summary judgment invoke the Rule of Law in arguing that the device is essential for allowing only those issues to reach juries where *factual* issues exist. See *Apex Oil Co. v. DiMauro*, 641 F.Supp 1246, 1257 (S.D.N.Y. 1986), *aff'd in part, rev'd in part on other grounds*, 822 F.2d 246 (2d Cir.), *cert. denied*, 484 U.S. 977 (1987). To allow juries to hear issues where there are no strictly factual questions is to run an unnecessary risk of their deciding the cases by invoking norms other than those embedded in the law, and so the jury instructions. After all, the defenders of the procedure argue, not only does summary judgment consume fewer resources, but it allows an official with a professional commitment to the Rule of Law, the judge, to decide the case. The contending parties often see the issue as one involving access to the "democratic" jury. The thrust of my argument will be to suggest that the real bite of summary judgment is to deny litigants a trial, whether before a judge or before a jury. On the history of the idea that juries were limited to deciding "issues of fact," see Abramson, *We, the Jury*, 88–90.

ber of distinct tasks.[22] The jury will listen to the evidence presented. Excluding from consideration any material that the judge rules inadmissible, the jury will attempt to construct the most probable sequence of events, usually including states of mind such as intention, knowledge, and motive.[23] This will require an evaluation of the credibility of witnesses and the reliability of other forms of admitted evidence. The jury will be guided here by its common sense, construed as a reservoir of judgments of the relative probability of events' occurring this way or that in the real world, under the circumstances established by the most reliable evidence presented. This process does *not*, fortunately for the Rule of Law, require the jury to inject its own moral or political judgments into the legal process. Otherwise the Rule of Law would be seriously threatened.

Once the jury has constructed the most probable narrative of what occurred, it is in a position to perform its final task. Having construed the most likely story of what occurred in the past, it must then make a determination as to whether or not that sequence of events falls within the authoritative categories contained in the jury instructions. This is properly a question of classification and basically requires the jury to make a judgment about the fair meaning of the words in the instructions.

It may be that certain of the categories in the instructions are identical with some episode in the most probable version of "what happened." Then no additional act of categorization will be necessary. In a murder case, for example, the jury may be instructed that, in order to find the defendant guilty, it must find that she shot the victim, and that the victim died as a result of the wound. It may well have found that both of those facts are episodes in the story it has already constructed. At the other extreme, the jury may be instructed that it may find for the plaintiff only if it finds that the defendant failed to exhibit the level of care that a reasonable person would have exhibited, and that, but for the defendant's lack of care, the plaintiff would have been uninjured. The jury's initial version of "what happened" may not have answered either of the questions implicit in the latter instruction, thus requiring an additional operation after the determination of what occurred. Between those extremes, the jury must decide whether it has "already" decided the mixed questions that the instructions identify as elements, a decision that can raise quite subtle issues.

In some cases, the jury may not be able to determine what more probably happened or what happened beyond a reasonable doubt. This will require a judgment for the defendant. Or it may reach a determination as

---

[22] I follow the account of Hastie, Penrod, and Pennington, *Inside the Jury*, 18–21.

[23] These may be "elements" of the cause of action, ultimate facts that the legal definitions require the party with the burden of proof to establish ("intent to kill"), or they may be, in the Received View, steps in causal chains leading to such elements (motive to kill as a consideration warranting the conclusion that the defendant did the killing). See Twining, *Rethinking Evidence*, 241 (on chains of inference at trial). See also Finkel, *Commonsense*

to what occurred, but be unable to reach a determination as to whether that occurrence fairly falls within a crucial legal category in the instructions; this too will require a judgment for the defendant (or a hung jury if the decision is not shared by the number of jurors the law makes necessary for a verdict).

The important point for the Received View is that the jury constructs its version of what occurred without recourse to value judgments not legitimized by the Rule of Law. So the major premises[24] by which the jury concludes that this or that version of events occurred are value-free factual generalizations about the way things happen in the world. Those premises, like all commonsense generalizations, have the form "Generally and for the most part . . ."; a further insight into the facts of the case is required to determine whether or not they apply in this specific case.[25] When the judge instructs the jurors that they are to rely on their "common sense and experiences in life," he or she is invoking this reservoir of empirical generalizations by which the jury may construct its account of what occurred. This notion of common sense poses no danger of infecting the Rule of Law with idiosyncratic value judgments potentially discontinuous with the preexistent, publicly announced, authoritative norms embedded in the language of the instructions. And, of course, the jury will have already sworn to render a verdict based on the law found in the instructions. In the authoritative language of the approved instruction in the Ninth Federal Circuit:

> Ladies and gentlemen: You now are the jury in this case and I want to take a few minutes to tell you something about your duties as jurors. . . . It will be your duty to decide from the evidence what the facts are. You, and you alone, are the judge of the facts. You will hear the evidence, decide what the facts are, and then apply those facts to the law which I will give to you. That is how you will reach your verdict. In doing so you must follow that law whether you agree with it or not.[26]

Justice, 49–50 (on jurors' tendency to compress elements like intent with circumstantial evidence like motive to move "closer to a moral conception of intent").

[24] The dominant tradition in evidence scholarship holds that logical relevance is constituted by a general factual proposition linking evidence offered (the *probans*) and the fact to be proven (the *probandum*). Since those generalizations serve as the premises in the processes of proof, the latter is in this limited sense "deductive." The classic article remains George F. James, "Relevancy, Probability, and the Law," *California Law Review* 29 (1941): 689.

[25] Bernard J. F. Lonergan, *Insight: A Study of Human Understanding* (New York: Philosophical Library, 1957), 173–81. I am conceding for the moment that common sense is composed of flexible "theoretical" generalizations, generalizations about how things *are* in the world. Later I will argue that, at a certain level, common sense is constituted by coping skills that do not represent states of affairs or objects in the world but are fundamentally practical. See chapter 8, below.

[26] Commission on Model Jury Instructions, Ninth Circuit 1992, *Manual of Modern Criminal Instructions for the Ninth Circuit,* nos. 1.01 and 3.01.

How the Devices of the Trial Support the Rule of Law

The Received View emphasizes that the legal system does not rely solely on the judge's pretrial rulings which screen out cases that do not present true issues of fact. Nor does it rely fully on the jury's sworn obligation to honor the Rule of Law. The constitutive rules of the trial, those rules that do not merely regulate the trial but actually make it what it is,[27] assure that trials operate consistently with the Rule of Law. *How* they do so is a fascinating story in the highly practical utopianism of the Anglo-American legal profession.

VALID LAW AND RELIABLE FACTS

Most obviously, it is the judge's task to instruct the jury as to the content of the law it must apply in deciding the case. Attorneys are not generally permitted even to *inform* the jury of its clear power, most dramatic in criminal cases where double jeopardy forbids retrial, to disregard the instructions and decide the case using its own best lights, much less to urge juries to exercise what the Received View takes to be an illegitimate power.[28] Nor may attorneys attempt to define or directly explain the meanings of the terms in the instructions.[29] It is permissible for a lawyer to read an instruction to the jury and "argue the facts," that is, argue that the most probable version of events falls fairly within the legal categories found in the instructions, but he or she may not implicitly suggest criteria other than those in the instructions—may not, for example, remind the jurors in the penalty phase of a capital case of the high cost of incarcerating a convicted murderer for life.[30]

The law of evidence seeks to ensure that the material from which the jury builds up its value-free narrative of what occurred is reliable. Constructing a version of what happened from unreliable evidence would threaten the Rule of Law by reducing the accuracy of fact-finding. Thus exhibits must be "authenticated";[31] only the originals of documents may be presented;[32] and witnesses may not report the hearsay assertions of

---

[27] John Rawls, "Two Concepts of Rules," *Philosophical Review* 64 (1955): 3–32.
[28] *United States v. Wiley*, 503 F.2d 106 (8th Cir. 1974) (affirming the trial court's refusal to give a jury nullification instruction).
[29] Richard H. Underwood and William H. Fortune, *Trial Ethics* (Boston: Little Brown, 1988), 366–68.
[30] Ibid., 367.
[31] *Federal Rules of Evidence*, Rules 901–903.
[32] Ibid., Rules 1001–8.

others,[33] since this would deprive the opponent of the opportunity to cross-examine the person who allegedly perceived the relevant occurrence. After all, as Wigmore put it in his most-quoted remark, cross-examination was "beyond any doubt the greatest legal engine ever invented for the discovery of truth."[34]

THE DEEP STRUCTURE OF TRIAL TESTIMONY: THE LANGUAGE
OF PERCEPTION

The law of evidence does not, however, stop at assuring the reliability of evidence. The advocates are not permitted to call just any witness and put just any reliable evidence before the jury. Evidence law requires that nonexpert witnesses testify based on their own "personal knowledge" and in the "language of perception."[35] Witnesses come to court to report to the jury what they have perceived, a requirement that all the byzantine twists and turns of the hearsay rule seek to protect. Witnesses must testify in a highly conventional style, quite difficult to master, often enforced by the judge's orders, "Just tell us what you saw" or "Just tell us what you did." The court is not interested in the witness's interpretations of what occurred, or his opinions of states of affairs he could not perceive through one of his five senses. And even a witness with the wisdom of Solomon will not be asked his or her opinion as to what the proper resolution of the disputed question before the court should be.[36] That would, of course, "usurp the province of the jury" and threaten the Rule of Law by resolving the dispute according to criteria other than those embedded in the instructions. This basic requirement, more a first principle than a rule of evidence, is of much deeper significance than any of the specific exclusionary rules that are usually thought to constitute evidence law.

Within the Received View, the importance of testimony in the language of perception runs even deeper. Our daily conversations and descriptions of events are suffused with opinion, interpretation, and evaluation. Often

[33] Nor may they repeat even their own prior statements, *Tome v. United States*, 115 S. Ct. 696 (1996), something long thought odd, since the declarant and the witness are the same person, and that person *is* available for cross-examination. See Robert P. Burns, "Foreword. Bright Lines and Hard Edges: Anatomy of a Criminal Evidence Decision," *Journal of Criminal Law and Criminology* 85 (1995): 843, 859–63.

[34] John H. Wigmore, *Evidence in Trials at Common Law*, vol. 5, sec. 1367 (Chadbourn rev., 1974), 32. See *California v. Green*, 399 U.S. 149, 158 (1970) (quoting Wigmore on the importance of cross-examination to assure reliability).

[35] See *Federal Rules of Evidence*, Rules 602 and 701.

[36] The early common law ensured that even an expert witness could not offer such an opinion by a rule (partially rejected in the federal system by Rule 704) that prohibited an expert from giving an opinion "on the ultimate issue before the jury." See, e.g., Wigmore, *Evidence*, vol. 5, sec. 1920.

we are allowed only to agree (or more rarely, disagree) with the leading questions of our conversation partners, questions themselves suffused with assumptions, opinions, interpretations, and evaluation. Such conversations are about matters of interest (*inter est*, it is between [the speakers]) but are, much more, occasions by which the speakers constitute and reform their relationship, an enterprise often well served by the sharing of opinions and judgments. The factual accuracy of the accounts is usually of less significance than self-revelation and invitations to reciprocity.

By contrast, testimony in response to nonleading questions in the language of perception provides the jury exactly what it needs to decide the case according to the norms embedded in the instructions: an artificially stripped-down, value-free account of the witness's perceptions. These perceptions are a kind of "prime matter," as Aristotle put it,[37] utterly plastic to both the jury's empirical generalizations and, more important, *to the legal norms embedded in the instructions*. Testimony in the language of perception reduces the likelihood that the jury will simply adopt the moral or political judgments smuggled into the "descriptions" by an authoritative or sympathetic witness.

NOT THE WHOLE TRUTH, NOTHING BUT LEGAL TRUTH: MATERIALITY

The Rule of Law reaches into the conduct of the trial in another way. Thayer, one of the early giants in the law of evidence in America,[38] announced as "a presupposition involved in the very conception of a rational system of evidence" that only relevant evidence will be admissible and all relevant evidence will be admissible.[39] The law of relevance has two important aspects, which were at common law termed materiality and logical relevance.[40]

Logical relevance focuses on the link between the evidence offered and the proposition the proponent of the evidence seeks to prove. Evidence is logically relevant if that link is supported by "experience or science,"[41] or, somewhat more technically, if that link, which constitutes the "probative

---

[37] Aristotle, *Metaphysics*, 110.

[38] James B. Thayer, *A Preliminary Treatise on Evidence at the Common Law* (Boston: Little Brown, 1898).

[39] Ibid., 264–65.

[40] The notion of "legal relevance" was sometimes thought to comprise materiality, logical relevance, and some further requirements. These latter have variously been argued to include a higher quantum of probative value than that which common sense would specify (Wigmore's "plus value") or conformity to specifically legal rules that govern permissible inferences. See Wigmore, *Evidence*, vol. 5, sec. 1367.

[41] *Federal Rules of Evidence*, Rule 401 (advisory committee's note).

value" of the evidence presented, is secured by a "major premise" that exists in our common sense (the "web of belief") and which a reasonable jury could conclude was applicable to the evidence submitted. For example, if the proponent wants to submit evidence that the defendant had consumed five beers within a half hour of a shooting of which he is accused, he or she will invoke the commonsense generalization, "Generally and for the most part, people who consume large amounts of alcohol will be less inhibited for a period of time after drinking."

It is materiality, however, which the Received View emphasizes as the key to assuring that the trial renders operational the Rule of Law. A lawyer will be permitted to present evidence before the jury only if the proposition he or she seeks to prove is one that is germane to the case under the applicable law. For example, under the traditional law of "independent covenants" applicable to an eviction action for nonpayment of rent, a landlord's failure to maintain the premises up to code will not excuse the tenant's nonpayment of rent; thus the tenant will not be permitted to introduce evidence of the deplorable condition of his apartment. To do so would tempt the jury to decide the case based on moral or political norms other than those embedded in the instructions and will thus endanger the Rule of Law. Even in cases where the proponent of the evidence can demonstrate its materiality by pointing to an element of a claim or defense specified by the legal rules, the judge may still exclude the evidence if this legitimate value of the evidence is "substantially outweighed" by the threat of the jury's considering the evidence under a norm other than that contained in the instruction.[42] Thus the version even of the factual truth that the jury sees will surely not be the "whole" truth: it might be called the "legal truth" or, to beg most of the important questions for the moment, a "political truth." As Clifford Geertz put it, "Whatever law is after, it is not the whole story."[43] Law's truth is most obviously "political" because it is partial and is shaped by a political decision to effect the Rule of Law by pushing the jury into deciding the case

---

[42] For example, assume a case in which a household employee claims that her employer libeled her by accusing her of stealing jewelry. The defendant claims the defense of truth (that the employee actually did steal the jewelry) and offers evidence of the plaintiff's "nervousness" on the morning in question. The plaintiff seeks to explain her anxiety by describing an earlier incident in which the defendant violently shoved another employee. Though the evidence is (1) logically relevant by virtue of a commonsense generalization about the bases of fear and (2) material because the substantive law makes evidence on the issue of the truth of the allegation legally significant, the judge may *still* exclude it because it tempts the jury to punish the defendant for being a bully.

[43] Clifford Geertz, *Local Knowledge: Further Essays in Interpretive Anthropology* (New York: Basic Books, 1983).

based on the instructions, and not by other available ("political" or "distributive") norms. This is a wonderful paradox, the political avoidance of the political.[44]

JUDICIAL CONTROL OF THE TRIAL

Finally, the judge must make a number of determinations in the course of the trial that are aimed at preserving the Rule of Law. At the end of the plaintiff's or prosecution case, the judge will decide whether a reasonable jury could, based on the evidence, rule for the plaintiff or prosecution. At the end of all the evidence, the judge will decide whether the jury could reasonably rule for the party with the burden of proof, and even after the jury has rendered its verdict, the judge may enter judgment notwithstanding the verdict if he or she believes that the jury could not reasonably have decided the case based on the norms stated in the instructions. The final protection for the Rule of Law is afforded by appellate review of trial-level findings of fact, whether by judges or juries.[45] Appellate courts will review determinations made at the trial levels, except for verdicts of not guilty in criminal cases that are protected by the double jeopardy clause. Judgments that could not have resulted from accurate fact-finding followed by fair application of the legal norm will be reversed.

The Received View thus understands the trial as the institutional device for the actualization of the Rule of Law. Pretrial practices assure that the law recognizes the right or obligation which the plaintiff claims, and that there actually is a question of fact for the jury. Evidentiary rules assure

[44] Hannah Arendt, "Truth and Politics," in *Between Past and Future* (New York: Penguin Books, 1977), 227, 260–64. Arendt argues that even the political realm, "its greatness notwithstanding," requires the support of other realms, such as the courts and the university, which do not give allegiance to specifically political principles.

[45] The stated standard for the review of jury findings of fact, the "substantial evidence test," is said to be more deferential to the jury's conclusions than is the standard for the review of a trial judge's findings of fact, the "clearly erroneous test." The former asks whether any reasonable finder of fact could have reached the jury's determination, while the latter inquires as to whether there is on balance a firm conviction that a mistake has been committed. Clark and Stone, "Review of Findings of Fact," *University of Chicago Law Review* 4 (1937): 190. Is it anomalous for the Received View that the judgments of the legal professional receive *more* scrutiny than that of the lay jury? It does seem to reflect a view that the legitimacy of the jury's verdict is not strictly a function of its "accuracy." Of course, in both criminal and civil cases the jury has constitutional status reflected in the Fifth, Sixth, and Seventh Amendments. The extent to which that status limits judicial control of verdicts is a very complex matter. See *Galloway v. United States*, 319 U.S. 372, 391 (1943); Frank W. Hackett, "Has a Trial Judge of a United States Court the Right to Direct a Verdict?" *Yale Law Journal* 24 (1914): 127.

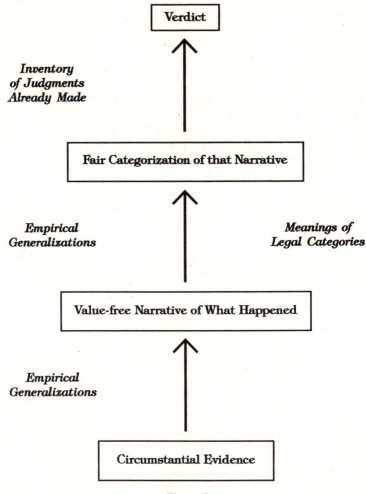

Figure 1

that evidence is reliable and is ready for easy imprint by the legal norms alone. The law of materiality requires that every piece of evidence be justified by a link to those same norms and will keep from the jury even material evidence that too strongly invokes other moral and political values, even implicitly. The jury can then construct a value-free narrative version of "what happened" based on the empirical generalizations that constitute its common sense, and render a verdict dependent on the "fit" between that account and the norms embedded in the instructions. The trial can be represented by figure 1.

In this schematization, the operations that the jury must perform in order to move from the circumstantial evidence to the verdict are different at each step, and so the arrows running up from Circumstantial Evidence to the Verdict have different significance at each step. However, it is fair to say that in different ways the lower levels *determine* the upper in ways that the upper do not determine the lower—each level is complete before the next step up is taken, and no lines of causality or justification run from the upper levels to the lower. For example, the jury does not determine its value-free narrative of what happened *in order to* reach a judgment that one of the legal elements had been established at the level of Categorization: they do not engage in "result-oriented" findings of historical fact. At Level 1, the warrants,[46] or justifications, that support moving from circumstantial evidence to narratives of events are empirical generalizations about what is likely to have happened, given the proof of other events (the circumstantial evidence) or about the believability of witnesses claiming to have seen events that "directly" prove a relevant fact. For example, the inference from the fact that the witness is the defendant's mother to the conclusion that she is shading the truth to help him is supported by the generalization "Generally and for the most part, mothers will do almost anything to help their children when the latter are in serious trouble." At Level 2, the warrants that justify moving from the narrative of events to the fair legal categorizations of that narrative are more complex: (1) insofar as the element in the instruction requires a further factual inference from the value-free narrative constructed at the second level, another empirical generalization is required; and (2) insofar as the meaning of the terms in the instructions are normative or evaluative ("maliciously" or "reasonably"), a judgment about the meaning of words and concepts is also necessary. The last step, the verdict, follows from the jury's merely inspecting the earlier steps to see whether the required categorizations have been made.

This notion of the trial is very powerful. It is, in the main, an account of those constitutive rules that are designed to support the Rule of Law and which do in fact play an important role in the trial, though not in the way the Received View would have it. I argue below that this view, for all its power, commits the error of misplaced concreteness. It takes one subset of rules and claims that they exhaust the reality of the enormously more complex and more admirable practices that actually constitute the contemporary trial. Nonetheless, since the Rule of Law is an important ideal, and the constitutive rules of trial are embraced and enforced by those who respect the Rule of Law, this ideal affects behavior. It is, how-

---

[46] Steven Toulmin, *The Uses of Logic* (Cambridge: Cambridge University Press, 1958), 98.

ever, so partial as to be a serious distortion of what we have allowed and designed the trial to be. This conclusion emerges from a more nuanced philosophical understanding of the trial's practices and linguistic structure, a more "phenomenological" study of what actually occurs at trial, and the social scientific findings on the trial. I devote chapters 2 through 5 to those tasks. To encourage the skeptical reader to follow along with me, I will describe a number of anomalies in the very rules of the trial which suggest that something more than the Received View is at work.

Anomalies in the Legal Structure of the Trial

The Received View, then, seems to capture much of what the American trial has become. It gives an account that invokes the deeply held American commitment to the Rule of Law and attempts to create "a government of laws, not of men." It explains some of the most striking and basic of the constitutive principles of the trial, principles that generate most of the more detailed edifice of the law of evidence.

There are, however, problems with this understanding of the trial, some of which are visible even in its legal structure. Indeed, they reflect a considered, though muted, public determination to preserve the trial as something other than that envisioned by the Received View. These features are likely candidates for what Rawls calls "considered judgments of justice"[47]—that is, judgments "about the basic structure of society which we now make intuitively and in which we have the greatest confidence[,]" judgments that may have genuine moral force.[48] Other problems emerge from reflection by participants and social scientists on the actual practice of judges, lawyers, witnesses, and juries. These may, of course, be dismissed as mere deviations from the ideal expressed by the Received View, deviations that await the next wave of reform. On the other hand, they may reveal a genuinely normative vision of the institution that is simply inconsistent with the Received View.[49] I discuss those anomalies here.

First, juries usually render "general verdicts." They do not write screenplays of "what happened." If the prime task of jury members, as judges

---

[47] Rawls, *A Theory of Justice*, 19–20.

[48] In Rawls's understanding, they are also judgments internal to creating a theory of justice, including a normative theory of the trial. My project here can be understood as an extended effort to reach "reflective equilibrium," a situation where intuitively approved practices (and their implicit principles) are brought into harmony with more general principles consistent with broader moral commitments. Ibid., 19.

[49] On the inevitability of implicit normative "frameworks" for understanding human practices and institutions, see Charles Taylor, *Sources of the Self: The Making of the Modern Identity* (Cambridge: Harvard University Press, 1989), 3–24.

of the facts, were to construct a relatively value-free narrative of what occurred, juries could be asked to agree on an account of what occurred and then turn the task of "applying the law" over to the judge. After all, this task of application inevitably involves interpretation,[50] and legal interpretation seems preeminently within the province of the judge. It is the judge who has legal training, who has a professional commitment to the Rule of Law,[51] who has access to the results in other cases,[52] and who has access to interpretive materials such as case law and legislative history of which the jury is kept ignorant. In short, the judge is more likely to have that respectful passivity toward the law's meaning and purposes which allows for genuine *interpretation*.[53]

Second, the legal rules prohibit official scrutiny into the actual mental processes of individual jurors or into the actual processes of jury deliberation.[54] The only allowable "jury poll" is whether the decision "was and is your verdict." Even an admission by an individual juror or the entire jury that it reached its decision based on a consideration other than those embedded in the instructions will not be grounds for reversal or a new trial.[55] Though the orthodox view is that a jury's *obligation* is to follow the judge's instructions, it is recognized that the jury clearly has the unreviewable *power* not to.[56] Do we insulate a jury's actions from effective scrutiny solely out of practical concerns, an appreciation of the need for finality, a concession to the shortness of life? Or is it, as I believe, a conscious legitimization of a kind of decision making, of which I hope to give an account, that is inconsistent with the Received View?

Third, juries have more than just the direct examinations "in the language of perception" before them when they make their decisions. Lawyers are permitted to address the jury in both opening statement and in

---

[50] Hans-Georg Gadamer, *Truth and Method*, trans. and ed. G. Barden and J. Cumming (New York: Crossroad Publishing, 1975), 274–78.

[51] See H. L. Hart, *The Concept of Law* (Oxford: Oxford University Press, 1976), 76–114, for an account of the "the law of the officials."

[52] In many jurisdictions, "jury reporters" provide very general descriptions of the nature of cases at the trial level and give the terms of jury verdicts and settlements. Judges may have access to both published and unpublished orders of other trial judges. And, of course, trial judges have regular access to the results in the somewhat skewed sample of cases that come to be described in appellate opinions.

[53] Gadamer, *Truth and Method*, xiii–xiv.

[54] See *Federal Rules of Evidence*, Rule 606(b); Christopher B. Mueller, "Jurors' Impeachment of Verdicts and Indictments in Federal Court Under Rule 606(b)," *Nebraska Law Review* 57 (1978): 920.

[55] *Tanner v. United States*, 483 U.S. 107 (1987) (upholding district court's refusal to hold an evidentiary hearing based on a juror's statement that several jurors had consumed alcohol and drugs and otherwise misbehaved during trial).

[56] Abramson, *We the Jury*, 85–95.

closing argument in ways that inevitably invoke norms that may bear little resemblance to those in the instructions. In opening statements, attorneys describe not what the evidence will be but what the "evidence will show." Lawyers tell stories that contain episodes to which there will be no testimony in the language of perception at all. These rich narratives will ideally be "vivid and continuous dreams"[57] that describe human motives, intentions, and actions of which there could in principle be no testimony in the language of perception. They will be "compelling" for reasons that have little to do with the jury's purely empirical generalizations, and may invoke all manner of moral and political values.[58] Closing argument as well, in many different ways, even if delivered in a manner that transgresses no rule of trial procedure, may invoke values that go well beyond the instructions.[59] If the jury's task were solely to find the facts to which the instructions were to be applied, it would seem that these two powerful rhetorical devices would never have evolved to their present shape. Their presence in the trial suggests that the Received View has captured only a portion of the normative resources available at trial.

Fourth, in civil cases the plaintiff in most American jurisdictions need only file a complaint that puts the defendant on notice of some set of facts that *would* entitle him to relief *if* the jury followed the law as stated.[60] It is still easy to "get a jury." We saw that the jury need not produce a screenplay of past events for the trial judge or the appellate court to review intelligently whether those events "fairly" could be held to fall within the legal categories found in the instructions. Neither may the trial judge require the plaintiff to allege specific facts entitling him to relief *before* the case gets to the jury. All that is necessary is that the plaintiff might be able to prove some set of facts that would entitle him to relief.

It is true, as I noted above, that at various points in the course of the trial, the judge is required to make independent evaluations of the evidence under the appropriate legal standards. The judge, however, need only determine whether, under the evidence presented, and making all

---

[57] The phrase is from John Gardner, *The Art of Fiction* (New York: Vintage Books, 1983), 31. Gardner argues that the creation of such a "dream" serves specifically moral ends. See chapter 6, below.

[58] W. Lance Bennett and Martha S. Feldman, *Reconstructing Reality in the Courtroom: Justice and Judgment in American Culture* (New Brunswick, N.J.: Rutgers University Press, 1981): 29–37 (providing examples of the way in which specifically *normative* judgments make one story more or less compelling than another).

[59] Anthony G. Amsterdam and Randy Hertz, "An Analysis of Closing Arguments to a Jury," *New York Law School Law Review* 37 (1992): 55–121.

[60] *Conley v. Gibson*, 355 U.S. 495 (1957). The issues here have been long debated among legal scholars and judges. See Richard L. Marcus, "The Revival of Fact Pleading under the Federal Rules of Civil Procedure," *Columbia Law Review* 86 (1986): 433, 439. The "liberal ethos" still prevails, with pockets of resistance. See, e.g., *Sutliff, Inc. v. Donavan Companies*, 727 F.2d 648, 654 (7th Cir. 1984).

inferences against the party attempting to keep the case from the jury, a rational fact-finder *could* find that each of the elements of the claim or defense had been proven. Trial judges are generally reluctant to find that evidence is so insufficient that a jury verdict is *irrational*, especially since such a finding begs for reversal. More significantly, a competent lawyer will virtually always be able to prepare and present a case that resists judgment as a matter of law even where he or she is seeking and expecting a verdict based on norms discontinuous with the instructions.[61] In criminal cases, motions for directed verdicts, even on a single element of a charge or defense and even when the defendant presents no evidence, are constitutionally impermissible. The judge's policing of the procedural protections for the Rule of Law seems very light indeed.

Fifth, the same sort of deference that applies to a trial judge determining whether to grant a motion for directed verdict applies to appellate courts reviewing verdicts, a deference that seems to have increased.[62] An appellate court may reverse a jury finding of fact only if reasonable persons could not have reached the verdict on the evidence presented.[63] Again, there is no inquiry permitted as to whether the jury actually *did* follow the instructions in reaching the verdict it reached. The court may inquire only into whether a reasonable jury that followed the instructions *could* have reached the verdict it did based on the evidence presented.[64] This leaves plenty of room for a jury actually to decide the case based on norms that have no place within the Received View.

Sixth, doctrines that make reversals of jury verdicts inconsistent with the values underlying the Received View less likely have become dominant. Increasingly, appellate courts have adopted the principle that evidentiary determinations are not questions of law to be freshly redetermined ("de novo review"). Rather, they are determinations delegated to the "sound discretion of the trial court," traditionally the *most* deferential standard of review.[65] This is significant for my purposes because, within the Received View, evidentiary doctrines are designed largely to keep the

[61] See chapter 2, below.

[62] Martin Louis, "Allocating Adjudicative Decision Making Authority between the Trial and Appellate Levels: A Unified View of the Scope of Review, the Judge/Jury Question, and Procedural Discretion," *North Carolina Law Review* 64 (1986): 993, 1005–6.

[63] There are various formulations of this standard, typically "not supported by substantial evidence" or "against the manifest weight of the evidence." In a given jurisdiction there may be subtle differences between those formulations, which are more likely to be verbal than real.

[64] See, e.g., *Jackson v. Virginia*, 443 U.S. 307 (1979) (review of record most favorable to the prosecution showed that a rational fact-finder could have found the petitioner guilty beyond a reasonable doubt).

[65] See, e.g., *General Casualty Insurance Companies v. Holst Radiator Co.*, 88 F.3d 670, 672 (1996) (a court of appeals will not disturb a trial court's evidentiary ruling absent clear and prejudicial abuse of discretion).

trial on the track dictated by the substantive legal standards, that is, to narrow the normative focus of the proceeding. When appellate courts fail, to any extent, to police the application of those evidentiary rules, to that extent an important pillar of the Received View crumbles.

Seventh, even in cases where evidence tending to invoke norms discontinuous with the legal standards has been erroneously admitted, reversal has become increasingly unlikely. After all, it is often said, a party is "entitled to a fair trial, not a perfect one."[66] Appellate courts have often embraced doctrines of harmless error that allow them to affirm jury verdicts where evidentiary rulings have permitted the jury to hear evidence that the Received View would proscribe.[67]

Traditionally, a trial judge's evidentiary rulings would be the basis for reversal if the evidence improperly included or excluded could have affected the verdict.[68] Most often such an "effect," particularly for evidence improperly admitted, was that the evidence—for example, improper evidence of a criminal defendant's "character"—invoked norms discontinuous with the instructions. More recently, courts have tended to affirm judgments in the face of improperly admitted evidence with the explanation that "putting aside the improperly admitted evidence, there remained evidence sufficient to support the verdict," or, at least as often, that the remaining evidence was "overwhelming."[69] Notice that saying that the properly admitted evidence was "sufficient to support a verdict" is only an assertion that a reasonable jury could have reached that verdict after putting aside the improperly admitted material. It says nothing at all as to whether the jury did in fact consider the improperly admitted evidence and, more important, nothing about whether *this* jury would have reached the verdict it reached if the improperly admitted evidence had been excluded. Appellate courts' increasing toleration for error often comes at the expense of the values underlying the Received View.

Eighth, until recently the Received View could point to the care with which appellate courts scrutinized the jury instructions as proof of its vision of the trial. Months of trial could come to naught if even one of the jury instructions misstated the law applicable to the case.[70] More recently, however, appellate courts have adopted a "harmless error" standard even

---

[66] *Rose v. Clark*, 478 U.S. 570, 579 (1986).

[67] Roger J. Traynor, *The Riddle of Harmless Error* (Columbus: Ohio State University Press, 1970). Jack B. Weinstein et al., *Weinstein's Evidence: Commentary on Rules of Evidence for the United States Courts and Magistrates* (New York: M. Bender, 1996), sec. 103[06] (limited review of error in rulings on evidence).

[68] *Kotteakos v. United States*, 328 U.S. 750, 764–65 (1946).

[69] *United States v. Short*, 947 F.2d 1445, 1455 (10th Cir. 1991).

[70] Traynor, *The Riddle of Harmless Error*, 4–12. *People v. Moore*, 43 Cal. 2d 517, 275 P.2d 485 (1954).

for the statement of the law that the trial court provides the jury and by which the jury, under the Received View, was to decide the case. Statements dismissing the importance of the misstatement of instructions after a lengthy trial are finding their way into appellate opinions with the blessing of the Supreme Court.[71] This reflects a renewed realism among appellate courts about the limited role that jury instructions play in the decision of cases, a realism long common among trial lawyers[72] and, of course, deeply inconsistent with the Received View.

Ninth, there has been, for at least the past twenty years, a strong drift toward admissibility in the law of evidence. The common law of evidence sought to keep the jury focused on the "jugular"[73] issue by permitting only that evidence which could "make the existence of any fact that is of consequence to the determination of the action more probable or less probable than it would be without the evidence."[74] It was the jury instructions, of course, that determined rigorously what is "of consequence." There are a number of reasons for the more recent relaxation of the rigor of the law of evidence that I discuss in chapter 3, but for the moment I want only to note one important consequence. The greater the range of evidentiary material the jury sees, the greater range of moral and political considerations available to the jury for the decision of the case. The broader the range of such considerations, the more will it be true that the legal norms will be merely *one* set of the considerations before the jury. There simply is no way for the court to control the meaning (or "semantic incommensurability")[75] of the evidence that the jury will see. In the lan-

[71] *Yates v. Evatt*, 500 U.S. 391, 402 1991) (harmless error analysis applicable to erroneous burden-shifting instruction); *Carella v. California*, 491 U.S.263, 266 (1989) (erroneous mandatory presumption instruction); *Pope v. Illinois*, 481 U.S. 497 (1987) (error in statement of element); *Rose v. Clark*, 478 U.S. 570 (1986) (erroneous rebuttable presumption instruction). But see *Sullivan v. Lousiana*, 508 U.S. 275 (1993) (erroneous burden of proof instruction not subject to harmless error analysis).

[72] Frankly, the jury instruction conference is often understood by trial lawyers as simply a formalistic trap for the unwary, requiring the trial judge precisely to state the appellate court's version of the law, even though there is little reason to believe that distinctions held dear by appellate courts will figure in the actual decision of the case. The danger is getting "favorable" instructions that do not help at all with the jury but sow the seed of reversible error. See chapter 5, n. 77, below (jury instructions are not well comprehended).

[73] John H. Langbein, "The German Advantage in Civil Procedure," *University of Chicago Law Review* 52 (1985): 823, 830 (describing the Continental judge's method of focusing on the question the law makes central).

[74] *Federal Rules of Evidence*, Rule 401.

[75] George Steiner, *Real Presences* (Chicago: University of Chicago Press, 1989):

A sentence always means more. Even a single word, within the weave of incommensurable connotation, can, and usually does. The informing matrix or context of even a rudimentary, literal proposition—and just what does *literal* mean?—moves outward from specific utterance or notation in ever-widening concentric and overlapping circles. These comprise

guage of the trial courtroom, when a judge lets in questionable evidence "for what it's worth," he cannot control what the jury will make of the evidence and the sort of importance the jury will confer on it.[76] The more rigid and formalistic the law of evidence, the greater the likelihood that the jury will be confined to the kind of adjudication envisioned by the Received View.

What does all this mean? These features of the contemporary trial have a cumulative force that is deeply perplexing for the Received View. They are especially puzzling because they are aspects of the very constitutive rules of the trial itself, the enacted rules that make the trial what it is, the "law of the officials." Some lawyers, judges, and commentators agree that the Received View fails to do justice to what occurs in the trial courtroom. Speaking of trial advocacy, they wearily remind us that rhetoric has always been "a weapon called upon to gain victory in battles where the decision hung on the spoken word."[77] Of course, they tell us, lawyers appeal to the emotions and prejudices of jurors and with effect. Of course, they say, jurors are prey to this sort of manipulation and are incapable of understanding, let alone following, the instructions. It's not without reason that prosecutors who cannot reach a plea bargain often conclude negotiations by saying, "Well, then, let's roll the dice." Didn't Learned Hand say that he could imagine no fate worse, save sickness or death, than having an important matter turn on the outcome of a lawsuit? The only virtue of this situation, we are told, is that outcomes are so unpredictable that most sane people will settle rather than resort to trial.[78] The trial, then, still is what it was when revulsion from it caused Plato to conclude that no good man could participate[79]—stylized combat where only the skill of the fighter and the fortunes of war determine the result.

---

the individual, subconsciously quickened language habits and associative field-mappings of the particular speaker or writer. . . . No formalization is of an order adequate to the semantic mass and motion of a culture, to the wealth of denotation, connotation, implicit reference, elision and tonal register which envelop saying what one means, meaning what one says or neither. . . .

Ibid., 82–83.

[76] Limiting instructions are generally thought to be ineffectual or worse. "Comment. Other Crimes Evidence at Trial: Of Balancing and Other Matters," *Yale Law Journal* 70 (1961): 763, 777; Hoffman and Brodley, "Jurors on Trial," *Missouri Law Review* 17 (1952): 235, 243–45.

[77] Paul Ricoeur, *The Rule of Metaphor: Multidisciplinary Studies of the Creation of Meaning in Language*, trans. Robert Czerny (Toronto: University of Toronto Press, 1975), 10.

[78] William Fellner, *Probability and Profit* (Homewood, Ill.: R. D. Irwin, Inc., 1965), 140–42 (uncertainty about probabilities and grave risks to important interests suggest a conservative strategy).

[79] Plato, *Republic* 592b.

Abandoning an uncritical version of the Received View does not force us to accept this nihilistic conclusion. My view is that we will have even more reason to embrace the trial as a great cultural achievement when we have attained a more accurate normative understanding of what the trial is about. Such an understanding would afford us a set of *situated* ideals[80] that may provide guidance for its continual reform, a different normative vision of what the trial is and a richer understanding of what it is that the trial has become for us.

To achieve that we have to start over, embark on a "second sailing."[81]

---

[80] On the importance of truly *situated* ideals, ideals that are actually embedded in practices and institutions, see Taylor, *Hegel*, 537–71.

[81] Seth Benardete, *Socrates' Second Sailing: On Plato's Republic* (Chicago: University of Chicago Press, 1989).

II

The Trial's Linguistic Practices

The actions of men cannot be measured with
the straight ruler of the understanding, which is
rigid. . . . The imprudent scholars, who go
directly from the universally true to the singular,
rupture the inter-connections of life. The wise
men, however, who attain the eternal truth by
the uneven and insecure paths of practice, make
a detour, as it is not possible to attain this by a
direct road.
  (Giambattista Vico)[1]

Out of the conjunction of activities and men
around the law-jobs there arise the crafts of law,
and so the craftsmen. Advocacy, counseling,
judging, law-making, administering—these are
the major grouping of the law-crafts. . . . At the
present juncture, the fresh study of these crafts
and of the mastery of their best doing is one of
the major needs of jurisprudence.
  (Karl Llewellyn)[2]

Introduction

One of the fixed points of the social scientific study of the trial is that the
juror makes his or her decision after an intense encounter with the evidence, and it is the evidence in the case, more than any other factor, that
determines the outcome.[3] The juror performs his or her task only after

---

[1] Giambattista Vico, *On the Study Methods of Our Time*, trans. Elio Gianturco (Indianapolis, Bobbs-Merrill, 1965), 35.

[2] Karl Llewellyn, "My Philosophy of Law," in *My Philosophy of Law*, ed. A. Kocourek (Boston: Boston Law Books, 1941), 181, 188.

[3] As I suggested above, this encounter will be fundamentally misunderstood if the evidence is viewed as the "stimulus" that "causes" certain behaviors on the part of the jury. Such a view may provide a methodological postulate for research programs that may prove fruitful. A social scientist who has been disappointed by his failure to produce reliable correlations between juror demographics and outcomes may understandably search for other "independent variables," and there is no harm in that. The distortion occurs when a researcher turns such a postulate into a metaphysical statement about what "really" happens at trial, implicitly denying the normative status of real intelligence and moral judgment. As

this highly structured language-centered event: the trial itself. The trial is usually over immediately after this encounter, since jury deliberation "changes" the result in fewer than one in ten cases. The initial majority almost always prevails.[4] Before we focus in greater detail on the *kinds* of judgments the jury must make,[5] we must examine the rules, practices, and performances that make the trial what it is. Trial rhetoric and trial evidence are far from "raw data." As we have begun to see, they are the result of rules and practices, fraught with normative judgments,[6] that create this decisive encounter. These create "the evidence," the engagement with which, the social scientists tell us, determines the results in most trials. The juror performs his intellectual operations in the encounter with these rule-bound practices.

In this chapter, I focus on what lawyers *do*. Ultimately, I will argue that what we may call the moral significance of the trial transcends the conscious purposes of the participants. Good lawyers usually understand this. They derive some satisfaction from the purely Promethean joy that attaches to effective performance; but their deeper satisfaction comes from participating in an important practice best described as "substantial," in the specific sense that it serves to realize the "ethical substance"[7] of a community.

What lawyers do is important, however, and fundamental to an understanding of the nature of the contemporary trial. Trial law is a communal social practice that, like all such practices, involves neither "acquiring a repertoire of routine responses to routine situations, nor grasping a general proposition (let alone a systematic theory) logically independent of the practice activities."[8]

---

in the philosophy of science, what is necessary is not a "causal account" of the inquiry that occurs at trial, but a "rational reconstruction" which demonstrates the *kind of validity* the determinations made at trial may claim.

[4] This is one of the most important social scientific findings about the trial. See chapter 5, below.

[5] See chapter 5, below.

[6] The rules and practices are sometimes the results of the conscious imposition, if you will, of a philosophical conviction. We should never forget Lord Keynes: "Practical men, who believe themselves quite exempt from any intellectual influences, are usually the slaves of some defunct economist. Madmen in authority, who hear voices in the air, are distilling their frenzy from some academic scribbler of a few years back." However, those convictions are more often deep convictions that provide the implicit public philosophy of an era, worked out implicitly in the process of debates over institutional realities. After all, many of the greatest of Lord Keynes's scribblers have stated in theoretical terms these basic constitutive commitments of an era or a civilization.

[7] The term is Hegel's; he uses it in distinction from a morality of abstract rules. See Taylor, *Hegel*, 365–88.

[8] Brian Leiter, "Heidegger and the Theory of Adjudication," *Yale Law Journal* 106 (1996): 253, quoting Gerald Postema, "Protestant Interpretation and Social Practices," *Law and Philosophy* 6 (1987): 283, 303.

Rather, it involves learning a discipline or mastering a technique. It involves the capacity to relate different items in the world of the practice and to locate apparently new items in that world, to move around with a certain ease in the web of relationships created by it. This is interpretation, in the straightforward sense that it involves a sure grasp of the "meaning" of the various actions in the repertoire in question through their places in the practices, and a grasp of how the practice fits together, how it makes sense.[9]

It will turn out (in chapter 5) to be essential to the nature of the trial that a human being actually "performs" his or her interpretation of events in a public forum.[10] I now explore the essentials of that interpretive discipline.

Pretrial Practices: The Double Helix of Norms

In preparing a case for trial a lawyer creates a double helix of norms. One strand is dominated[11] by narrative and the other by informal logical inference or argument. Narrative is the story of events, actors, backgrounds, actions, and motives organically related to express a moral-political significance, a human meaning. As one might hear it in the beginning of an opening statement, "This is a case about loyalty and betrayal." "This is a case about keeping promises." "This is a case about a very wealthy man's abuse of an employee." Argument is a logical pattern of propositions, in this case leading to assent to a final proposition (a "legal element") that must be proven or disproved. Argument, like all rhetoric, can have multiple audiences. In jury trials, there are two important audiences, the judge and the jury. (For reasons I will describe shortly, there are still multiple audiences in bench trials.)

It is this double helix of narrative and argument that a lawyer calls "my theory of the case." Concretely, it will have its most systematic expression in the combination of opening statement (narrative) and summation (argument). *It is necessarily abstract.* It omits much of the concreteness of what the trial will reveal; it is a "cut" into the evidence. Good lawyers understand what "cut" to make, which inspired simplification to pursue. They also understand that the trier of fact will come to understand that even the best "factual theories" are rather *too* simple.

---

[9] Postema, "Protestant Interpretation," 303–4.

[10] See chapter 5, below.

[11] I say "dominated" for two reasons. There is an informal logical dimension to the relationship between the norms embedded in the opening statement (even if those norms are discontinuous with the legal elements) and the evidence presented. There is also, as we have seen, a narrative dimension to the intellectual processes, even as the Received View under-

The theory of the case is thus a simple, plausible, coherent, legally sufficient narrative that can easily be integrated with a moral theme.[12] Two rhetorics, one narrative and one "logical," are embedded in the presentation on which the jury must rely.[13] The narrative rhetoric appeals to the jury or the trial judge as the actual decision-maker in the case. By contrast, the argumentative rhetoric appeals primarily to the trial judge and the appellate court insofar as they perform the light policing of the Rule of Law I described in the first chapter. These arguments and the evidence on which they rely are usually calculated not to move these secondary triers of fact to judgment but simply to supply them with a kind of formal assurance of the "reasonableness" of the decision of the primary trier of fact. Given the deferential standards with which the trial judge and the appellate courts review jury determinations, the need to convince them that a reasonable jury *could* have employed those norms to decide the case is not overly demanding.

The argumentative rhetoric also appeals to the primary trier of fact in those cases, a minority, where argumentative processes are likely to be important. There are two such situations. First, both parties' narratives may carry such little normative force that the jury can decide the case only in the manner described by the Received View: by constructing an accurate and value-free account of what occurred, followed by judgments of legal categorization that respect the meanings of the words of the instructions. For reasons described below, this is rare. Second, it may be that an initial majority on a jury needs to invoke the authoritative norms found in the instructions to persuade several jurors who may not have been persuaded by the norms embedded in the narratives and need to be

---

stands them, by which even the most value-free account of "what happened" is understood before the legal norms can be applied to that factual account.

[12] I follow the convention of distinguishing between "theory of the case" and "theme." See Steven Lubet, *Modern Trial Advocacy: Analysis and Practice* (Notre Dame, Ind.: National Institute for Trial Advocacy, 1993), 7–9. Some writers distinguish a "factual theory of the case" from a "persuasive theory of the case" to express roughly the same notion. Of course, concretely there is but one story told, which should exhibit both epistemological and moral power. Probably the most adequate treatment of pretrial practices for attorneys describes the narrative theory of the case this way:

> The ultimate aim of developing, selecting and adorning theories with evidence is to produce at trial what we might term a complete theory of the case. A complete theory of the case combines legal theories and descriptive and explanatory hypotheses in a story which has both rational and psychological appeal. It is a theory that describes what happened and why in a way that is persuasive both to the mind and to the heart.

David A. Binder and Paul Bergman, *Fact Investigation: From Hypothesis to Proof* (St. Paul, Minn.: West Publishing, 1984), 184.

[13] Twining, *Rethinking Evidence*, 239 (describing Wigmore's view that narrative and informal logic were the two means of organizing trial evidence).

persuaded to join the majority. The argumentative strand in the theory of the case provides the majority with a relatively "neutral" set of rhetorical resources with which to convince the minority.[14] (Here, of course, if the majority reaches its decision by intellectual operations other than "argument," the norms imbedded in the instructions will not have "caused" the verdict, since that decisive initial majority will have been constituted for reasons other than their allegiance to those norms.)

Choosing a Theory of the Case

How does a lawyer reach that theory of the case? Most cases begin with a client interview, typically in three stages. The first is explicitly practical: the lawyer asks the client a set of open-ended questions to determine how he defines the problematic situation in which he finds himself and what resolution he seeks. That definition and that desired result are not absolutes—they are subject to refinement and modification in dialogue with the attorney—but the ethical rules give the client's ultimate definition of his problem and expected solution hegemony over any attempt by the lawyer to dictate the goal of the representation.[15] Second, the lawyer asks the client another set of somewhat more directive questions in order to construct a relatively comprehensive chronological reconstruction of the central events, identified from the first portion of the conversation.[16] Finally, the attorney begins to ask specific questions that serve to test the viability of possible factual theories that may form aspects of a unified theory of the case. These questions are "theory-driven"— they seek to verify or falsify possible narratives to an acceptable degree of probability.[17]

There are limits on the stories the lawyer may tell. The possible narratives are constrained, with increasing concreteness, by (1) the criminal laws against client perjury and attorney subornation of perjury and disci-

[14] I will not say "pressure" the minority. Although social scientists sometimes view this interchange between the initial majority and the minority as "social pressure," there are significant philosophical problems with that concept. Jury deliberation approaches an "ideal speech situation" where a better argument should have an unusually strong likelihood of prevailing. Or, to put it differently, "He forced me to do it: he used logic on me!" shouldn't usually be considered the *kind* of coercion that is normatively problematic. After all, as Arendt put it, truth is inherently coercive, and Euclid was a veritable tyrant. Arendt, "Truth and Politics," 240 (quoting Mercier de la Rivière).

[15] *Model Rules*, Rule 1.2 (the client should determine the goals of the representation).

[16] David A. Binder and Susan C. Price, *Legal Interviewing and Counseling: A Client-Centered Approach* (St. Paul, Minn.: West Publishing, 1977). *

[17] A theory that has been verified to an acceptable level of probability may create a "triable case." It is a case where at least one crucial "factual" question is debatable.

plinary regulations prohibiting attorneys from misrepresenting facts to the court or presenting known perjury; (2) the calculations of the party or the attorney that misrepresentation is likely to be implausible; and (3) the settled moral dispositions of client and attorney not to lie. At times the client's account of events also limits the stories that may be told at trial. At other times the client's story may be fitted easily within a number of possible full narratives. At still other times the client's initial story may be reshaped to allow its integration into factual theories that did not obviously present themselves. This last need not be a kind of manipulation that leads away from the truth, because the client's initial recollection may suffer from distortions of perception, memory, communication, or a misguided desire to tell what he falsely believes to be a helpful story. At other times, since different narratives have different legal consequences, it is the client's goals for the litigation that determine the theory.

The process of developing factual hypotheses runs something like this:

> One listens to a story, which triggers one or more potentially applicable legal theories. Contemporaneously, or subsequently, one reviews the story in light of each legal theory. If a story describes what happened in a way that completely coincides with a legal theory—that is, if the story can be termed a "legal story"—one *may* not bother to consider additional factual hypotheses. . . .
>
> But the comparison of a story with a legal theory may reveal that the story does not explain what happened in a way that fully activates or defuses the legal theory. Or the comparison may reveal that the story is but one of a number of reasonably possible ways that the legal story may be told. In either situation one is likely to "conjure up" other stories about what happened that might activate the legal theory. These factual possibilities then become the bases for ensuing investigation.[18]

As investigation proceeds, the possibilities are limited by the need to maintain the credibility of the client's basic story and by the increasing probability that there will be relatively more decisive contradictory evidence as the story becomes more fanciful. These further considerations, built into the trial, limit the rhetorician's natural desire to tell the most plausible story regardless of its truth. Plausible but false stories are also forbidden by rules that prohibit the client from telling or the lawyer from presenting evidence of stories about whose truth they have serious subjective reservations, *regardless* of whether those stories can effectively be attacked at trial.[19]

There are also what might be called extrinsic reasons to choose one among a range of possible stories to the jury. One story, but not another,

---

[18] Binder and Bergman, *Fact Investigation*, 171–72.
[19] See chapter 3, below.

might permit a desirable remedy, such as injunctive relief or punitive damages, or avoid an especially unwelcome consequence, such as commitment to a state mental institution.[20] One story but not another might allow for recovery against a certain defendant more able than another to compensate the plaintiff for his injury. One story but not another might pass muster under a statute of limitations. What allows the variation are variable facts subject to different plausible interpretations, such as "What was the defendant's state of mind at the time this occurred: innocent, negligent, reckless, malicious?" The advocate will not usually be asking the question "Well, what *was* his state of mind?" but rather "What are the consequences of alleging it was this rather than that?" and "Do we have sufficient evidence to survive a directed verdict on this point?" and also tell a persuasive story to the jury while not violating prohibitions on suborning or assisting perjury or presenting false evidence? What must be recognized are the practical considerations that dictate the factual statements made, often in the language of past occurrence. The very story of "what happened" is determined in part by a judgment about what is likely to be done in response to one or another version. As John Dewey put it approvingly, it follows an "experimental and flexible logic" that is "relative to consequences rather than to antecedents."[21] Facts are, to this limited extent, purposes.

After the initial interview with a client, a lawyer will set about the process of factual investigation. This is guided most generally by *both* strands of the double helix. If the client bears the burden of proof, the attorney must gather sufficient evidence that a secondary finder of fact, be it judge or appellate court, cannot say that there was insufficient evidence for a jury to have reasonably concluded that each element was established.[22] He will also seek to gather evidence—testimonial, documentary, or physical—that directly supports the theory and theme of the case, concretely presented in opening statement, of which he or she actually hopes to convince the jury, the primary finder of fact.

The attorney will follow a relatively straightforward hypothetico-deductive logic in his investigations. With regard to the theory of the case, he or she will ask this question: "If this fact (whether an element or simply a factually or normatively significant event) is true, what else would or

[20] Thus an emotionally disturbed person who has killed one of her children might decline to raise an insanity defense and focus on "obtaining" a conviction for involuntary manslaughter.

[21] John Dewey, "Logical Method and the Law," *Cornell Law Quarterly* 10 (1924): 7, 26–27.

[22] And so many lawyers will consult the jurisdiction's pattern jury instructions on each cause of action, which contains a summary statement of the legal elements. Often they will write their closing argument after reviewing those instructions.

might be true?" ("If my client really was at home, rather than at the crime scene, perhaps he made a telephone call of which there is a record or a witness . . ."). Just as in scientific inquiry,[23] this process can never lead to anything but probability, for there may be alternative descriptions or explanations for the evidence. Even in the case of so-called direct evidence, say eyewitness evidence, the alternative explanation may be the lack of credibility of the witness.[24] As a purely logical matter, this method, like all scientific method, commits the fallacy of affirming the antecedent ("If it was raining, the streets will be wet. But the streets are wet. Therefore, it was raining." *Quod non sequitur*). This inevitable "flaw" in empirical inquiry is what makes it possible to produce a rhetorically compelling mass of evidence for a proposition that is quite false.

The party who does not bear the burden of proof most often has his or her own version of events and will thus go through the same process as the party who does. And each will also seek to demonstrate that facts which ought to be true if the opponent's theory of the case were true are in fact not so, thus seeking to "falsify" the proposition that the opponent seeks to establish. Indeed, the party who does not bear the burden of proof may present a purely "negative" case, simply attacking the opponent's case and then arguing that he has not met his burden of proof, although the received wisdom is that presenting an alternative theory, if possible, is likely to be more successful.[25]

Factual investigation is thus theory-driven. Something may turn up in discovery or investigation that will cause the lawyer to revise his or her theory and redirect the inquiry consistent with a new set of hypotheses. After all, *one* of the bases of plausibility is the extent to which a theory is "supported" (to beg a thousand questions) by the evidence. But it is the felt necessity to present a full factual theory and theme—the concrete necessity to give an opening statement—that directs and structures the process.

As the evidence accumulates, the lawyer will continue to evaluate the theory and theme of the case and so the opening statement. *The* most important decision a trial lawyer makes is the precise cut, the inspired

---

[23] Vincent Potter, *On Understanding Understanding: A Philosophy of Knowledge* (New York: Fordham University Press, 1994). John Dewey noticed the similarity between a lawyer's and a scientist's methods in "Logical Method and the Law." He also noticed the difference: that the lawyer was not disinterested in the results of the inquiry as the ideal scientist is. Of course in scientific inquiry, the investigator is ultimately seeking to verify or falsify a universal law, not a historical fact. His investigation is inductive, not abductive. Potter, *On Understanding Understanding*, 52–57.

[24] See, e.g., Elizabeth Loftus, *Eyewitness Testimony* (Cambridge: Harvard University Press, 1979).

[25] The negative case is more common in the criminal context where the prosecution's burden of proof is higher and the prosecution cannot compel the defendant's testimony.

simplification, to make into the mass of evidence. (Similarly, the most important decisions made in the course of trial are what evidence to engage, what to "make an issue of.") For reasons I explain below, this will affect the lens through which the jury will "remember" and so understand the evidence. In short, historical truth is always mediated by the *meaning* of the evidence, and meaning is determined by how the evidence is remembered, that is, structured. As we will see, this organizing insight must be compelling *and* defensible. It requires a synthetic factual, legal, and moral judgment about the case and the witnesses. It seeks to persuade the juror on the single most important decision the juror will make: What is this case about; what is the issue? The choice of a "theory of the case" is one of the moments when the law reveals itself "as a continuing and collective process of conversation and judgment."[26] Choice of theory of the case is peculiarly a matter for *judgment* because the criteria for the choice of a compelling theory of the case are incommensurable, that is, incapable of being compared by the application of any one simple measure.

The Criteria for Theory Choice

First, the theory must be at least sufficient as a matter of law. There have been occasions, dreadful no doubt to their victims, where a motion for a directed verdict has been granted after a trial lawyer's opening statement. (The judge said, in effect, "If that's what even *you* say happened, then the law says you should lose the case!") To the extent that the trial lawyer believes that the jury will explicitly follow the instructions, he or she should develop a theory of the case that is more than "sufficient" under the law, but which can *fairly* be categorized within the legal elements because it is the fairness of that fit that will determine, in the manner the Received View postulates, the jury's verdict.

Second, the theory itself should have moral or political appeal, in that it provides the jury with a moral reason to rule favorably. Thus an action for breach of a complicated commercial contract is a case about "broken promises." Or an action that pits a large corporation against an appealing start-up company that made an ambiguous request for insurance on a lost shipment may find the lawyer for the former suggesting that the jury has to decide whether to reward the smaller company's sloppiness and inattention to detail. To anticipate slightly, *both* lawyers will be doing this, so that the case is inevitably about which of the norms invoked by counsel

---

[26] Dennis M. Patterson, "Law's Pragmatism: Law as Practice and Narrative," *Virginia Law Review* 76 (1990): 937, 983.

to structure the case is the more "powerful" or "important," as well as about "what happened."

Third, the story should not contain internal contradictions: the defendant cannot claim to have been in his mother's house in Chicago and in his brother's house in Boston at the same time.[27] Somewhat more complex are motivational inconsistencies such as those manifested in this story used by Binder and Bergman as an example:

> I was in the back part of the corner grocery store about 9 P.M.—they were getting ready to close. I was trying to decide what flavor yoghurt to buy when I heard a voice up front say, "Stay calm and I won't shoot. Just give me all your cash." I thought there was a robbery; I got very scared, but I decided it might be very important if I could identify the robber. I walked quietly toward the front of the store, next to one of the grocery shelves. As I walked, I got out a pencil and a piece of paper and wrote down what the robber and the clerk said, but later I lost the piece of paper. I can remember it anyway, just about word for word. Within about thirty seconds I was five feet from the robber, to his side and a little behind him. By looking out from in back of the shelf, I got a good look at his profile. I just stared at him the whole time he was there. Just before he left the cash register area, he fired a shot. I couldn't tell if it hit the clerk. Then the robber ran toward the back of the store, on the other side of the shelves I was standing behind. I immediately chased him and yelled at him to stop, but he kept running and I didn't see which way he went after he got out the back door. I know I'd recognize him if I ever saw him again.[28]

Here there is an inconsistency between the way the actor acts during a relatively short period of time, first claiming to be scared ("I got very scared") and then acting recklessly ("I immediately chased him . . ."), *and* inconsistencies with generalizations about the way people usually act ("As I walked, I got out a pencil and a piece of paper and wrote down what the robber and the clerk said . . .").

The theory should also have a kind of coherence that goes beyond lack of internal contradiction. It should avoid episodes that are extraneous, that are unrelated to the central meaning of the story:

> It is also important to consider that since most audiences for stories (e.g., jurors) have not been directly exposed to the events or actions in them, they have little recourse but to base their judgments about the credibility of stories on assessments about story structure. . . . To the extent that these assessments yield ambiguities, the story will be both difficult to interpret and regarded as implausi-

---

[27] This, of course, is not a logical contradiction, unless translated into "I was in my mother's house at a certain time" and "I was not in my mother's house at that time." This requires a premise from science or metaphysics about space and time.

[28] Binder and Bergman, *Fact Investigation*, 136.

ble. . . . The higher the frequency of ambiguities, the more variation there will be in the interpretations of those members of the audience who do make sense of the story. . . . Finally, as the number of ambiguities increases, the chance that the audience will accept the story as it stands as plausible or true decreases.[29]

Thus each detail of the story ought to add something that furthers its central meaning. Otherwise the jury may lose track of this central meaning and, even more dangerous, come to believe that the lawyer needs to prove matters which he believes are immaterial.

Fifth, the story should, to the extent possible, follow the "rule of probability."[30] A theory is superior to others if it portrays persons acting in ways that are consistent with deeply held commonsense beliefs about the way persons "generally and for the most part" act under similar circumstances. Because of the overwhelmingly circumstantial nature of proof at trial, even in cases where there is direct evidence, the trier of fact must inevitably rely on commonsense generalizations when assessing testimony. There is often simply no *reason* to believe that events occurred in a way inconsistent with the way things go, despite the universal belief that surprising things happen all the time. To the extent possible, the lawyer will try to avoid theories, however factually accurate he believes them to be, that ask the jury to accept as true a generally improbable event or action.

Sixth, the theory of the case will also seek to portray the client acting in ways that exhibit good character and the opponent in ways that exhibit bad character. Most "triable" cases depend on witness credibility, and parties are most often witnesses. Parties who are shown to act in a trustworthy manner are most likely to be believed as witnesses. That's fair enough even within the Received View.[31] But evidence suggests that juries are simply reluctant to hand a victory to a person who has acted badly.[32] Jurors may understand the distinction between what Aristotle[33] called compensatory justice and distributive justice, between honoring legally defined rights and honoring moral uprightness, but a theory is superior

---

[29] Bennett and Feldman, *Reconstructing Reality in the Courtroom*, 68. The authors' empirical investigations using simulated situations tended to confirm the assertions in the text.

[30] Louis Nizer, *My Life in Court* (Garden City, N.Y.: Doubleday, 1961), 9–13. Aristotle's advice to the dramatist is probably the most extreme version: "A probable impossibility is to be preferred to an improbable possibility." Of course, a dramatist does not have to worry about the presentation of evidence after the play. See chapter 6, below.

[31] The law of evidence distinguishes between evidence offered on witness credibility and on general character to act this way or that in the world, but at trial the two inevitably merge.

[32] See chapter 5, below.

[33] Aristotle, *Nicomachean Ethics* 1131a–1132b: 122–28.

to the extent that it relieves jurors of the normative dissonance produced by injury of the virtuous and vindication of the wicked.

Seventh, the theory should also be supported by admissible, credible, and ethically presentable evidence. The rules of evidence may preclude the presentation of strong evidence that suggests one version of events rather than another.[34] One theory, but not another, may rely on testimony given by the opposing party or a witness aligned with the opposing party, thus virtually eliminating issues of witness credibility. On the other hand, an extremely persuasive theory of the case, immune to successful attack, may be precluded by a client's resigned statement, "Well, it just didn't happen that way."[35] Once those words are spoken, by virtue of the operation of the ethical rules I will discuss below, legal creativity receives a shock from which it cannot easily recover.

Eighth, the theory of the case must anticipate the opposing party's positions and attempt to blunt the power of his or her theory and theme. The "truth" presented by each party's theory is always already a *comparative* truth: it has been "chosen" because of its normative superiority over the *particular* theory that the party anticipates his or her opponent's presenting.[36] Somewhat similarly, a theory should not "open the door to" (render relevant) evidence that weakens the moral appeal of the case or portrays the client as untrustworthy. These are two of the ways in which the basic narrative contains game-theoretical features—in both cases what appears to be a simple factual narrative of what occurred has actually been chosen, in part, to anticipate and neutralize the expected evidentiary and normative strengths of the opponent. Of course, each party is shooting at a moving target, in that his opponent is engaging in exactly the same enterprise, and, in fact, anticipating what he is likely to anticipate and move to counter, and so on into potential infinity.

Finally, in a way I illustrate more concretely below in chapter 4, each theory of the case implicitly invites the trier of fact to determine *what mode of social ordering is appropriate for this case*, a clearly "metalevel" practical judgment about the problematic situation that has led to the

---

[34] See Robert P. Burns, "A Lawyer's Truth: Notes for a Moral Philosophy of Litigation Practice," *Journal of Law and Religion* 3 (1985): 229, 258–63 (on the factors that create a discontinuity between actual events and the picture that emerges during trial). See Robert Burns, Thomas Geraghty, and Steven Lubet, *Exercises and Problems in Professional Responsibility* (Notre Dame, Ind.: National Institute for Trial Advocacy, 1994), 123–30.

[35] The latter, by the way, suggests the special difficulties in defending fully innocent people. Lies may be tailored to the needs of the moment, while truth has a stubbornness that may defy widely shared notions of probability.

[36] Bennett and Feldman, *Reconstructing Reality in the Courtroom*, 111–13, illustrate the principle through the choices made by defense counsel in the Angela Davis case.

trial. This is one form of what Bernard S. Jackson has called the "narrativization of pragmatics,"[37] the structuring of a story so as to encode a normative judgment. As we will see, the very way a story is told can suggest that a situation ought to be considered from a moral point of view, as a strictly legal case, or as an opportunity for political reconstitution of a community.

Unfortunately, these criteria for the choice of theories[38] of the case are incommensurable. A morally compelling story may raise serious issues of legal sufficiency. It may have to rely on self-serving testimony from the client, rather than evidence from unbiased sources. It may suffer from "inferential gaps" for which there is the weakest of circumstantial evidence. A story that is well supported by credible evidence, on the other hand, may rely on the jury's following closely a legal rule that does not easily square with common sense, or believing a third party witness with whom the client would not want to be associated. A story that portrays the client as acting virtuously may present him as too good to believe. And so on. What deepens the difficulty of the situation is that virtually all the evidence must be chosen and shaped in order to support a dominant conception, at the risk of the ambiguity which spells implausibility.[39] You usually can't have it both ways. A lawyer must rely on an imaginative anticipation of how a possible theory will "play out" in the distinctive context of the trial, guided by something like a dramatic sense.[40] Once the choice is made, it must be rigorously followed at the risk of incoherence and a lack of persuasiveness. Much of the trial lawyer's struggle, in fact, is to keep testimony from squirming into the watery ambiguity that almost seems to be the natural level it seeks. Without a single factual theory and theme to which to relate the testimony, the struggle is hopeless. Since it is ultimately inevitable that the "squirming facts exceed the squamous mind,"[41] only a single theory will yield anything that looks like "a case."

It is easy to be cynical about the lawyer's tasks in this pretrial enterprise. This cynicism is undeserved. From a broader perspective, a lawyer is pro-

[37] Bernard S. Jackson, *Law, Fact, and Narrative Coherence* (Merseyside, England: Deborah Charles, 1988), 161.

[38] I have spoken here as if theories were each homogeneous, such that only one choice had to be made. In fact, each general narrative presents an enormous number of "subsidiary" choices: choices among descriptions, characterizations, and interpretations.

[39] See chapter 5, below.

[40] See Francis Fergusson, *The Idea of a Theater. A Study of Ten Plays: The Art of Drama in Changing Perspective* (Princeton: Princeton University Press, 1949), 236. Fergusson uses the unhappy term "histrionic sensibility" for this feel.

[41] Wallace Stevens, "Connoisseur of Chaos," in *The Collected Poems of Wallace Stevens* (New York: Knopf, 1954), 215.

viding an indispensable service[42] in mediating among the perceived needs and desires of the client and public norms embedded in commonsense morality, in the official norms lodged in the jury instructions, and in our sense of public identity and purpose. These mediations are indispensable for the achievement of justice,[43] certainly in a pluralistic society, but also, I suspect, in any decent society. They move in all directions, something that the somewhat strategic cast of my description here may cloak: what a client may claim is also modified, usually in the processes of counseling and negotiation, by the results of his lawyer's understanding his "best case" in the ways I have suggested. Societies are surely imaginable in which private and public norms and interests are sought to be made fully continuous with each other. When Hannah Arendt complained that Plato wholly eliminates politics, which assumes an irreducible diversity and discontinuity of perspective and purpose, from the *Republic*, she is pointing to this kind of Order in his "city in words." This is not our society, nor do we want it to be.

---

[42] Academics (in particular) are sometimes tempted to feel superior to such professional labors. They should not do so. Those labors serve our needs, which are often the deepest we have—the need for a social order, among others. If those needs are essentially served by some activity or institution, such as a profession, then there is nowhere to go to be superior to that institution, except by climbing out of oneself. The only decent direction in which to move is into thought about how things might be otherwise, thoughts in which one is quite likely to be joined, indeed led, by members of the profession itself.

Bernard Williams, "Professional Morality and Its Dispositions," in *The Good Lawyer: Lawyers' Roles and Lawyers' Ethics*, ed. David Luban (Totowa, N.J.: Rowman & Allanheld, 1983), 269.

[43] Hanna Pitkin, "Justice: On Relating Private and Public," in *Hannah Arendt: Critical Essays*, ed. Louis P. Hinchman and Sandra K. Hinchman (Albany: State University of New York Press, 1994), 261. Milner Ball puts it this way, invoking the notion of the "story of origins," the historical narratives of the constitutional events that define the nation:

A lawyer forms the story of his client, first for himself and then for judges and juries, by discerning and emphasizing or deemphasizing given elements under the influence of earlier courtroom stories. Story is the way a lawyer understands, makes sense of, and presents a case. Courts arrive at a decision about a case by replaying it in their minds in search of the fit of its parts and the fit of the whole with prior stories. Story is the way courts come to and explain judgments.

In this process, the story of origins may be more or less near the surface but is always controlling, a possibility that can be explored by understanding that the juridical telling and connecting of stories is a kind of typology. The typological enterprise requires the story of beginning for its point of departure and for a continuing basis of interpretive selection.

Milner S. Ball, *The Promise of American Law* (Athens: University of Georgia Press, 1981), 23.

The lawyer's attempt to construct a case in which the private goals of the client can be defended or advanced has effects both on the client's goals and on the legal language and culture in which those goals are enmeshed. This is true because "our ends are themselves inextricably situated in a rhetorical medium, and are constitutionally shaped by this medium. Our ends are not merely pursued rhetorically, they are themselves constituted rhetorically. . . . Pursuit of the end is 'always already' embedded in the medium of its pursuit: discernment of what I want is inseparable from the words and manner of expression in which I express what I want. . . ."[44] Concretely, a lawyer's imagining the case that can be constructed in support of one or another of the client's goals may lead, through the process of legal counseling, to a reformulation of those goals; this may happen in a number of different ways. The weakness of that case may well convince the lawyer and then perhaps the client that his initial goals should be reexamined in light of the strong countervailing social or legal norms that spell weakness. This may be true because those norms may in a sense be the client's own. Difficulties in "making his case" may reveal to him that he has unreflectively tried to "make himself an exception."[45] Or the client's reevaluation may be more instrumental. His chances of success may simply be too low. In either case the client and the lawyer have been somewhat transformed:

> Drawn into public life by personal need, fear, ambition, and interest, we are there forced to acknowledge the power of others and appeal to their standards. We are forced to find or create a common language of purposes and aspirations, not merely to clothe our private outlook in public disguise, but to become aware ourselves of its public meaning. We are forced, as Joseph Tussman has put it, to transform "I want" into "I am entitled to," a claim that becomes negotiable by public standards. In the process we learn to think about the standards themselves, about our stake in the existence of standards, of justice, of our community, even of our opponents and enemies in the community; so that afterwards we are changed.[46]

But the opposite movement is at least as important. The consistent and willful, though thankfully often unsuccessful, effort to stretch, even manipulate, the language of moral, political, and legal evaluation to accommodate private interest and purpose has important benign consequences. This effort

---

[44] Ronald Beiner, *Political Judgment* (London: Methuen, 1983), 95.
[45] Hannah Arendt, *The Life of the Mind* (New York: Harcourt Brace Jovanovich, 1978), 188.
[46] Pitkin, "Justice," 261–88.

ensures, as nothing else could, that congruence between the terms and assumptions of our language and the conditions of social and natural reality that is essential to the survival of a language of justice and the culture it enacts. . . . For in the law, our language of facts and law is constantly being tested against the real world, against common sentiment, against cases and argument, and remade in light of what is discovered. This means that the law is a way in which the community defines itself, not once and for all, but over and over, and in the process it educates itself about its own character and the nature of the world.[47]

The consistent attempts on the part of lawyers, however willful, to construct a case in aid of private goals serve "to convert the raw human materials of greed and fear and the desire for power, and the like, into questions presented in the language that we maintain," and thus to "preserve and improve a language of description, value, and reason—a culture of argument—without which it would be impossible even to ask the questions . . . about the nature of justice in general or about what is required in a particular case."[48] Lawyers force judges and juries continuously to redefine the range of applicability, and so the meaning of legal rules in the context of the most compelling description of individual needs and the most pointed arguments that those rules *cannot* reasonably have been intended to frustrate *these* needs. This effort, however partial, serves as a bulwark against the process of ossification of overgeneralized public norms that ham-fistedly frustrate important private interests. These processes are going on in literally millions of conversations between lawyers and clients, all of which take place in the long shadow of the trial.

The lawyer's pretrial task is the development of possible theories of the case and a final choice among them. The theory has both "narrative" and "logical" elements. The narrative will be an artificially definite account of events, designed to achieve the result sought by the client, chosen in light of a set of often incommensurable rhetorical strengths. Each lawyer will construct a case that appeals to the most powerful norms with which he can plausibly, and consistent with the trial's constitutive rules, relate his case. *Each* lawyer is doing this. In some cases, there will in fact be relatively little range of choice; in others there may be a much larger range. That choice will be made in anticipation of the distinctive linguistic practices of the trial itself.[49] It is to those practices that I now turn.

[47] James Boyd White, "The Ethics of Argument: Plato's *Gorgias* and the Modern Lawyer," *University of Chicago Law Review* 50 (1983): 882.

[48] Ibid., 880.

[49] It will also be made in light of the constitutive rules of the trial, both ethical and evidentiary. I will address those in chapter 3.

Trial Practices

Opening Statement

The first step to a more adequate version of the opening statement is to understand that it presents to the juror what the evidence will *show*, not what the evidence will *be*. As such it is a complete "God's-eye" narrative of the events that have led to the trial. The narrative is "omniscient" in that it includes, as episodes or facts, truths which could be reached only by inference from circumstantial evidence, most prominently, intentions, beliefs, and other states of mind. So long as these are stated as mere episodes in a narrative, and the *reasons* why the jury should conclude that these actually occurred are not marshaled in argumentative form, the lawyer will not be "arguing," the most important legal restriction on opening statement. The opening has an "argument," but it is like the argument of a novel, deriving from all the sources of plausibility that pure narratives can have.

In triable cases, the battle for the jury's imagination that begins with opening statement is not simply an argument about "what happened." It is a battle about the frameworks within which events should be understood—whether, for example, through the lens of traditional morality, on the one hand, or that of psychiatry, on the other. It is a battle about what kind of "social ordering" the situation demands: legalistic, moral, bureaucratic, political. At another level, the opening invokes social and cultural values embedded in authoritative "scripts" and invites the jury to finish the story.

What is a story? Paul Ricoeur emphasizes the way the individual episodes of a story power the overall structure: "A story describes a sequence of actions and experiences of a certain number of characters, whether real or imaginary. These characters are represented in situations which change . . . [to] which they react. These changes, in turn, reveal hidden aspects of the situations and the characters, giving rise to a new predicament which calls for thought or action or both. The response to this predicament brings the story to its conclusion."[50] Or again, "a story is a detailed, chronological narration of interrelated events with a beginning point, connecting points and a termination point. It normally focuses on substantively critical events and surrounds such events with details of happenings that came before and after."[51] Opening statement does its work

---

[50] Paul Ricoeur, "The Narrative Function," in Ricoeur, *Hermeneutics and the Human Sciences*, ed. and trans. John B. Thompson (Cambridge: Cambridge University Press, 1981), 277.

[51] Binder and Bergman, *Fact Investigation*.

by creating a "vivid continuous dream"[52] in the minds of the jurors, something that creates the conditions for moral judgment.[53]

We must appreciate the *distinctive* nature of the narrative told in opening statement. It is quite different from other stories.[54] For now, let me mention three central features. Perhaps the most important is that it takes place in a legal proceeding. Problematic situations find their way to trial only if judgment is necessary. The inevitability of legal judgment and subsequent action demands that the story contain a single or at least a dominant significance. Normally there is no need for human beings to be so peremptory as to assign a dominant significance to a human event. Many works of fiction derive their richness from the ambiguities of human meaning that are woven into their narratives. By contrast, all theories of the case suffer from "legalism,"[55] the assignment of some single dominant meaning to the situation, whether or not that meaning is the one which the *legal* norms suggest should be the most significant.

Second, since different legal consequences may follow from different stories, and the constitutive rules of the trial (ethics and evidence) allow for a significant measure of attorney choice,[56] the stories told have a further pragmatic or purposeful element to them. In this context, *facts are purposes.*[57] This is, as we have seen, because defined and different consequences flow from the likely judgments suggested by different stories. The parties who control the "objectives of the representation" are usually most interested in those consequences, not in other measures of narrative quality.

Third, and in some tension with the foregoing, the stories told at trial are disciplined by the commonsense belief that "something happened."[58] That "something" is necessarily something definite, something determinate, and it appears[59] that its determinate reality is the criterion, or at

---

[52] Gardner, *The Art of Fiction*, 31 (speaking of the basic technique of the novel).

[53] See chapter 6, below.

[54] Much of the recent explosion of literature on narrative in law, especially written from a literary perspective, fails to appreciate these distinctive qualities. I believe that a good deal can be learned about trials from the study of literary forms, such as novel and drama, so long as the distinctive differences of the trial are kept in mind. For a representative selection, see Peter Brooks and Paul Gewirtz, *Law's Stories: Narrative and Rhetoric in the Law* (New Haven: Yale University Press, 1996).

[55] Judith Shklar, *Legalism: Law, Morals, and Political Trials* (Cambridge: Harvard University Press, 1964; reprint, 1986).

[56] See chapter 3, below.

[57] This is true for both the "ultimate facts" that are the legal elements and the normatively significant suggested conclusions.

[58] Paul Ricoeur, *The Reality of the Historical Past* (Milwaukee: Marquette University Press, 1984) (on the difference between history and fiction).

[59] See chapter 6, below.

least one criterion, by which any story told at trial is to be judged. Derivatively, and put with deliberate vagueness, this means that the "quality" of the real story presented at trial has, *at least in part*, to do with its relationship with the rest of the trial, including its evidentiary phase. To put it baldly, *a lawyer can't just tell the best story.*[60] The opening statement has a performative dimension: it is a promise. The attorney implicitly promises the jury that he or she will supply reliable evidence to support the God's-eye story which is told in opening. It is one of the standard rhetorical devices of closing argument to suggest that an advocate has "broken his promise," thus invoking against him the deeply significant morality of the trial itself.

So much for the form of opening statement. What about its contents? But we already know the answer to that question. For the opening statement is precisely the time in the trial when each lawyer presents, as a "vivid, continuous dream," his or her narrative theory of the case. The story told in opening statement must achieve the optimum integration of the factors that serve as the criteria for the choice of the theory of the case. It will do this in a way that expresses or reveals the complex norm, inseparable from the details of the story he tells, and on which he relies. That norm, not otherwise expressible, is what gives the case life, allows it to "hang together," to "ring true."

One way to suggest how these different issues can be embedded in what are, after all, only simple stories is to recount an edited version of two opening statements in a murder case tried quite a number of years ago, along with my commentary, written shortly after the trial. This forms chapter 4, below. The commentary tries to articulate precisely the significance of the major features of each of the opening statements in the full context of the trial. What was apparent to me at the time was the ways in which these competing narratives were actually arguments made across a number of levels. The openings said in the language of storytelling that the most important issues in the case were not narrowly factual at all. Rather, those issues forced the judge to decide what *kind* of event had occurred and, more important, what form of social ordering[61] was appropriate to the case. These pragmatic "metaissues" would be presented to the court in the language of "fact-finding," but they actually required a decision that was truthful to the situation in a much richer way.

[60] This is worth saying because of a tendency among some investigators to draw conclusions about the trial from findings about "stand-alone" storytelling exercises in which, for example, some audiences cannot, under some circumstances, reliably distinguish between true and false stories.

[61] Lon Fuller, "The Forms and Limits of Adjudication," *Harvard Law Review* 92 (1978): 353.

Direct Examination

The storytelling of direct examination stands in stark contrast to that of opening statement. The contrasts are real and important, though not quite for the reasons the Received View would suggest. Direct examination does not provide the "pure data" from which reliable determinations of fact and unsullied judgments of law may be made. It does set a number of the extreme tensions within the trial that are the key to an understanding of its nature. It is the second of the "consciously structured hybrid of languages"[62] that make the trial what it is.

First, the witness is required to testify in the language of perception, a requirement which can be enforced by objections that the witness is offering "conclusions" or "opinions." This makes it relatively harder for the witness to supply a version of events so highly interpreted that it is *impervious* to reinterpretation in light of competing theories of the case. Requiring a witness to recount, to the extent possible, a precise version of his perceptions will produce an account whose meaning is open to honest debate. Memories about perceptions are *less* likely to be products of purposeful reconstruction than are opinions. For example, in the case from which the opening recounted below is taken, the key question concerned the defendant's state of mind at the time she killed a young child. A policeman who had arrived on the scene shortly after the child's death continually sought to testify to "what apparently happened," and so to present a version of events that was relatively comprehensible from a commonsense standpoint. When he was forced to testify to what he recalled perceiving, a more bizarre and incomprehensible version of the defendant's actions emerged. Indeed, in an example of an aspect of the trial that is pervasive, the contrast between what he wanted to say "apparently happened" and what he actually saw and heard starkly demonstrated how bizarre the defendant's behavior had been. The requirement of testimony in the language of perception, described above, keeps the direct examination *available* for the whole range of its possible meanings, not merely the meaning the witness wishes to give it. In one sense, then, the Received View's view of direct examination is correct. Direct does take place under conditions that allow for the understanding of the case in light of norms other than those embraced by the witness. Where it goes wrong is in supposing that direct is designed to accommodate only the norms of pure factual accuracy, on the one hand, and the Rule of Law, on the other.

[62] Mikhail M. Bakhtin, *The Dialogic Imagination: Four Essays by M. M. Bakhtin*, ed. Michael Holquist, trans. Caryl Emerson and Michael Holquist (Austin: University of Texas Press, 1981).

Not only must the witness testify in the language of perception, but he must also testify, in the main, in answer to nonleading questions. This does not, we will see, mean that there is no art to the presentation of direct examination, but it does have some significant consequences. First, even a well-prepared witness has to *choose*, throughout the examination, what words to use in the description he gives. How he puts it tells the jury who he is to such an important extent that the formal evidentiary rules prohibiting "evidence of character" are almost trivial. Even testimony in the language of perception involves perceptual *judgments* and not merely the offering of sense-data.[63] Certainly when the witness is allowed to offer an opinion, but also when he offers a perception (sometimes even without cross-examination), the jury can understand any gaps between how he *wants* to put it and how he is *justified* in putting it.

Direct examination has what might be called a standard structure, though it is subject to many variations. First, the witness is introduced, providing personal background—relatively more in the case of parties, relatively less on the part of others. This introduction is both ubiquitous and, from the standpoint of the Received View, indefensible. It supplies officially prohibited "character evidence," going to both credibility and propensity to act in the world in this way or that. It violates the fundamental principle that a witness is not to be accredited before he is discredited. It is, however, universally accepted, so long as kept within very fluid limits. In a civil rights case I tried, for example, the plaintiff had been publicly charged with infractions that were particularly humiliating, charges the jury eventually found to have been racially motivated. His introduction to the jury showed him working his way up from poverty in public housing, doing combat duty in Vietnam, and, probably most important, rising in the ranks to positions of public authority in the United States Army. That introduction had significance radiating through the case in a large number of *different* ways. It is only after the witness is introduced that the scene is set and the story told.

There is considerable art to setting the scene and telling the story, only a few aspects of which I mention here. The process involves devices that, in the full context of the trial, allow the truth to appear in a contested public context, a result which sensitive observers have understood to be enormously difficult, demanding art and, yes, artifice.[64] As is true with all the elements of the trial, these devices must be evaluated in their full rhetorical context.

---

[63] In Peirce's famous example, we *see* an azalea, that is, an already-interpreted perception, not merely a pattern of shapes and colors.

[64] Arendt, "Truth and Politics," 250–51.

One set of devices clusters around *simplification*.[65] The direct examiner understands her theory, her theme, and the requirements of legal adequacy. Though the use of nonleading questions makes it difficult to exclude any detail the witness believes important,[66] the examining lawyer can ask questions that suppress irrelevant detail and encourage the provision of detail which contributes to the case. In the words of a widely used trial advocacy text by Steven Lubet: "Ask what it contributes to the persuasiveness of your story. Does it supply a reason for the way that someone acted? Does it make an important fact more or less likely? Does it affect the credibility of a witness? Does it enhance the moral value of your story? If all of these answers are negative, you're looking at clutter."[67] Simplification allows almost each bit of evidence to add something to the case offered, eventually, we will see, increasing the intellectual forces within the tension that the trial creates. Notice that, in Lubet's account, evidence can make a contribution to the factual theory of the case *or* the credibility of witnesses *or* the moral significance of the story told. Simplification also embodies the lawyer's crucial determination about what to make an issue of. This form of simplification counsels the exclusion of what Lubet calls unprovables (facts that may well be true, but which may damage a witness's credibility because not capable of convincing proof), implausibles (facts that may well be true, but which share that continually disturbing feature of the real world, its unpredictability), impeachables (facts that may well be true, but of which there is strong contrary evidence), and door openers (facts that bestow arguable legal relevance to otherwise irrelevant material). So, for example, counsel in the murder case described below excluded any mention of a defendant's postarrest abuse at the hands of the police, because it did not contribute to his theory of the case, it was unprovable by physical evidence, and the client had not immediately complained about it. In "Rockfield" at least,[68] police witnesses would likely be believed in the inevitable denial, an outcome likely to damage a client's credibility far beyond the particular issue.

Simplification allows *each* lawyer to present only that evidence which bears directly on the core issues in the case, and to present an enormous

---

[65] Lubet, *Modern Trial Advocacy*. Lubet's book is easily the most comprehensive discussion of the rhetorical devices of the trial.

[66] This intrusion of the irrelevant itself has a function, that of reminding the trier of fact that it is the real world which is being discussed. The real world resists the sheer coherence of art, as it resists any other form of unifying intelligence. Lonergan, *Insight*, 590–94 (there is an "empirical residue" remaining after any intelligent grasp for which no form of abstract intelligibility fully accounts).

[67] Lubet, *Modern Trial Advocacy*, 23.

[68] I have read that is no longer true in all American cities. See generally Morgan Cloud, "The Dirty Little Secret," *Emory Law Journal* 43 (1994): 1311 (on police perjury).

amount of evidence that does so bear in a relatively short period of time. This is one of the reasons, again, that almost all the authorities warn against multiple or alternative factual theories. The shaping and organizing process is difficult enough in relation to one theory. It is probably impossible and certainly confusing when directed by alternative theories.

The other set of devices clusters around the *structure* of the direct examination.[69] These devices, too, serve to heighten the significance of the examination for the issues before the court, issues that are themselves chosen from a limited range of possible issues. The rules of "primacy and recency" counsel beginning and ending the narrative with a memorable and dramatic point. Apposition allows for sequential questioning on matters where a causal connection is suggested. Significant events can be repeated. It is possible to expand and contract the duration of the examination to suggest a slower or faster pace of events or observations in the real world. Questioning can follow a topical rather than a strictly chronological order.

These last two devices raise both ethical and epistemological questions that cannot be answered until considered in the context of the entire trial. Is it a distortion of the truth to "slow down" the time in which a witness had an opportunity to observe an assailant, for example, by asking a large number of questions each of which seeks only a small bit of information? Such a strategy may consume ten or fifteen minutes in describing a five-second event, imparting the impression of a significant opportunity to observe. By the use of topical organization, rather than purely chronological organization, a lawyer may question a harried emergency room physician only about the tasks she performed for a single patient, the plaintiff, so as to impart an impression of a careful and systematic attention to the plaintiff's case.[70] In general the lawyer here is not asking, "Did it happen this way?" She is asking, "Can the witness's memories and convictions stand this interpretation within the ethical, evidentiary, and rhetorical context of the trial?"

There is nothing automatic about the translation from the real-world event to the presentation in the courtroom. Most certainly, it is not the case that the most unrehearsed or spontaneous presentation is for that reason the most true to the underlying event. Nor is it the case that the sequential presentation of the witnesses's unadorned perceptions, which are in any case almost infinitely divisible, Zeno-like, in response to potential questions, will convey the meaning of the encounter. Indeed, social scientific studies of memory suggest that our recollection ("re-collection,"

---

[69] Lubet, *Modern Trial Advocacy*, 25 ff.

[70] The example belongs to James McElhaney, *Trial Notebook*, 2d ed. (Chicago: American Bar Association, 1987), 239.

"re-membering") of an event is a feeling-tinged dominant gestalt around which even the most sincere attempt at accurate memory selects details to support.[71] In the case of the assailant, the victim may have gotten a *very good* look at her attacker. In the case of the ER physician, the attention she gave to the plaintiff may well have been thoroughly focused and professional, despite the intervening demands on her time. In both cases, *some* omission of possible detail is inevitable, and the meaning is in the details. There is an enormous range of possible accounts that could be given of the two events, and the choice of inclusion or exclusion is almost infinite.

There is no neutral way in which language can simply mirror accurately an important real-world event. Any account will be given sequentially, and the "information" it contains will be doled out to the listener piece after piece. A human encounter that lasted a second may be enormously complex. A longer encounter may be simpler. We have no access to such an encounter except through description and narrative, the length and structure of which can in no simple, or pictorial, sense be "congruent" with the event it narrates. The medium *cannot* be the message. Our access to the human events on which trials focus is, as with all historical events, "mediated by meaning." The task of the linguistic practices of the trial, its "consciously structured hybrid of languages," working together, is to convey that meaning.

Direct examination, then, conveys the witness's understanding of the meaning of a past event, embedded in the perceptual judgments he makes. The rhetorical practices of the lawyer serve mainly to allow the witness to convey that meaning effectively. Pretrial interviewing and witness preparation usually allow the witness to sharpen his understanding of the meaning of the event and structure his testimony to convey it. It must be the witness's conviction that ultimately structures the testimony, or, as we will see shortly, the testimony will collapse under cross-examination.

In short, direct examination provides testimony in a much stronger sense than is implicit in the Received View.[72] The jury inevitably hears not the report of the imprinted sense-data of a witness but his interpretation of what occurred. This makes credibility in a deeper sense much more central to the trial than the Received View suggests. Likewise, this makes the perceived moral character[73] of witnesses more important. What direct examination provides is the witness's judgment about the meaning of a past event expressed in a way (the language of perception) that allows for

---

[71] Bruner, *Acts of Meaning*, 58–59.

[72] C.A.J. Coady, *Testimony: A Philosophical Study* (Oxford: Clarendon Press, 1992), 133–77.

[73] Alan Donagan, *The Theory of Morality* (Chicago: University of Chicago Press, 1977), 52–57. Donagan calls these "second level" moral judgments, judgments about persons, not acts.

honest debate about that meaning. As we will see shortly, the meaning of the witness's perceptions may be reinterpreted in a number of ways.

The presentation of testimony at a high level of particularity does not remove interpretation but rather allows for more effective reinterpretation. It also has another very important effect. It pushes the level of inquiry downward, to a level of particularity, which, I argue later, is the natural home of *moral* evaluation: "in practical life, particular facts count more than generalizations."[74] The details supplied on direct examination are exactly the sorts of details that we are hungry for when we are making important moral decisions in daily life. They invoke a set of familiar norms (usually echoing the narrative ethics of opening statement) that may be quite distant from the official norms found in the instructions. By focusing so much of the trial on the sorts of events about which we feel generally competent to judge in the world of ordinary life (the "life world"), we legitimize the ordinary moral values and judgments of judge or jury. This simple fact is of enormous significance to the understanding of the trial.

Perhaps an artist could listen with the greatest care to the witness and create a direct examination that precisely manifested the significance of the witness's account of what occurred. But art it would be. It would require first an utterly true understanding of what the witness was saying and then the construction of an examination that, with refinement and precision, manifested exactly that chaste understanding. We do not ask this of our attorneys, and with good reason. The necessary gifts are too rare, and the enforcement of such an approach is so utterly impossible that it might prove the greatest misfortune to have an attorney who actually embraced this ideal. And even these considerations assume that the understanding of our artist *is* true.

We take a different tack in the law. We impose significant evidentiary and ethical restrictions on attorneys and then allow them, within those strictures, to construct the most favorable possible narrative the witness can provide. There is, of course, more. The direct examination must be constructed with the anticipated cross-examination and closing argument in mind. Thus the process of selection and simplification must be defensible. The omission of significant details is so distorting that it cannot help but be resented by the jury if explored on cross-examination. Thus the examination is the most favorable possible construction of the key events that the constitutive rules and the anticipated deconstruction in cross and argument will allow. It has a *normative* basis: the appeal to or invocation of the meaning of an event that is the most compelling in light of the most powerful norms available to the attorney.

---

[74] Aristotle, *Rhetoric* 1392a12–18, trans. Beiner, in Beiner, *Political Judgment*, 93.

If the devices of the adversary trial are working, the final picture of the key events that emerges will bear some resemblance to the version that might have been presented through the utterly fair questioning of our witness by our artist-lawyer. But not quite. The picture of events that emerges from the adversary trial will turn out to be far more helpful. Likewise, the peculiar rules that apply to direct examination serve purposes different from and far more important than those suggested by the Received View. Direct examinations do not function primarily to provide uninterpreted raw data, Aristotelian prime matter, for the imprint of probabilistic generalizations and official norms. In other words, testimony in the language of perception does have important functions, but they are different from and more interesting than those the Received View postulates.

When a witness tells a story "in his own words," he reveals his own identity,[75] which is important in the trial for many reasons. He begins to uncover the tension, one of the most important of many, between what he *wants* to say and what he *can plausibly* say within ordinary language and the life world in which he and the jury share a common sense. The artifice that lawyers bring even to this least adorned of trial exercises is shaped not by the question "How exactly did it happen and in what order?" Rather, the lawyer asks, "Can this witness's testimony support the interpretation I wish to put on it?" That "support" or lack of it comes in many ways and from the combined significance of all the evidence.

Cross-Examination

The methods of cross-examination stand in stark contrast to the heavily characterized, fully God's-eye, narrative of opening statement and the apparently simple narrative of direct. It is the most prominent of the deconstructive devices of the trial. What opening and direct examination build up, cross-examination can destroy or profoundly reinterpret.

In any of its forms, the heart of cross-examination is the sequencing of short, clear, crafted statements that cannot plausibly be denied and which, in sequence, suggest an inference that supports, in one way or another, the cross-examiner's theory or theme of the case. Cross-examination "questions" are statements. They do not seek information[76] but rather

---

[75] Occasionally a witness can "fake sincerity," but the practices of the trial make it very difficult.

[76] Except such information that the lawyer needs to create yet another deconstructive line of statements. In the United States, where pretrial discovery in criminal cases is very limited, cross-examination must serve this limited discovery function.

serve to remind the jury of aspects of the truth of the situation that the witness has chosen not to reveal. Of course, this has significance for the jury's assessment of the facts and also of the witness. Questions must be short because the assumption is that the witness disagrees globally with the examiner, *wants* to disagree. The questions are like watertight compartments on a ship: the examiner can lose one or two without total disaster's engulfing him. Thus the attorney must keep each question limited to achieve damage control. Questions must be clear because the jury will and should hold ambiguity against the lawyer, and any ambiguity may fairly be exploited by a witness who, by the time cross comes around, is committed to a story now under attack. They must be as crafted as possible because they are designed to suggest a conclusion that the witness will resist.[77] But the craft must not compromise the last feature of the cross-examination question: that the witness simply not be able plausibly to deny the statement that each question contains. Finally, the entire purpose of the sequence of questions is to suggest to the jury a conclusion consistent with the examiner's theory of the case.

The key to effective cross-examination is control. In contrast to direct examination, the lawyer is permitted in cross-examination to proceed in leading fashion. Control is central because of the purpose of cross-examination. Its premise is that the witness (or the examining lawyer) has made a more or less conscious decision to testify in a certain manner, that he has cut into the great booming, buzzing confusion of his own relevant experience and *decided* to testify in one certain way. He has decided which details to include and which to exclude. He has decided, within the limits on the form of examination described above, to describe a scene one way and not another, to tell a story one way and not another. He has told his story in such a way as to obscure the *real* significance of aspects of the story. He has failed to describe spatial and temporal relations in a full way. He has presented a story that has the appearance of completeness, that is "autopoetic"—it appears to fully represent the reality about which he seeks to testify. But it is not complete; or at any rate the purpose of cross-examination is to demonstrate that it is not. After a successful direct, the deconstructive shock of an effective cross-examination can be stunning.

While opening statement and direct examination are two different forms of constructed narrative, cross-examination is the first of the devices by which the trial deconstructs narratives. It is the succession of narrative construction and deconstruction, reconstruction and decon-

---

[77] My own method is first to create a sequence of short, clear, unambiguous, and undeniable propositions and *then* to try to craft them to suggest the partisan conclusion, but without losing clarity, univocity, or deniability.

struction, that lies at the heart of trial discourse. Deconstruction is the last word in the sequence because, I believe, it is rare that a jury will have accepted a complete narrative surrounding the events that have occurred. In a "triable case" there will often be large patches of uncertainty on past events. These patches are filled in by different *sorts* of (1) judgments of probability of purely historical events, (2) moral judgments, and (3) judgments of human and political significance. To anticipate, it is *because* jurors are justified in saying they are unsure (by a degree of probability that is affected by the *normative* judgments concerning the importance of failing to find this rather than that, for this to go undetermined rather than that) that they can take a global moral approach to the case.[78] In a well-tried case, there is often a large swath of this indeterminacy to be resolved, as we will see, through a practical-moral judgment, not a judgment of purely factual probability.

To the extent that jurors feel justified in saying they just don't know what the sequence of movements or the precise meaning of the events was, the jury may move into a sphere where the conscious relationship between factual and normative is undefined, where judgments of fact, of specific personal culpability, and of moral or general public significance relate to one another without full conscious control. Cross-examination can move a jury into this sphere by showing that a witness who has told a lucid, coherent, and complete story has made a series of choices based on more or less self-interested or casual assumptions. Even questions of fact are issues for choice, usually made in an interested way.

Cross-examination can shock a jury into understanding that there exists a series of (often unasked) questions the answers to which will transform the reliability and the meaning of a particular account. It can provide a jury with the experience of a radical reconceptualization of an account of what occurred, reminding them that, finally, they may rely only on their own assessment of what happened and how it should be judged. Ultimately, they must depend on their own insight and reflective judgment.

I now describe in the most compressed way some of the devices that a cross-examiner may use to achieve her deconstructive purposes. Cross-examination may rely on alternative narrative construction. It may go over the same narrative terrain that the witness has traversed, but do so to exhibit the possibility of an alternative inference. This is relatively easy and can be extremely effective. In the murder case recounted below, the cross-examination of the state's attorney who took the defendant's statement consisted in presenting in a coherent order those aspects of the de-

---

[78] This shows the inevitable pervasiveness of Kalven and Zeisel's "liberation hypothesis" in "triable cases." See chapter 5, below.

fendant's statement that portrayed her behavior on the night of the killing as bizarre and disoriented. And just as in direct examination, a cross-examination that is this kind of "positive" examination may rely on simplification and restructuring to suggest alternative possible interpretation.

This can be powerful for a number of reasons. First, the story contained in the examiner's questions has a kind of spartan simplicity, punctuated every few seconds by the witness's admission that each fact is, in fact, the case. Second, it frequently happens that the witness will take the smallest liberties with the facts on direct examination. In a case where there was some dispute about the level of chaos that prevailed in the defendant's home, the state recounted that she lived with "several" unrelated people, when, in fact, the cross revealed that there were eight. In that same murder case, the detective who investigated the case testified that the defendant had told him that she had gotten "angry" at the child, when in fact neither her court-reported statement nor any of the police reports mentioned such a statement.[79] Revealing these small acts of willfulness demonstrates the element of construction in the direct as a whole. Third, and relatedly, it often happens in this sort of cross-examination that the witness will perceive the significance of the alternative story that the lawyer is, in effect, telling by the use of the cross-examination "questions," and will seek to resist it. I recall one case where I repeated back to the witness his own earlier statement that complaining witnesses seemed eager to testify against my client, which he promptly denied, claiming that they were reluctant to get involved, a proposition that supported his interpretation of the case. The impeachment that followed was doubly effective. For if the cross-examination has been well prepared, and the lawyer's statements are really undeniable, often because taken verbatim from a previous statement by the witness,[80] the witness's inevitable concession simply serves to underscore both the willfulness of the witness's original testimony and the significance of that willfulness.

There is an important difference between the language of direct and cross-examination. The nonleading character of the questioning on direct

---

[79] What was the truth of the matter? It may be that the witness remembered such a statement, but then such a memory may have been faulty. It may have been, on the other hand, that the witness's own need to present a coherent account, implicitly an explanation, of the events produced such a memory.

[80] It has always astounded me how willing expert witnesses in particular are to deny categorically statements they themselves have made often in relatively brief reports written shortly before trial when those statements are placed in a context which shows that they may support an alternative opinion. It is a testament to Madison's observation, "As long as the connection subsists between [man's] reason and his self-love, his opinions and his passions will have a reciprocal influence on each other; and the former will be objects to which the latter will attach themselves." *The Federalist*, No. 10 (Madison) (New York: Modern Library, n.d.)

means that the choice of words in the actual testimony is the witness's. On cross-examination the choice of words is that of the lawyer, an in-court actor who has not taken an oath to tell the whole truth. More important, the lawyer's framing of questions is not guided, as with an honest witness, by a recollection of events relatively independent of the rhetorical exigencies of the trial. In this regard, the witness's language of direct embodies a weakness and a strength. The weakness is that it is not highly crafted with an eye to the issues in the case but is constrained by the memory of those "brutally elementary data"[81] which, let us say, a novelist would omit. But this is also its strength, or may be if the witness demonstrates respect for "those things we cannot change at will," so enhancing his credibility. Cross-examination has precisely the opposite strength and weaknesses. It is obviously interested, something that a well-conducted redirect examination can show, and by conducting even the best cross-examinations, the lawyer shows herself a partisan. On the other hand, the cross-examiner has the novelist's advantage of choosing the language of each "question" for full rhetorical effect, subject only to the requirement that the examiner's statements not be subject to plausible deniability.

Sometimes the cross-examiner cannot retell through the witness on the stand the entire story from another perspective but will seek only certain limited admissions that are consistent with an alternative theory and which the witness consciously omitted. Somewhat relatedly, the examiner may multiply, often close to infinity, those things which the witness does not know or did not do. The suggestion, of course, is that the unknown fact, if known, ideally will (if there is other evidence of it) or at least could, radically change the understanding the witness has or the jury should have.

Second, cross-examination can more directly suggest facts or theories that provide explanations other than those suggested on direct examination. It may present to the trier of fact a series of additional facts that change the significance of the story the witness has told. It may show that the perceptual judgments made by the witness, what he saw the events *as*, are analyzable, in the best empiricist traditions, into more atomistic sense-data. Those could have been synthesized in some other way, an alternative perception. The examination may further suggest that this alternative perception was rejected, consciously or unconsciously, because of interests of one sort or another that the witness had in "seeing it his way." For example, a psychiatrist in a criminal case who has noted the defendant's pervasive sadness as a symptom of a borderline personality disorder may be asked whether the defendant was incarcerated at the county

81 Arendt, "Truth and Politics," 239.

jail on the two occasions when she was examined: "It would kinda make you sad to be in jail, huh, Doctor?" The same psychiatrist who testifies that the severity of the defendant's condition was manifested in her unwillingness to talk openly with anyone other than a single female intern may be asked, "Well, teenage girls feel more comfortable speaking with women, no?" More powerfully, the cross-examination may reveal the "other face" of a fact on which the direct examiner has relied. In a civil rights case I tried that addressed, in part, disproportionate discipline imposed on a black police officer, the defendant called a white officer to testify that he had received a similar level of discipline to that imposed on the plaintiff. The friendly cross-examination showed that the discipline in question was imposed after the white officer, alone on the force, voiced support for the plaintiff.

Third, the cross-examination may cast doubt on or qualify the opponent's story. The examiner may ask himself the same question as would the attorney preparing for trial ("If this testimony is true, what else would be true?")[82] and then proceed to show that the consequences are false or implausible. If the defendant used a racial slur in referring to the plaintiff, the plaintiff surely would have mentioned it to a close adviser and counselor. But he didn't. Therefore the slur didn't take place.

Fourth, many of the most important cross-examinations are of witnesses who are also parties or important actors in the real-world events that have led to the trial. Here the most important goal of the cross-examiner can be to allow the jury to see, in apparent qualification of the general principle that the common law trial does not permit examination of a party's character, the kind of person this is. Sometimes this involves simply gaining admissions from the witness about his or her own past actions and omissions in the real-world drama that led up to the trial, relevant perhaps only because they are "part of the story" that demonstrate one or another moral failure. Or parts of the direct examination can be reviewed in ways that show its inherent self-serving implausibility. In what I call the "long cross-examination," typically of a party opponent, the lawyer may simply require the opposing party to perform under circumstances where he is challenged with aspects of a situation he would prefer not to confront. How a person acts when he is not getting his way can be very revealing, especially when what is being challenged is the story he actually tells himself.

Fifth, and somewhat more subtly, the witness can be asked questions the very answers to which reveal relevant dispositions. A policeman who

---

[82] This logic is at least formally valid: If P, then D. But not D. Therefore, not P. This is in contrast to the implicit logic of case *construction* (and all of empirical science).

left a convenience store without paying for cigarettes can be asked whether a store owner might feel reluctant to insist on payment from the police. An affirmative answer involves a marginally helpful admission of fault, while a negative answer demonstrates an unwillingness to see things from another's perspective and a willfulness in the face of the truth that radiates through the case in many ways.

A witness can successfully navigate cross-examination if the factual and moral judgments he brings to the stand are sufficiently *definite* that they enable him to resist the impulse to say what appears advantageous under the shifting rhetorical grounds of cross-examination.[83] This is very difficult for a witness who is a party or who believes in the justice of a party's cause. One of the great strengths of what the trial has become is to provide a context within which a witness is tempted mightily to violate a moral first principle, as applicable in description as in prescription.[84] Put bluntly, and with what may be viewed as a tinge of Victorian moralism, a witness who survives this ordeal appears both credible and decent.

Sixth, there is available to the cross-examiner an entire repertoire of methods of "impeachment," the devices for undermining the credibility of the witness. These will attack his original perception, his memory of the event, his sincerity in swearing to tell the whole truth, the clarity of his mode of expression, and the ways, often subtle, in which these interact with each other. The examiner may draw admissions about the witness's meager opportunity to observe because of lighting, brevity of time, confusion of the circumstances, his own fear, or significant distraction. His memory may be challenged by the examiner's eliciting admissions about

---

[83] This is why it is important to prepare a witness to testify, and why the belief that preparation is mainly a form of distortion is naive. Responsible witness preparation simply allows a witness to present clearly his considered judgments while testifying.

[84] For Kant—and a parallel point could be made about many earlier moral philosophers—the difference between a human relationship uninformed by morality and one so informed is precisely the difference between one in which each treats the other primarily as a means to his or her ends and one in which each treats the other as an end. To treat someone else as an end is to offer them what *I* take to be good reasons for acting in one way rather than another, but to leave it to them to evaluate those reasons. It is to be unwilling to influence another except by reasons which that other he or she judges to be good. It is to appeal to impersonal criteria of the validity of which each rational agent must be his or her own judge. By contrast, to treat someone else as means is to seek to make him or her an instrument for my purposes by adducing whatever influences or considerations will in fact be effective on this or that occasion. The generalizations of the sociology and psychology of persuasion are what I shall need to guide me, not the standards of a normative rationality.

Alasdair MacIntyre, *After Virtue*, 2d ed. (Notre Dame, Ind.: University of Notre Dame Press, 1984), 23–24.

the length of time that has elapsed or the similarity of this incident to many others with which he may be confusing it.

The examiner may question the witness's sincerity by eliciting admissions concerning his affection for a party or his reasons to despise the opposing party. His attitudes toward the racial or ethnic groups to which a party belongs may be exposed. Any prior statements or actions of his that are inconsistent with his trial testimony may be explored. Any errors in his trial testimony, even on inconsequential matters, may be revealed. The witness will be required to reveal any conviction involving false statements or dishonesty, such as perjury, and, in many jurisdictions, any felony convictions in the recent past. In yet other jurisdictions, the witness will be required to admit to *any* previous conduct or statements that may reflect badly on his credibility: basically any false statements he may have made throughout his life.

In all these cases, in the absence of a previous admission, it will be the underlying facts from which these unfavorable conclusions about the witness's credibility may be drawn that will be put to the witness. For now, the jury is simply invited to draw the inference in question. Because there will be *some* reason, some justification for disbelieving any one part of the witness's testimony, the jury may choose to disbelieve any or all of it because of the circumstantial evidence of one sort or another that it is not credible. This is what is meant by the saying of trial lawyers to the effect that there is direct evidence and circumstantial evidence, but the probative force of all evidence is circumstantial.

Often the same persons are both witnesses and parties. Though a different set of rules applies to the impeachment of witnesses than applies to evidence probative of the alleged actions of parties, no jury is likely to distinguish sharply between the credibility of a party as witness and the deservingness of a witness as party. The exclusive moral rule of the relationship between the witness and the jury is one of truthfulness. A party treats the jury decently or not, depending solely on his truthfulness. A jury that believes it was mistreated by a party, prevented from doing its duty, will be inclined to think badly of that party. The jury knows, too, that a person's attitude toward the simple factual truth, his accuracy or fairness, is not a bad indicator of that person's fairness in general, his willingness to subject his own desires and projects to a standard beyond them, a trait that we generally call "decency."

The structure of the trial itself elevates the importance of witness and party credibility. For as the trial progresses through plaintiff's rebuttal case, and sometimes defendant's surrebuttal, parties are limited in presenting evidence that attacks or qualifies. The trial itself easily becomes the moral event to which the judge or jury responds.

Of course, much more could be said about cross-examination. It is one of the most fascinating of the rhetorical arts. But it can fairly be said that its general purpose is to allow the jury to look through the narratives of the witness's direct examination. It is a method to break the selectivity, the willfulness, the manipulativeness that inheres in self-interested story-telling, or perhaps in any story told by men or women. In conjunction with the other devices of the trial, it may serve to reach toward a truth that lies beyond storytelling.

Cross-examination can reveal other possibilities that, once identified, become, in light of all the evidence, more plausible than the one suggested. It may reveal not another factual possibility but a personal reality, in the way in which a witness who is also an important real-world actor performs an important public duty, the duty to tell the truth at trial, where the jury is relying on that truth in a matter of public significance. What a witness takes to be the "whole truth" of a situation says a great deal about who that witness is. When the jury imagines the events that have led up to the trial and casts in that real-world drama the particular people whom they have come to know as witnesses, the significance of the case may well be altered deeply.

The constitutive rules of the trial elevate the importance of a past event. But they cannot elevate the importance, the significance, of that event, which can be reached only through narrative, over the importance of the way witnesses actually tell their stories. For the trier of fact, the undeniable reality is the trial itself. The trial's the thing. The fairness of the way in which witnesses testify is often the actual basis for the jury's judgment. "Juries rule for those they like and trust." What that slogan means, I think, is that juries trust those who have treated them decently and have shown respect for the important task they have, especially under the intentionally difficult and demanding circumstances of cross-examination.

Closing Argument

In opening statement the lawyer provides a full narrative of the events that have brought the case to trial, a God's-eye account. That account has the internal plausibility that comes from structural elements of the story, its consistency with factual and normative commonsense generalizations, and it should invite the jury to finish the story so that the dimly perceived harmonies of the moral world are restored.

By the time closing argument begins, each lawyer cannot but be aware that the enabling simplicities of opening have largely disappeared. The "vivid and continuous dream" is only a memory, now more distant than the patchy and ambiguous presentation of events that has emerged in the evidentiary phase. The jury has now seen the case from innumerable perspectives, and the lawyer's task is to coax[85] the jury back into seeing it sufficiently from his perspective, into accepting his "theory and theme" just enough that they will be prepared to act in precisely the way that the advocate urges. The closing argument is the time when the lawyer will address directly the difficult relationships between theory and theme, on the one hand, and the evidence, on the other. In the most effective closings, he will directly and reasonably deal with the inevitable factual and moral difficulties that a triable case presents. He will be both *reconstructing* the narrative he provided in opening and *deconstructing* the narrative offered by his opponent. Occasionally he may present a compelling argument; much more often he will be more than pleased to have discovered an appealing argument. And to anticipate the later chapters, in closing the lawyer is moving between the *significance* of events and their *truth*.

Most basically, the advocate will "argue the evidence." Here he moves beyond the theory and theme struck in opening, to argument that the evidence presented in their support is believable. Here there is a rough hierarchy in the relative strength of supporting evidence: admissions are the strongest, the opponent's failure to dispute evidence is next, followed by a strong basis in common sense and experience, with arguments about relative credibility of witnesses at the bottom.[86] It is *argument* because of the employment of a range of devices that, in *quite different* ways, urge what we might most broadly call the relative strength of the advocate's position, now on the axis of truth as well as the axis of significance.[87] Thus the advocate may explicitly draw conclusions or inferences from the evidence presented that serve to demonstrate the truth of his theory of the case. He may carefully assemble a range of supporting detail that has been scattered intentionally throughout the case and whose significance may only have been hinted. He may invoke the allusions and analogies that have become part of trial lawyers' lore, or that his own imagination conjures up: "the greatest weapon in the arsenal of persuasion is the analogy, the story, the simple comparison to a familiar object" since "[n]othing can move the jurors more convincingly than an apt compari-

---

[85] And so it is said that "you cannot persuade jurors to do what they do not want to do. The goal of argument is to help the jury want to do the right thing, to feel comfortable in making the proper judgment." McElhaney, *Trial Notebook*, 499 (quoting trial lawyer Jack Liber).

[86] Lubet, *Modern Trial Advocacy*, 446–68.

[87] I closely follow Lubet's account here. Ibid., 452–64.

son to something they know from their own experience is true."[88] So on circumstantial evidence: "If you go into the woods and find a turtle on a tree stump, you know he didn't get there by himself!" On the witness caught in a lie: "If you order beef stew and the first bite of meat is rancid, you're not expected carefully to remove that bite and accept the rest!" And on and on.[89]

Because closing is the final engagement in the battle for the jury's imagination, and because, for reasons I discuss below, a theory is accepted or rejected as a whole, both sides will be careful to stay "within" their theories and themes. Even the plaintiff's rebuttal[90] argument will be organized according to the structure of his affirmative case. Even the defendant, after an initial denial of the plaintiff's or prosecution's claims, will almost always move quickly to reconceive the case from his own perspective. Part of closing argument will be devoted to a small number of crucial "turning points"[91] in the case, those key issues which, once resolved, cause everything else to "fall into place." Trial lawyers know that these issues are not purely factual. And so, especially in the rhetorically most important moments of closing, the beginning and the end,[92] the advocate will focus on "making the jury *want* to decide the case in your favor."[93] He may invoke the jury instructions at this time or he may revert to narrative—retelling a portion of the full story he told in opening, perhaps at a higher pitch of descriptive-evaluative intensity. Take this example, offered by Lubet, of a patch of closing argument from an automobile accident case in which the defendant crashed into the back of plaintiff's car when the latter stopped to let a fire engine go by:

The defendant was "too busy to be careful." We know that from his actions and their consequences. But what was he busy doing? He was rushing to a meeting for the sole purpose of increasing his income. He was worrying about money, not about safety. It is true that he was late, but that was no one's fault but his own. And once he was late he was so obsessed with getting to the meeting that he threw caution out the window. He was so "busy" that he didn't

---

[88] Craig Spangenberg, "Basic Values and the Techniques of Persuasion," *Litigation* 4 (Summer 1977): 16.

[89] The examples are from McElhaney's *Trial Notebook*, 484, 510.

[90] The usual practice is for the party with the burden of proof (the plaintiff or prosecution) to speak first, the defense to respond, and the burdened party to finish with a rebuttal that is limited to the points made by the defendant. (The latter limitation is often interpreted very liberally.)

[91] Lubet, *Modern Trial Advocacy*, 473.

[92] The advocacy literature speaks of "primacy" and "recency"—the importance of the first thing a decision-maker hears and the very last thing.

[93] Lubet, *Modern Trial Advocacy*, 477.

even care to see whether or not the plaintiff was injured. No, that business meeting was all that mattered. We, everyone is at risk when drivers behave that way. No one is safe on the road when people care more about their meetings than they do about the way they are driving. You cannot allow someone to think that it is all right to be "too busy to be careful."[94]

The kind of moralism embedded in this description ("too busy," "rushing," "worrying about money," "obsessed," etc.) is designed to motivate the jury to condemn the action in its verdict. It is available, however, only if all the evidence allows the description to ring true. The advocate here is moving "between facts and norms," relying on both the "logical" strength of the factual inferences he offers and the importance of the norms he invokes.

Closing is argument as well because of the advocate's ability explicitly to address and directly to criticize the opponent's inferences, analogies, theory, and theme. In this mode, closing argument is, like much of cross-examination, a deconstructive device, in two different ways. First, it can attack the internal coherence, both factual and normative, of the opponent's case, arguing usually that both the factual generalizations and the normative principles on which it is built are crudely overgeneralized and misstated. Second, it can attack the relationship between those generalizations and principles, themselves unassailable, and the *evidence* that this case falls within them. (Here the advocate may directly urge the lack of credibility of the opponents' witnesses, their motive to lie, and their untrustworthy demeanor while testifying.) Here the advocate can say of his opponent's opening, in effect, "Pretty story, but it just isn't true!" That opening was the lawyer's *promise* to produce evidence to establish the important assertions she made. The trial shows that the promise has been broken!

It is worth anticipating[95] here the complex ways in which the few rules surrounding closing situate the trial in a web of public meanings. It is the *lawyer*, not the client, who addresses the jury. He is prohibited from directly expressing his personal opinion on the justness of the cause or the credibility of the witnesses. He must accept the law as given in the instructions and may not paraphrase that law, misstate it, or urge the jury to disregard it. The analogies, allusions, and stories he tells in order to make both factual and normative arguments are all drawn from the jury's common sense. The advocate is prohibited from addressing a juror by name or from urging the jury's self-interest or lessening the responsibility the jury bears by mentioning the possibility of appeals or of commuted

---

[94] Ibid., 463.
[95] See chapter 5.

sentences. Closing dramatizes the transformation of private desire into public right. When "I want" becomes "I am entitled to," the claimant must submit to the complex public norms by which the latter claims are determined.

Just as in opening, the advocates in closing almost inevitably and performatively pose for the jury metalevel issues concerning what is important about the lawsuit. Amsterdam and Hertz have written an analysis of the closing argument in a New York murder trial that parallels in important ways my analysis of the opening statement given below in chapter 4.[96] In their case, the issue for the trier of fact was also the mental state of the defendant. What they noted in their detailed and careful study was, once again, the metalevel argument between the attorneys about what was at issue. The prosecutor's argument said implicitly that it was important to take historical facts seriously, and that the jury had in common sense the means to attain the morally significant goal of achieving factual truth. The prosecution's closing employed the narrative form of history, reasserting the God's-eye view of the standard opening, and "muting" the jury's action in reaching a judgment. The implicit message was that "reality does not need to be created . . . it is already out there in events. It is knowable. Indeed, having heard the prosecution's evidence and being capable of using common sense, the jury already 'knows' the relevant reality."

The defense argument implicitly presented a drama in which the jury is the protagonist. The issue is not what happened back then, but rather whether the jury will now keep its promise to insist on proof beyond a reasonable doubt, even though it will be tempted not to by its negative emotions toward the defendant. So the defense tells "vignettes," not "tales," since no one story "is sustained for long enough to build up an engrossing narrative momentum."[97] "Plainly, the prosecutor is telling a tale about how David shot Mary in 1987, and is asking the jury to accept that tale as true in 1991. Equally plainly, defense counsel is telling a tale about how the jurors in 1991 are deciding where the truth lies after listening to the testimony of witnesses and the arguments of lawyers anent an intriguing but intangible murder mystery set in 1987—a play within a play, and one in which Gonzago's poisoning is of considerably lesser consequence than the catching of Claudius' conscience."[98] The authors noted that notwithstanding the almost complete identity of the "underlying" facts in defense and prosecution closings, "the lawyers told com-

---

[96] Anthony G. Amsterdam and Randy Hertz, "An Analysis of Closing Arguments to a Jury," *New York Law School Law Review* 37 (1992): 55–121.

[97] Ibid., 63.

[98] Ibid., 73.

pletely different stories, with completely different plots, completely different themes, completely different narrative structures. They evoked different stock scripts. They used different metaphors and different grammars. Despite their acceptance of the same legal and logical canons—or perhaps because of it—they created different worlds that gave those canons different meanings."[99] The prosecution invoked the moral centrality and epistemological security of the task of declaring an objective truth that had been demonstrated, "already out there now real." The defense focused on the moral denseness of what the jury was actually doing now. The inevitable task for the jury was to decide how the entire case, including their own judgment, should be viewed.

The trial is constituted as a "consciously structured hybrid of languages," each quite different from the others. Together they build up an enormous, almost unbearable, set of tensions of different kinds. Both lawyers must locate the most powerful norms, from any source, that support the client's case, and demonstrate how those norms are what *this case* is about. The trial is the crucible in which what is most important about norms and facts is determined.

[99] Ibid.

III

The Trial's Constitutive Rules

> GORGIAS. And I claim too that, if a rhetorician
> and a doctor visited any city you like to name
> and they had to contend in argument before the
> Assembly or any other gathering as to which of
> the two should be chosen as doctor, the doctor
> would be nowhere, but the man who could speak
> would be chosen, if he so wished. And if he
> should compete against any other craftsman
> whatever, the rhetorician rather than any other
> would persuade the people to choose him, for
> there is no subject on which a rhetorician would
> not speak more persuasively than any other crafts-
> man, before a crowd. Such then is the character
> of rhetoric. . . .
>
> SOCRATES. And what kind of man am I? One
> of those who would gladly be refuted if anything
> I say is not true, and would gladly refute another
> who says what is not true, but would be no less
> happy to be refuted myself than to refute. . . .
>
>   (Plato)[1]

THE RULES of the trial are Plato's revenge on the rhetoricians. The great
sophists who inhabit the dialogues fully understand that in an organized
society rhetorical technique can be the most powerful device for the assertion of pure will, utterly indifferent to the common good, indifferent to
the truth, indifferent to what we would call moral judgment. Rhetoric as
Plato knew it "was a weapon, intended to influence people before the
tribunal, in public assembly . . . a weapon called upon to gain victory in
battles where the decision hung on the spoken word."[2] It had "savage
roots," and its potential citizenship was in "the world of the lie":

[1] Plato, *Gorgias* 456c–458a, in *The Collected Dialogues of Plato*, 239–41.
[2] Ricoeur, *The Rule of Metaphor*, 10–11.

[I]t is always possible for the art of "saying it well" to lay aside all concern for "speaking the truth." The technique founded in the knowledge of the factors that help to effect persuasion puts formidable power in the hands of anyone who masters it perfectly—the power to manipulate words apart from things, and to manipulate men by manipulating words. . . . What distinguishes persuasion from flattery, from seduction, from threat—that is to say from the subtlest forms of violence?[3]

The Athenian trial courts as Plato described them were precisely these uncontrolled rhetorical battlefields, on one of which, of course, Plato's great teacher lost his life.[4] It is probably not too extreme to assert that Plato's perception of the dangers and power of uncontrolled adversary presentation in democratic societies pushed him toward "authoritarian" forms of government which arguably eliminated politics altogether.[5]

The American trial is a highly rule-bound form of rhetorical practice. It is an inheritance of centuries during which a balance between the "Platonic" and the "democratic" aspects of our tradition was struck. All the values intertwined with the Rule of Law, which the Received View celebrates, stem from the Platonic inheritance, as does, most fundamentally, the importance of focusing the trial on a legal evaluation of a past action.[6] Our democratic legacy finds expression in other aspects of the trial, including the litigants' control of the presentation of evidence,[7] those attorney ethical rules and approved practices which counsel the importance, if not primacy, of the client's interests, and, of course, the jury system itself.[8]

---

[3] Ibid.

[4] On the Athenian trial and its resistance to what we would call legal norms, see R. E. Allen, *Socrates and Legal Obligation* (Minneapolis: University of Minnesota Press, 1980). For a full account of the central place of the jury-courts within Athenian democracy, see Martin Ostwald, *From Popular Sovereignty to the Rule of Law: Law, Society, and Politics in Fifth Century Athens* (Berkeley and Los Angeles: University of California Press, 1986).

[5] See Brian Vickers, *In Defense of Rhetoric* (Oxford: Oxford University Press, 1988), 83–147. On the elimination of politics in the Platonic vision, Beiner, *Political Judgment*.

[6] The American trial's relative aversion to character evidence in favor of evidence of specific past actions is often thought to have its basis in the modern liberal notion that law controls only external behavior in the interests of mutual peace or maximum freedom (in the sense of noninterference). See, e.g., John Stuart Mill, *On Liberty* (New York: W. W. Norton & Co., 1975). However, Aristotle's notion of commutative justice, restoring to a litigant his legitimate expectations regardless of his moral desert, implies a notion of legal proceedings relatively indifferent to moral character. See Aristotle, *Nicomachean Ethics*, bk. 5.

[7] For the contrast with more "authoritarian" Continental systems, see Damaska, *The Faces of Justice and State Authority*, 47–70.

[8] See generally Abramson, *We, the Jury*.

The constitutive rules of the trial look to both its Platonic and its democratic inheritances, though they tilt toward the former. Those rules are designed to transform what would otherwise be sophistic battlegrounds into Platonic dialogues. And just as our constitutional structure is designed to produce results consistent with a government by statesmen long after George Washington is gone, so the trial's rules try to effect that kind of dialogue without Socrates or any other agent intent on the appearance of the truth. The political judgment embedded in those rules is that in a democratic society the legal realm and the moral realm need added protection; individual interest and political purpose will take care of themselves. The balance is so complex and subtle, however, that a fairly full account of the different sorts of rules is necessary if we are to appreciate the contexts of and the constraints on the trial's practices.

The Rules of Ethics

The law of evidence contains the most obvious set of rules that make the contemporary trial what it is. More easily overlooked, especially by scholars whose principal interest is the extent to which the law of evidence promotes or hinders accuracy in fact-finding, is the pervasive effect of the law of professional responsibility on the trial. Just as surely as the law of evidence, legal ethics, both as a set of precise disciplinary rules and as an expression of the ethos of the practicing bar, forms a decisive part of the constitutive rules of the trial. Someone who is interested in answering the question "What is a trial?" cannot leave them out of account.

In Service to Client Autonomy

First, except for the special case of the prosecution in criminal cases, the client decides whether or not to proceed to trial. After all, a "lawyer shall abide by a client's decision whether to accept an offer of settlement of a matter."[9] (The office of the prosecutor has unreviewable discretion not to file or to decline to prosecute a criminal case. A settlement in the form of a plea bargain must be approved by the judge.) This decision is a corollary to the lawyer's duty to "abide by a client's decisions concerning the objectives of representation" and to "consult with the client as to the means by which they are to be pursued."[10]

[9] *Model Rules*, Rule 1.2(a).
[10] "In a criminal case, the lawyer shall abide by the client's decision, after consultation with the lawyer, as to a plea to be entered, whether to waive jury trial and whether the client will testify." Ibid.

But the client's right to set the objectives of the representation reaches decisively into the trial itself. Concretely, those objectives will often determine the opening statement that the lawyer gives, where the crucial "theory of the case" is presented. For example, a mentally competent criminal defendant charged with first degree murder may decide that his primary objective is to avoid indefinite detention in a state mental hospital. He may well decide, after consultation with his lawyer, that the goal of the trial is to obtain a conviction for involuntary manslaughter and a relatively short prison sentence, most of which he may already have served awaiting trial. What his lawyer says "is the case" in opening statement will be a function of that client goal, as will all the evidence presented, the way it is organized and shaped.

I tried a criminal case many years ago where the defendant initially claimed to be an innocent bystander to a crime allegedly performed by his codefendant. He gave a plausible account of the encounter in which his codefendant was the only perpetrator and in which he was not an accomplice. We dutifully prepared to try the case on that theory and to allow him to testify to his account. Minutes before trial, our client told us that he would be killed if he blamed his codefendant and ended up in the penitentiary. He refused to testify. Since a plea bargain was, for a number of reasons, out of the question, the only remaining theory of defense was mistaken identity, the "really" false story that the client was not present at the crime at all. Of course, he could not testify to that false story;[11] but, duly qualified by the prefix, "The evidence will show . . . ," it could, under prevailing norms, serve as the theory of the case.

It is, in effect, the criminal defendant's privilege against self-incrimination that makes such a situation possible. In the civil context, a party can be required to testify. If he gives testimony that his lawyer knows to be false, even on the basis of privileged communications, the lawyer will be duty-bound to disclose the falsehood of the testimony to the tribunal. But the theoretical point is that the opening statement's assertions of weakly qualified fact can be a direct function of the client's objectives in the trial. And, to anticipate, the opening statement in the criminal context is also a function of the *political* decision, embedded in the Fifth Amendment, to allow a defendant to decline to testify.

Another example comes from the materials we use to teach professional responsibility to trial lawyers.[12] The case involves a murder charge based on a problematic eyewitness identification against one Joe Mitchell. Mitchell is charged with the drive-by shooting of his estranged wife. His

---

[11] Ibid., Rule 3.3(a)(4). *Nix v. Whiteside*, 475 U.S. 157 (1986).

[12] Burns, Gerghty, and Lubet, *Exercises and Problems in Professional Responsibility*, 49–56.

lawyer thinks him innocent. His landlady saw him return to his room shortly before the shooting, and he was in his room when the police arrived shortly thereafter. It is barely possible, though quite unlikely, that Joe left his room, slipped by the landlady, did the shooting, and returned to his room. The problem is that Joe admits to his lawyer that he did, indeed, leave his room for a breath of air after reading a deeply disappointing business letter. If Joe does not take the stand, the lawyer may give an opening statement in which she claims that "the evidence will show" that Joe never left his room. Further, the lawyer may conduct a destructive cross-examination on any witness, however truthful, who claims that Joe was seen outside his room at the time.

These are dramatic and troubling examples. There is no intrinsic reason why lawyers could not be forbidden to present an opening statement that they knew to be false, or to conduct a cross-examination on an actually false premise, though there are serious practical problems with such a rule. More common is the situation in which a lawyer in a civil case may choose a theory of the case, and thus give an opening statement, based on a client's preference for one form of relief rather than another. These situations emerge because civil and (especially) criminal trials are constituted by public rules, *almost all the way down.* (I say "almost" because of the moral core of the criminal law.) Wherever political power is constrained by general rules, there always exists a serious likelihood of anomalous results in individual cases. And where it is truly political power that is being constrained, the rules are likely to be more general and more rigid, precisely because freezing the (often benign) exercise of discretion is our conscious purpose. These inevitably overgeneralized rules are, in large part, a function of the fact, branded on the consciousness of the founding fathers during the colonial experience, that (especially) the criminal trial is a *political* institution, one of whose most important goals is the control of state power. In no existing nation is that power unambiguously identical with moral authority. In Tocqueville's classic formulation, "The jury is, above all, a political institution, and it must be regarded in this light in order to be duly appreciated. . . . He who punishes the criminal is . . . the real master of society."[13]

This political function of the trial generates patterns of counterpoised overgeneralized rules where an apparently broad advantage to one side, usually the defendant, designed to control state power, is often offset by other rules, which give the state a specifically unreasoned advantage. The state must prove the defendant guilty beyond a reasonable doubt. The defendant need not speak to the police (if he knows how to assert the

---

[13] Alexis de Tocqueville, *Democracy in America*, trans. Henry Reeve (New York: Vintage Books, 1945), 293.

right) or testify at trial.[14] The defendant's admissions to his lawyer may not be disclosed, though they will prevent the lawyer from presenting the defendant's otherwise plausible denials inconsistent with those admissions. In all but a handful of states, however, the defendant does not have the right to compulsory pretrial process. (I am among those many lawyers who have begun a serious felony trial with only the vaguest notion of how the state's witness will testify.) If a defendant calls a witness whom he believes to have been the actual perpetrator and that witness refuses to testify on the grounds that his testimony will tend to incriminate him, the defendant may not even inform the jury of what has occurred. In some jurisdictions a defendant may not present any evidence in support of a factual theory unless he has accumulated enough evidence to push the theory, in the judge's estimation, over an ill-defined threshold of plausibility. The defendant's past crimes are not admissible to show bad character but may be presented to impeach his credibility should he choose to testify. And so on and on. These are, again, inevitably overgeneralized rules which operate so clumsily that they can entangle the innocent more easily than the guilty. Many of them stem from a formally overblown (and practically unavailable) version of the privilege against self-incrimination, followed by judicial and legislative tolerance of a host of prosecutorial advantages taken to "offset," mechanically and in gross, this advantage. The general point, for our purposes, is that one cannot evaluate the wisdom of any particular rule of professional responsibility, even when it may frustrate the achievement of accuracy on a particular matter, outside this enormously complex, even bewildering, kaleidoscope of competing rules.

To return to my main point, the factual theory of the case is determined in part by the client's objectives, and the lawyer is bound to present the theory that is most consistent with the client's objectives. Client control of the key factual theory of the case, toward the establishment of which an effective advocate will rigorously marshal everything she does in the courtroom,[15] is a feature of the Anglo-American trial system that is strongly at odds with its Continental cousins, where there is a much higher level of judicial involvement in the determination of issues both of fact and of law.[16] On the Continent "the law" as interpreted by the judges ultimately determines what the relevant factual questions are, and hence what the "ultimate facts" can be. Nothing so ephemeral, so

---

[14] Marvin Frankel, *Partisan Justice* (New York: Hill and Wang, 1980) (on the irrationality of the current balance of advantages and disadvantages and how it may injure especially the innocent).

[15] MacElhaney, *Trial Notebook*, at 47–54.

[16] Damaska, *The Faces of Justice and State Authority*, 111–16.

political, so individual as a given party's "objectives" should interfere with that process.

Further, the ethical rules both enjoin and reflect an ethos with which the business of theory construction and evidence presentation is to be carried out. It is the spirit of "warm zeal" for the client's interests. Probably the "classical expression"[17] of the conviction that this ethos contributes, through the adversary system, to discovery of truth is the report of the Joint Commission of the American Bar Association and the Association of American Law Schools issued in 1958, of which Lon Fuller was the principal author.[18] That document notes a sharp distinction, apparent in the 1969 *Model Code of Professional Responsibility* and again in the 1983 *Model Rules of Professional Conduct*,[19] between the lawyer as counselor and the lawyer as advocate. As counselor, the lawyer is expected to offer the client his best judgment as to what seems to him in the client's best interests, even if the client is disinclined to listen. Moreover, the lawyer is encouraged to share with his client his own moral perspectives on the situation the client faces. In this way, the ethos of the profession recognizes a discontinuity, a gap, between the world of individual conscience and the harsher, more mechanical, world of the working of public rules and processes, which should be bridged only by the informed, free choice of the client.

It is the client who chooses.[20] The lawyer's task is to protect the client's autonomy from the threat posed by the complexity and alien nature of

[17] Charles W. Wolfram, *Modern Legal Ethics* (St. Paul, Minn.: West Publishing, 1986), 565 n. 8.

[18] "Professional Responsibility: Report of the Joint Conference," *American Bar Association Journal* 44 (1958): 1159.

[19] *Model Rules*, Rule 2.1: "In representing a client, a lawyer shall exercise independent professional judgment and render candid advice. In rendering advice, a lawyer may refer not only to law but to other considerations such as moral, economic, social and political factors, that may be relevant to the client's situation." The Comment to the Rule goes further: "Advice couched in narrowly legal terms may be of little value to a client, especially where practical considerations, such as cost or effect on other people, are predominant. Purely technical legal advice, therefore, can sometimes be inadequate. It is proper for a lawyer to refer to relevant moral and ethical considerations in giving advice. Although a lawyer is not a moral advisor as such, moral and ethical considerations impinge upon most legal questions and may decisively influence how the law will be applied." Ibid., Comment 2.

[20] William Simon's suggestion that the lawyer should exercise his own moral judgment in the choice of objections and means is well outside the consensus, as he recognizes it to be. William H. Simon, "Ethical Discretion in Lawyering," *Harvard Law Review* 101 (1988): 1083. See David B. Wilkins, "In Defense of Law *and* Morality: Why Lawyers Should Have a Prima Facie Duty to Obey the Law," *William and Mary Law Review* 38 (1996): 269. See generally David Luban, *Lawyers and Justice: An Ethical Study* (Princeton: Princeton University Press, 1988).

the legal system. If the choice is to litigate, to go to trial, the lawyer becomes less the philosopher and more the fighter,[21] or at least the very single-mindedly loyal diplomat. He or she puts partisanship, fellowship, competitiveness, and ambition at the service of presenting the most morally and factually compelling version of a client's story. Or perhaps I should say "position," because the narrative will be the result of a set of conversations in which the story that the client claims to be true is confronted by the lawyer's judgment about what is factually plausible and morally compelling. The result of this effort is the presentation of a case imagined and researched with the care that only the most delicate conscience and rigorous intelligence could muster. It is even guided by a kind of fair-mindedness,[22] the imagined perspective of an impartial juror.

By providing this energetic form of partisanship, the legal system says something like the following: There is really a great deal to say on behalf of any person, and of most causes. We sometimes don't imagine so because of the main enemy of human compassion, sloth. We cannot count on compassion's overcoming sloth, but desire for victory, for status, for public display, and for wealth can defeat even that formidable adversary. In a serious matter, in which a man's life or liberty is at stake, he ought to have the benefit of the more energetic springs of human effort, not the more noble or the more seemly. This is a perspective James Madison understood.

Thus a trial advocate may and often must make the most impolite or embarrassing suggestions,[23] even if they are offensive to the powerful. By the law of professional responsibility, the client's interests supersede every code of silence. This enforced brashness is enormously important and deeply antiauthoritarian. As Arendt has explained, in totalitarian regimes

---

[21] In his great essay, "Politics as a Vocation" (trans. H. H. Gerth and C. Wright Mills [Philadelphia: Fortress Press, 1965]), Max Weber recognized this rigorously strategic quality of the Anglo-American lawyer as something rare in Germany. Weber thought that the disparity in strategic spirit contributed to the defeat of Germany in the First World War.

[22] See Burns, "A Lawyer's Truth," 229. In that article I contrasted the "fairness" germane to the specifically moral point of view with the strategic and public imagination of the trial lawyer.

[23] Of course a lawyer may not "engage in conduct intended to disrupt a tribunal," *Model Rules*, Rule 3.5(c). The Comment to Model Rule 3.1 forbids a lawyer to bring or defend a proceeding or even assert or controvert an issue if "the client desires to have action taken primarily for the purpose of harassing or maliciously injuring a person." The ABA standards for both the prosecution and the defense function provide, "The interrogation of all witnesses should be conducted fairly, objectively, and with due regard for the dignity and legitimate privacy of the witness, and without seeking to intimidate or humiliate the witness *unnecessarily* [emphasis added]." *American Bar Association Standards relating to the Administration of Criminal Justice* (1992): Prosecution Standard 3–5.7; Defense Standard 4–7.6.

the number of things that are known by everyone but unspeakable everywhere, especially in public forums, increases without limit.[24] The parties' control of what story to tell, of what fact to put in issue, is an important bulwark against the invulnerability of One Big Story.

The theoretical significance of this control is that the trier of fact is never asked to determine what is the fairest or truest account of events. Implicitly, the trier of fact decides instead between human purposes, because only those versions of events organized to support a party's "objectives" may permissibly be presented to the trier of fact. Close to its core, the trial is a practical decision between the considered purposes of the parties, each mediated both actually and rhetorically, by public norms whose comparative relevance to a highly specific factual context is played (and fought) out.

But there are limits. Those limits contribute to the powerful tensions that pervade the trial. They respect "those things that man cannot change at will,"[25] and ensure that the trial is not *only* a political event. A lawyer may not herself make a false statement of material fact or law in the trial court.[26] Nor may a lawyer offer evidence that he knows to be false. If a lawyer has offered evidence that he learns to be false while the action is still pending, he has a duty to "take reasonable remedial measures."[27] The most dramatic example occurs when the lawyer's own client has testified falsely and refuses to correct the false testimony. In the civil context, and probably in the criminal as well, that includes "disclosing the existence of the deception to the court or to the other party," even where the source of the lawyer's information is a confidential communication with the client.[28] There are difficulties surrounding "what a lawyer knows," but the

[24] Arendt, "Truth and Politics," 227.

[25] Ibid., 263–64.

[26] *Model Rules*, Rule 3.3(a)(1). This can extend to requiring the lawyer actively to correct a judge's misunderstanding, at least where there is some reason to believe that the judge is relying on the lawyer's silence as an endorsement of the view he falsely holds. Prosecutors are prohibited from prosecuting a charge that the prosecutor knows is not supported by probable cause. Rule 3.8(a). Lawyers in civil cases are prohibited from bringing "frivolous" cases, urging frivolous defenses, or arguing frivolous grounds, all subject to the provision that a lawyer may make a "good faith argument for an extension, modification, or reversal of existing law." Federal Rule of Civil Procedural 11, amended in 1983, and then again in 1993, has been a center of significant controversy and extensive litigation. It now requires that a lawyer certify that factual allegations in pleadings and motions have "evidentiary support" or are "likely to have evidentiary support after a reasonable opportunity for further investigations or discovery." For an account of the controversies surrounding the 1983 rule, see E. Wiggins, T. Wilgig, and D. Stienstra, *Report on Rule 11* (Federal Judicial Center, 1991).

[27] *Model Rules*, Rule 3.3(a)(4).

[28] Ibid., Rule 3.3(a)(4). See Geoffrey C. Hazard, Jr. and W. William Hodes, *The Law of Lawyering*, vol. 1 (New York: Aspen Law and Business, 1998): 610–614.4.

authorities address that problem with a common sense that tries to avoid sophistry, on the one hand, and a too-cavalier readiness to find a client, especially one charged with a criminal offense, to have committed perjury, on the other. Nor may a lawyer "counsel or assist" a witness, including a client, to testify falsely.[29] Once the lawyer knows that potential testimony, however helpful, is false, he may not offer the testimony or prepare the witness to present it effectively. Even if he only "reasonably believes" the evidence is false, he may choose not to offer it.[30]

There are some very delicate ethical questions surrounding the manner in which a lawyer may prepare a client or witness to testify. "Horseshedding" a client is a hallowed tradition. Every viewer of *Anatomy of a Murder* knows that a lawyer may provide a reasonably intelligent client with the legal standards ("the speech") and await a story that conforms to those standards. Some research indicates a high level of perjury in some quarters, some of it inevitably lawyer-assisted.[31] These are clear abuses.

Still, the ethical issues here can be delicate for a number of reasons. A client or a witness may have consciously or half-consciously manufactured a distorted story based on a misunderstanding of the legal standards. For this reason, or in order to motivate a client to remember important details, a lawyer may be justified in explaining the legal issues. Furthermore, the processes by which a lawyer can reconstruct events from a limited memory bear a close resemblance to those by which he can construct events—both involve the use of imagination and common sense to determine the probable course of events. When reconstructing events, the lawyer bothers to inquire seriously whether that is *actually* the way things happened; when constructing events he is concerned only whether the story is plausible and not obviously inconsistent with other credible evidence.

There is also what might be called the range of fair characterization across legal categories, the classical subject for acceptable "horseshedding." The standard example is an issue that arises in the workmen's compensation area.[32] Did the worker "slip" or "trip?" In one case he recovers; in the other he doesn't. Should the client be allowed to decide how to characterize the event with a full understanding of the conse-

---

[29] *Model Rules*, Rule 3.4(a).

[30] The troubling feature of *Nix v. Whiteside*, 475 U.S. 157 (1986) is that it apparently involved this lower standard. The court held that a defendant is not deprived of effective assistance of counsel when a lawyer who reasonably believes that the defendant intends to testify falsely threatens to reveal the perjury to the court and thereby "coerces" the defendant not to testify.

[31] Cloud, "The Dirty Little Secret."

[32] Monroe H. Freedman, *Understanding Lawyers' Ethics* (New York: Matthew Bender, 1990), 158–59. See generally ibid., 143–60, for a good discussion of the issues.

quences of what otherwise might be an overcasual choice of words? Or consider a case in which an attorney is sure that his opponent will attempt to show that his client, the owner of a small business, hired his employees without regard to their qualifications. In preparing the client for testimony, the lawyer asks his client why he hired his vice president, Peter Jones. The client responds, "Because he was my friend." A competent American lawyer will not remain content with that answer. Further inquiry may well lead the client to respond the next time, "Because I have known and respected him for a long time, and I knew that he had many qualities that the job required." Is the less considered answer the "truer" answer?[33]

One should not underestimate the force of the prohibition against assisting a witness to testify falsely. Most lawyers take it very seriously, including those who are sophisticated in the methods I have just described. There is a real line between reconstructing the past and constructing it. The prohibition is strongly reinforced by criminal sanctions for suborning perjury. It has a major effect on the evidence presented at trial. The accounts of events given by witnesses impose real and stubborn limits on the lawyer's ability to shape the trial to manifest a preferred human meaning. The ethical rules we are considering protect that relative stubbornness, some would say sacredness, of simple fact, the importance of which will engage us below.

Just as a lawyer may not himself make false statements or offer false evidence, he has certain kinds of obligations to the other side's evidence as well. An attorney may not "unlawfully obstruct another person's access to evidence or unlawfully alter, destroy or conceal a document or other material having potential evidentiary value."[34] He or she must make a "diligent effort to comply with a legally proper discovery request by an opposing party."[35] And if she is a prosecutor, she must comply with her constitutionally based[36] obligation to "make timely disclosure to the defense of all evidence or information known to the prosecutor that tends to negate the guilt of the accused or mitigate the offense."[37]

---

[33] Recall that the client will be cross-examined. His friendship will be exposed at that time, when the comparative fairness of the two answers can be evaluated. Where adversary proceedings will not take place, the ethical rules impose higher burdens of "fairness" on the *individual* attorney: "In an ex parte proceeding [one where the opposing party is not present], a lawyer shall inform the tribunal of all material facts known to the lawyer which will enable the tribunal to make an informed decision, whether or not the facts are adverse." *Model Rules*, Rule 3.3(d).

[34] Ibid., Rule 3.4(a).

[35] Ibid., Rule 3.4(d).

[36] *Brady v. Maryland*, 373 U.S. 83 (1963).

[37] *Model Rules*, Rule 3.8.

The prohibitions on a lawyer's making a false statement, however un-detectable, or presenting false evidence, however effective, are examples of the way in which the constitutive rules of the trial incorporate the lawyer's "natural" or full knowledge of events. They are, in a sense, limitations on the trial's artifice. By contrast, other constitutive rules require that a lawyer put aside his own full knowledge and judgment and defer to the trial's artifice. By prohibiting a lawyer from alluding during trial to "any matter the lawyer does not reasonably believe is relevant or that will not be supported by admissible evidence,"[38] the rules enjoin, as a matter of ethical obligation, deference to all of the policies embedded in the law of evidence, to which I will soon turn. An attorney may neither assert a personal knowledge of the facts, except under those very rare occasions on which a trial attorney may testify, nor state her personal opinion as to "the justness of a cause, the credibility of a witness, the culpability of a civil litigant, or the guilt or innocence of an accused."[39] It is only what can be proven subject to the public rules of the trial that affects the outcome.

Though the privileges, including the lawyer-client privilege, are part of the law of evidence, the lawyer's duty of confidentiality goes beyond the attorney-client privilege, which applies only to confidential communications from the client and prevents compelled disclosures at trial. The duty of confidentiality prohibits the lawyer from revealing anything, whatever its source, "relating to the representation." This affects the trial as well. It allows a lawyer to rely on what can be dozens of often slight misunderstandings by witnesses and opposing counsel that are helpful to his case. He does not have to tell the court that they "don't quite have it right." This is unlike the singular instance of "false testimony" offered by a witness whom she herself calls, where she has a duty to take "remedial measures" based on her own knowledge, whatever its source. Here, again, it is the artifice of the trial, embedded in the ethical and evidentiary rules operating together, that reigns.

Hence the law of professional responsibility pushes the trial in two very different directions. It imposes on a lawyer an *ethical* obligation to bend all his imagination and effort to present a case, tell a story, that serves his client's own perceived interests. Facts are purposes. Yet against this general obligation stand specific and limited prohibitions: the client deserves counsel on the wisdom of his perceived interests in light of how the legal order will view those interests; access to evidence should not be obstructed; false statements should not be made nor false evidence pre-

---

[38] Ibid., Rule 3.4(e).
[39] Ibid.

sented; and the lawyer should respect the principles and policies embedded in the evidentiary rules. Purposefulness must respect those things which we cannot, or should not, change at will. The tension is between energy and respect. In any case, the rules of professional responsibility, both in reinforcing and limiting the trial's artifice, make it what it is.

The Law of Evidence

I have alluded to the law of evidence in describing the Received View's understanding of its contribution to the Rule of Law. I want to provide a somewhat fuller, though still quite compressed, account of evidence law here that attempts a fair account of both the truth and limitations of that understanding. I have suggested that broad developments in evidence law are problematic for the Received View. Here I will try to view those same developments as an important part of a fuller understanding of the trial.

I will necessarily be painting with a broad brush here. Evidence law is, after all, a vast body of doctrine that has developed over centuries, and, despite recent simplification and rationalization, it still bears many vestigial organs from that evolution. Here, an ounce of history truly is worth a pound of logic. In the wonderful words of the Supreme Court written a half century ago:

> We concur in the general opinion of courts, textwriters and the profession that much of this law is archaic, paradoxical and full of compromises and compensations by which an irrational advantage on one side is offset by a poorly reasoned counterprivilege to the other. But somehow it has proved a workable even if clumsy system when moderated by the discretional controls in the hands of a wise and strong trial court. To pull one misshapen stone out of the grotesque structure is more likely simply to upset its present balance between adverse interests than establish a rational edifice.[40]

---

[40] *Michelson v. United States*, 335 U.S. 469, 485–86 (1948). One example. In many jurisdictions, the law of evidence permits a lawyer to discredit a witness by proving that he has been convicted of a violent felony. Though rationalizations are available, impeachment with prior crimes, even if they show no inclination to false statement, is a child of history. Originally, felonies were capital crimes, and so there *were* no felons who could later be witnesses! Then, as more exceptions to the execution of felons arose, the "civil death" of total incompetence to testify seemed like a fair compromise. Finally, felons were permitted to testify (were no longer "incompetent") but could be confronted with their past crimes "solely to impeach their credibility." Such impeachment is usually permitted, despite a slight tilt in some evidence codes against it (see *Federal Rules of Evidence*, Rule 609), even where the prospective witness is a criminal defendant charged with a violent felony, and, if the defendant is so

Although all of evidence law cannot easily be understood as emerging deductively from one or two generative principles, its broad purposes have a unity I hope here to identify.

The law of evidence provides the "grammar" of the trial. Only those truths that can be said "grammatically" can become part of the legal world. A very important part of the significance of that grammar is incorporated in the Received View's understanding of evidence law, but other important aspects are omitted.

Recall the perspective of the Received View. The requirement that a witness testify in the language of perception lies close to the heart of the law of evidence.[41] A witness's testimony, with narrow exceptions, must be the report, under oath, of an event that the witness once saw, touched, tasted, felt, or heard and now remembers. Only thus, the Received View tells us, can we be sure that the norms embedded in the instructions, and not the moral and political beliefs of the witness, will be used to decide the case.

Regardless of the norms by which the jury decides the case, the requirement of testimony in the language of perception has a deep moral basis. Opinions and conclusions are *more* likely than are perceptions to be part of the "anxious, usually self-preoccupied, often falsifying veil" that our "fat relentless egos"[42] weave to serve our own interests and illusions. Of course, we often "see what we want to see." But perceptions have *more* of a tie to events that are independent of our interests, desires, and expectations than do our opinions. This is something, once again, that Madison understood: "As long as the reason of man continues fallible, and he is at liberty to exercise it, different opinions will be formed. As long as the connection subsists between his reason and his self-love, his opinions and his passions will have a reciprocal influence on each other; and the former will be objects to which the latter attach themselves."[43]

Contemporary evidence law recognizes, however, that the world is not neatly divided up between "pure description" of "facts," on the one hand, and interpretations, evaluations, opinions, and conclusions, on the other.[44] Seeing is "seeing as." Even scientific observation is "theory

---

bold as to take the stand and exercise his constitutional right to testify, where the jury will almost inevitably consider the prior crime for what the law of evidence says is the "wrong" purpose.

[41] This is embodied, in the *Federal Rules of Evidence*, in the following prohibition: "A witness may not testify to a matter unless evidence is introduced sufficient to support a finding that the witness has personal knowledge of the matter." Rule 602.

[42] Iris Murdoch, *The Sovereignty of Good* (London: Routledge, 1991), 52.

[43] *The Federalist*, No. 10 (Madison), 55.

[44] Rule 701 of the *Federal Rules of Evidence*, controlling lay-witness opinion testimony, is a significant liberalization of the common law's restrictions on those opinions.

laden."[45] Ordinary perceptions are not merely "sense-data" but are filled with expectations and interpretations. We do not see a patch of colors and shapes; we see an azalea. There is nothing purely given. There is rather a continuum from description to inference to interpretation to evaluation.[46] Assume a criminal case in which the prosecution is attempting to prove that the defendant tried to escape police custody. The desk sergeant may testify, "He walked toward the front door" or "He walked quickly toward the front door" or "He moved furtively toward the front door" or "He was making a break for it." The latter two are probably not going to be permitted in most American courtrooms. But notice that even the first statement, no doubt admissible in almost every American courtroom, contains a large degree of interpretation embedded in the selection. He was walking toward the "front door," and not toward the bench standing next to it or the phone on the wall or the men's room past the door in the corner. The interpretation may well be justified, but it is embedded in description itself.

As this example shows, there *are* important differences among forms of testimony, the real significance of which I hope to describe at greater length below. As testimony approaches the ideal of pure description, it becomes unproblematic. As it moves away from that ideal (and an ideal it is), it becomes problematic. In the language of the trial courts, it is no longer "based on personal knowledge." It becomes potentially objectionable as opinion testimony, as improper characterization, as reputation testimony, as unauthentic, as violating the best evidence rule, as hearsay. In each case the proponent of the evidence must look to some specific rule, with additional requirements, exceptions, and limitations, to admit the problematic testimony. The requirement of testimony in the language of perception, embodied in the requirement that testimony be based on "personal knowledge" and that it stay within the nonopinion rule, is one of the two fundamental principles of the law of evidence.

The nonopinion rule is, in the trial courtroom, supported by a range of objections "to the form of the question." Most prominently, these objections prevent the lawyer's "leading" most witnesses on direct examination ("The defendant then walked toward the door, didn't he?"), calling for conclusions ("Was he trying to escape?"), or assuming facts not [yet] in evidence ("Where did he begin his walk toward the front door?"). These rules prohibit some of the most common devices of ordinary conversation and have entangled thousands of young lawyers in their nets, reducing them to an embarrassed silence.

[45] See generally Richard J. Bernstein, *The Restructuring of Social and Political Theory* (Philadelphia: University of Pennsylvania Press, 1976), 1–54.

[46] Christopher Hookway, *Peirce* (Boston: Routledge & Kegan Paul, 1985), 151–66.

These rules were not constructed in order to enforce the legal profession's priestly prerogatives, to allow only the initiated to engage in the activities that invoke the power of the legal system. Rather, they enforce a certain vision of the form that direct examination, and so witness testimony, ought to have. They are rules that serve as "mere abridgement of the activity itself; they do not exist in advance of the activity."[47] The envisioned activity is lay witness testimony about any episode as a rhythm of physical description and then chronological narrative of events and actions. The first can be accomplished without leading questions and questions that call for conclusions or the assumption of facts not yet in evidence only because the witness testimony has an implicit structure— that of spatial relationships. In fact, one of the most common rhetorical devices for description of the scene is the "walk around." ("Now, as you entered the house and looked to your left, what did you see?" "And as your gaze came around to the area right in front of you, what did you see there?") The second step has its implicit structure as well—that of temporal relationships. The most common question in direct examination is simply, "What happened next?" Now this simplicity is deceiving: as we have seen, a fair amount of craft can go into the structuring of a direct examination. My point here is only that unless the examination is conducted as a rhythm of physical description, and chronological narrative, it will inevitably violate the strictures against leading, calling for conclusions, and assuming facts not (yet) in evidence. Basic elements of narrative structure are embedded in the evidentiary rules that constitute direct examination. In ordinary conversations, even those about past events, we *rarely* engage in this kind of sustained, disciplined storytelling. We *rarely* focus on detailed description of scene and narrative of past events in such a "formal" way.[48]

The other basic principle is the requirement that the evidence be relevant. The great scholar James Bradley Thayer summarized it thus, "(1) nothing is to be received which is not logically probative of some matter requiring to be proved; and (2) everything which is thus probative should come in, unless a clear ground of policy or law excludes it."[49] As we saw above, relevance has two aspects, logical relevance and materiality, and both, like the requirement of testimony in the language of perception, serve the Rule of Law.

---

[47] Michael Oakeshott, *Rationalism in Politics and Other Essays* (London: Methuen, 1962), 101.

[48] Thus legal interviewing is a learned art in which a narrative structure is often imposed by the lawyer on a major portion of the conversation. Binder and Bergman, *Fact Investigation*, 244–316.

[49] Thayer, *A Preliminary Treatise on Evidence at Common Law*, 530.

Materiality requires that the proposition which the evidence is offered to prove be a proposition that is "of consequence."[50] The substantive law, of course, determines whether the proposition is of consequence. Materiality is the notion that, more than any other, serves to limit the range of the inquiry at the trial, that keeps "every witness box from becoming a confessional."[51] Most broadly, it seeks to limit the trial to serving corrective or commutative justice, restoring a party to his legally legitimate expectations (or "rights"), without regard to broader inquiries concerning what we now call distributive or social justice, the fairness of the overall distribution of benefits and burdens between the parties.[52] In a liberal society, it serves specifically to suppress inquiry into the moral character, or desert, of the parties.

Materiality thus requires that every unit of evidence offered be related to an element of the crime, claim, or defense—the propositions that the party with the burden of proof must establish in order to prevail. It has a dark side. The dark side is the threat it poses to "the truth, the whole truth, and nothing but the truth." Materiality serves to assure that the truth which emerges at trial is a "legal truth," determined solely by those aspects of the case that the law deems "of consequence." Insofar as the legal perspective on the case deviates from a compelling moral perspective, for example, the trier of fact will be unaware of morally relevant aspects of the situation. Sometimes the gap between morally relevant and legally relevant may be justified, but ultimately it must be morally justified.[53] And even if justified, it risks absolutizing the legal artifice by detaching it from its moral foundations, and so forgetting "that man is only the master, not the creator of the world."[54]

The other element of relevance is logical relevance: the unit of evidence must actually *be* probative of (or disprove) a legally determined element of the claim or defense. Today, most scholars (and the *Federal Rules of Evidence*, the most influential partial codification) accept Thayer's view that this determination is made in light of logic and common sense. It is

[50] *Federal Rules of Evidence*, Rule 401.

[51] Patrick Riley, *Kant's Political Philosophy* (Totowa, N.J.: Rowman & Littlefield, 1983), 176.

[52] Rawls, *A Theory of Justice*. Aristotle supplied a specific notion of distributive justice, distribution according to moral desert. *Nicomachean Ethics*, bk. 5. Where such notions are not legally operative or legitimate, as in liberal societies, distributive justice will tend to follow some notion of equality rather than moral merit. See MacIntyre, *After Virtue*.

[53] See Donagan, *The Theory of Morality*, 184 (criticizing Max Weber for too sharp a dichotomy between moral and political).

[54] Hannah Arendt, *The Origins of Totalitarianism* (New York: Harcourt Brace Jovanovich, 1973), 302.

not primarily an issue of law[55] but the kind of determination a detective, a historian, or a responsible investigative reporter might make in deciding whether a piece of potential evidence really does prove the issue of historical fact before him. Logical relevance addresses a *relationship*, then, between the evidence offered and the proposition to be proved—the "warrant," in Toulmin's language, for a belief that the introduction of evidence increases the probability of the fact to be proven. The link between the piece of evidence and the fact to be proven is in most cases a commonsense generalization that forms part of the web of belief that in turn constitutes the world in which we live and act. It makes sense that judges, who presumably are learned in the law, should police materiality. It is paradoxical that judges, whose education and experiences and so common sense are unlikely to be congruent with those of most citizens, should police logical relevance.

But it is very light policing. To be logically relevant, a proposed piece of evidence need only make a proposition of consequence to the determination of the litigation (a "material" proposition) more or less likely than it would be without the evidence. It must ever so slightly[56] alter the balance of probabilities. Once it achieves that level of probative force, it can be excluded only for what are basically pragmatic reasons,[57] and only if those reasons "substantially" outweigh its probative force.

Thus evidence is relevant if it makes any material proposition ever so slightly more or less likely than it would be without the evidence, unless certain pragmatic considerations *substantially* outweigh its probative value. That is a strong tilt toward admissibility, a tilt which approaches the vertical if understood practically.

The human mind seeks to determine historical truth ("what happened") by constructing plausible narratives that are both consistent with

---

[55] The relevance of a particular kind of (usually inflammatory) evidence can come before an appellate court, usually accompanied by an argument from the opponent of the evidence that whatever probative value (logical relevance) the evidence has is substantially outweighed by its prejudicial effects. An appellate determination of the logical relevance of a class of evidence can thus come to have the force of law. For example, in *United States v. Abel*, 469 U.S. 45 (1984) the court held that gang membership would, in some circumstances at least, be relevant to the impeachment of the prosecution's witnesses.

[56] Contemporary evidence codes, such as the *Federal Rules of Evidence*, thus reject Dean Wigmore's notion that evidence must have some higher level of probative force, "plus value," as he put it. The only reason to reject evidence that has *any* probative force is because of one of the considerations embodied in Rule 403, none of which addresses pure probative force of the evidence, purely "epistemological" or "logical" matters. See John H. Wigmore, *Evidence in Trials at Common Law*, Tiller rev., sec. 28 (Boston: Little Brown, 1983), 969.

[57] Federal Rule 403 lists "the danger of unfair prejudice, confusion of the issues, or misleading the jury, or by considerations of undue delay, waste of time, or needless presentation of cumulative evidence."

the "web of belief" and supported by reliable evidence. The notions "consistent," "supported," and "reliable" are subject to varying interpretations and raise deep questions that I postpone. Since differing and contradictory narratives (concretely, opening statements) can be constructed from the same material, we need an institutional device that allows us to evaluate the relative plausibility of the competing narratives. A trial judge will not usually make his or her relevancy determinations by considering the direct logical relationship of the evidence offered to a material proposition. Rather, he or she will situate the evidence offered within the proponent's factual theory of the case. But an advocate will almost always have choices to make among theories of the case and always will have choices among details of the factual theory, "subplots" if you will.

As we have seen, the meaning or significance of bits of evidence is often indeterminate. As trial lawyers say, "Every fact has two faces."[58] The jury will determine the significance of bits of evidence as it decides which factual theory of the case to accept. Conversely, it will determine which factual theory to accept based on the individual bits of evidence offered to prove the theory. As I hope to show, the gaps between such theories go far beyond simple disagreements about "what happened." They include basic divides among worldviews and modes of social ordering, always implicit. For example, in a murder case like the one I describe below, the prosecution may offer evidence that the defendant was given to bursts of anger or exhibited anger near the time of the killing, in order to suggest that the killing was the result of a moral failure, the failure to exercise self-control. That same anger may, however, be offered as evidence, indeed, a classical symptom, of borderline personality disorder, itself a source of transient psychotic functioning. In the same case, evidence that shows the defendant is usually gentle and trustworthy can be presented. On the one hand, it may suggest, as a matter of "logical relevance," that she is not suffering from a "mental disease or defect" in the Victorian language of the criminal code. On the other hand, the same evidence may suggest that the violent act for which the defendant is being tried was not an expression of her "real" personality and thus must have been "caused" by her mental illness. The decision as to the *meaning*, hence "probative value,"

---

[58] For example, in a murder case, the fact that the defendant was drinking before a shooting may suggest that his self-control was reduced. On the other hand, it may suggest that he could not have had the coordination to aim and fire the lethal shot. Anger may provide a motive to kill or may be a symptom of a serious psychological disorder that may provide a defense. A witness's high level of certainty may enhance credibility or may be evidence of bias. Assume a defamation action. The fact that a wealthy homeowner had previously lectured a maid about eavesdropping may provide evidence that he had no reason to expect that his subsequent criticism of another maid would be overheard, or good reason to believe that it would be overheard. The examples are endless.

of such evidence is inevitably circular, since the part is being interpreted in light of the whole and the whole in light of the parts. This "hermeneutic" reality is reflected in the practice of judges' looking to the party's theory of the case to determine whether an individual piece of evidence is relevant. As I discuss in more detail below, the meaning or significance of a piece of evidence is determined not only by a judgment concerning what "is the case" but also by judgments about how we should treat the situation, "what is to be done." In the language of the trial courtroom, a lawyer will respond to a relevancy objection by recounting to the judge that portion of his or her opening statement which the evidence "goes to prove." A lawyer is generally given latitude to "try his own case."

But since the factual theory of the case will often determine what evidence is relevant, the advocate may choose the factual theory of the case in light of the potentially available evidence. This is also true for legal theories. Assume that a lawyer has the option of proceeding under a contract theory or a tort theory—for example, breach of a health insurance contract or tortious refusal to pay under the contract. Punitive damages are usually available in tort, but not in contract actions. The net worth of the defendant is relevant for purposes of determining the amount of punitive damages, but the fact that the defendant is an extremely rich company or man may alter the moral or political evaluation of the merits of the case in ways that go well beyond punitive damages. The lawyer may choose one legal theory rather than another in order to admit certain evidence whose significance may radiate far beyond its immediate "logical relevance." Assume that the lawyer is defending a libel case and considering raising the defense of truth, that is, that the statement the defendant made about the plaintiff, although damaging, is true. Defense counsel will weigh the large range of circumstantial evidence concerning the plaintiff's actions, much of it fraught with moral significance, that the defense of truth will render material. For example, if the alleged libel is an accusation that an employee has embezzled money, the defense of truth may make relevant, as a possible motive for the theft, the plaintiff's gambling debts or high-priced drug habit. Though there are rhetorical costs to proposing a defense that the jury does not accept, defense counsel may plead that theory, expecting that he will not finally establish it by a preponderance, in order to offer evidence whose significance emerges from broader moral norms.

There are deep reasons why most evidence has "multiple relevances," some legitimate and some illegitimate. The illegitimate inferences may invoke substantive moral or political norms outside the instructions for the ultimate decision of the case, or may involve lines of reasoning—from a party's "character" for example, or from a hearsay statement—that the law of evidence determines insufficiently reliable on which to base a

purely factual determination that must be made if the trier of fact is following the norms in the instructions. Recall that evidence may be excluded only if its probative value is *substantially* outweighed by the dangers of unfair prejudice, such as that from an "illegitimate inference," and
one can understand the inevitability of evidence whose significance can
overwhelm the substantive legal norms by invoking alternative values.

Thus the lawyer's control over both the legal and factual theory of the
case, the low standard for logical relevance, the high standard ("substantially outweighed") for exclusion of logically relevant evidence, and the
pervasiveness of the nonopinion rule all suggest that the rules of evidence
function more to structure than to exclude evidence. This is true, even
within the "rationalist" tradition in the law of evidence, which generally
understands the warrants that render a piece of evidence logically relevant
to be purely empirical, and so value-free, empirical generalizations embedded in the judge's common sense about what happens "generally and
for the most part."

But there is more to relevance. Most obviously, what constitutes "*unfair*
prejudice, confusion of the issues, or misleading the jury,"[59] possibly calling for the exclusion of logically relevant evidence, requires a normative
judgment on which purely legal considerations offer little guidance, and
to which appellate courts are especially deferential.[60] In many different
ways, normative considerations affect "pure" relevancy determinations,
both by rule and by judicial practice. This occurs in a self-conscious and
focused way and, more important, in a tacit and pervasive way.

Some of these "relevancy" rules embody deeply held views about the
importance of limited government. For example, evidence law prohibits
a lawyer's presenting proof of a witness's religious beliefs in order to show
that he is more or less credible. In my view, this has more to do with a
constitutionally rooted notion that no legal consequences *should* flow
from religious convictions than with empirical generalizations about the
actual probabilities that persons with this or that set of religious beliefs
are likely to be more or less trustworthy. I also believe that the common
law's historical aversion to "character evidence"[61] was intertwined with

[59] *Federal Rules of Evidence*, Rule 403.

[60] *United States v. Long*, 574 F.2d 761, 767 (3d Cir.), *cert. denied* 439 U.S. 985 (1978);
United States v. Robinson, 560 F.2d 507 (2d Cir. 1977), *cert. denied* 435 U.S. 905 (1978).

[61] "Character evidence" is evidence of a general moral disposition offered to show that
the person acted in conformity with that disposition on a specific occasion. The evidentiary
notion emerges from what can be described as a broadly Aristotelian perspective in which
persons have moral characters for which they are generally responsible. The very notion of
"character evidence" is in tension with a more scientific image of the personality in which
"personality disorders," for example, are, on the one hand, the results of genetic and envi-
ronmental factors, and, on the other hand, the "cause" of human behavior. This deeper

an Augustinian[62] belief that ultimate moral judgments of persons were a divine prerogative which political-legal institutions *ought* not to exercise, and was not based upon the weak rationalization usually offered that such evidence is "unreliable."

Other relevancy rules explicitly, and more directly, subordinate an empiricist notion of factual accuracy to "policy goals." Here we see the surest signs of the much maligned "social engineering," an engineering in many cases based on little social science. So, for example, evidence rules prohibit evidence of "subsequent remedial measures," such as the repair of a damaged sidewalk, when offered to prove that the owner was originally negligent in maintaining the area, lest the law discourage such repairs. Similarly, evidence of statements made in negotiation or of withdrawn pleas in criminal cases is inadmissible in most cases, as is evidence that a person has paid an injured person's medical expenses. In each of these cases, the law exludes evidence, notwithstanding the fact that it may alter the probabilities of some event "of consequence" to the determination of the action and so increase the likelihood of an accurate determination, in order to provide incentives for behavior that is judged socially beneficial.

The law of evidentiary privilege—attorney-client, therapist-patient, priest-penitent, and so on—also functions to exclude evidence that has probative value. Significant, and largely derivative,[63] controversies surround the philosophical justifications for the privileges. As is generally the case in contemporary moral philosophy, the arguments usually pit utilitarians against Kantians. The former argue that the privileges have consequences which generally further the sum of human happiness. Kantians argue that confidentiality is intrinsic to certain relationships, respect for which is intrinsic to equal respect for moral persons, and that forcing

---

conflict between language games, one moral and the other scientific, produces many of the conflicts and paradoxes in the area. The ascendancy of the scientific image is one of the factors that has led to the erosion of the protections against character evidence.

[62] Hannah Arendt, *The Human Condition* (Chicago: University of Chicago Press, 1958), 10–11. For the congruence between Augustinian skepticism about state power and liberal notions about limited government, see Graham Walker, *Moral Foundations of Constitutional Thought: Current Problems, Augustinian Prospects* (Princeton: Princeton University Press, 1990). Kant's liberalism and legal positivism can easily be seen as flowing in part from his Augustinianism, embedded in the Lutheran Pietism in which he grew up. See Ernst Cassirer, *Kant's Life and Thought*, trans. James Haden (New Haven: Yale University Press, 1981), 16–18.

[63] They are derivative in the sense that they tend to follow from the author's general philosophy of law. Thus Wigmore defended the attorney-client privilege on utilitarian grounds, and Fried would defend it on deontological grounds. Wigmore, *Evidence*, vol. 8, sec. 2285; Charles Fried, "Lawyer as Friend: The Moral Foundations of the Lawyer-Client Relation," *Yale Law Journal* 85 (1976): 1060.

disclosure is thus immoral. Kantians usually have problems making sense of any notion of "balancing" the good of respect for these intrinsically valuable relationships with general policy goals, for "[j]ustice is the first virtue of social institutions," and every "person possesses an inviolability founded on justice that even the welfare of society as a whole cannot override."[64] Regardless of its philosophical underpinning, privilege law represents a political-moral judgment that certain values are more important than accuracy in fact-finding. As such, it limits the truth that is allowed to appear at trial in favor of social goals which transcend the importance of factual truth. For example, the justifications for the privilege against self-incrimination lie closer to the concerns about limited government noted above, though here, too, arguments about what is intrinsically disrespectful to the moral person may appear.[65]

More subtle and more interesting are classes of evidence that are regularly admitted despite poor claims that they increase the factual likelihood of some material event. In many murder prosecutions, gruesome pictures of the deceased are routinely received into evidence, despite offers by the defense to stipulate or agree to the legal element of the death of the victim and all the details of the condition of the body. Although there are Received View justifications for this practice, none are really convincing. Wigmore, one of the great rationalists in the law of evidence, had to concede that this evidence was being offered and received for another purpose, in that it had "legitimate moral force."[66] What he meant was something like this. The defendant is physically present in the courtroom. The formality of the proceedings and the various precautions taken to protect his rights, visible to the jury, emphasize the moral significance for him and for us of a careful and just determination of the proceedings. The victim of the crime is not present, but he, too, has a moral claim for justice of which the jury should be aware. Admitting pictures of the victim serves to adjust what might be called the "moral balance" of the case. Regardless of whether this particular practice is justified, it serves as the most graphic example of a process that pervades a lawsuit, an attempt to admit evidence that illustrates the *moral significance* of the action which is at the heart of the suit.

Moreover, trial judges who are not doctrinal wizards are often viewed as fair and good trial judges. Though they may not go through any process that can be recognized as "legal reasoning," their moral compass directs the exercise of their considerable discretion to keep this balance more or less right. This is another way in which the law of evidence as one of the

---

[64] Rawls, *A Theory of Justice*, 1.

[65] Frankel, *Partisan Justice*.

[66] Wigmore, *Evidence*, vol. 9, sec. 2591.

constitutive rules of the trial must be understood in a manner inconsistent with the Received View.

In another class of cases, a weak legal relevance has been developed doctrinally that provides a justification for evidence whose overwhelming moral significance lies outside the legal norms. For example, in one state, evidence of previous child abuse is admissible when the attorney introduces it to prove that the lethal violence for which a parent is on trial was done with intent to kill or do great bodily harm or with the knowledge that death or great bodily harm was probable, justifying a conviction for murder rather than involuntary manslaughter. As a matter of appellate law, such evidence of previous abuse is admissible even when it did *not* result in death or great bodily harm, suggesting as a matter of logic that the perpetrator did not believe that the current abuse would have such a result either. I would suggest that the formal theory of relevance is merely the conduit through which evidence of "prior acts,"[67] otherwise inadmissible but morally significant, comes before the jury. This evidence is morally significant, and such moral considerations especially pressing, where the legally determined central "factual" issue—the perpetrator's "knowledge" during the moment or two of the abuse—is so elusive, almost a will-o'-the-wisp.

There is a more subtle but utterly pervasive manner in which relevancy determinations involve judgments that go well beyond assessment of the purely factual "strength" of an empirical generalization linking the tendered evidence to a material fact. I have mentioned the limited but real plasticity of individual pieces of evidence to conflicting interpretations. Because "every fact has two faces," many cases are "triable." The juror will consider the possible significance, the meaning, of an individual piece of evidence by locating it within one and then another of the competing factual theories of the case. One factual theory of the case is accepted in part because of the evidence supporting it, and all the evidence[68] is inter-

---

[67] See, e.g., *Federal Rules of Evidence*, Rule 404(a).

[68] This is not to deny that the juror may simply shrug in the face of one or another bit of evidence that cannot be integrated into the preferred theory of the case. Even investigators who accept an ideal of scientific knowledge which seeks absolutely universal "covering laws" may have to rest content for long centuries with anomalies that are unexplained. At trial, however, truly unexplained anomalies are less likely for two reasons. First, almost all evidence comes in through witness testimony, and thus evidence apparently inconsistent with a preferred theory can be dismissed because of doubts about the credibility of a witness. Second, unlike scientific experiments conducted to establish, or, more likely, falsify a universal theory, the focus even of scientific evidence at trial is an individual event; scientific evidence must bear on that single event. This almost inevitably raises issues not only of witness credibility (the notorious "bloody glove") but also of different sorts of honest mistakes in the handling of samples. And even if the "chains of custody" of the sample were to be utterly unimpeachable, the testing procedure itself may not, in contrast to scientific experimentation in quest for general laws, be repeatable.

preted in light of the accepted theory. The process is inevitably circular. The judge must respect that process in making his or her relevancy determinations. If there are normative elements (other than strict legal materiality) in the plausibility of one *entire* theory of the case, or in the plausibility of what we can call one of its subplots, then there will inevitably be normative elements in the relevancy determinations that the judge makes. For the meaning of the evidence is conferred by the entire theory or the subplot, and it is the meaning of the evidence that provides the "probative value" of the individual piece of evidence. I will show below that there are in fact normative elements in the plausibility of any theory of the case.[69]

The nonopinion rule and the relevance rule are the two most important and most "generative" of the rules of evidence. They are "generative" in the sense that most of the other evidence rules can be derived from them. There are basically four other categories of evidentiary rules, which have limited theoretical interest because of their derivative nature, but I deem them worth mentioning to round out the picture. The so-called best evidence rule requires only that the originals of documents be offered if available. The requirement of authenticity applies to all evidence that is not what I called the "unproblematic" form of testimony in the language of perception. Therefore, evidence as diverse as documents, physical evidence, telephone calls, and scientific processes all must be authenticated, unless it belongs to a class of evidence where there is no serious reason to doubt that evidence "is what it purports to be."[70] Authentication is usually fairly undemanding, the available methods virtually without limit, and the standard for admissibility relatively low.[71] Though it is possible that some potential evidence can be excluded because the requisite "foundation" as to authenticity is unavailable, such exclusions are relatively rare.

Evidence must also be "competent"—broadly speaking, "eligible to be received as evidence." For example, a judge is incompetent to testify in a trial over which she presides; a juror is incompetent to testify as to his own intentions during deliberation in order to "impeach" or overturn his verdict; it is still said that a witness who has not perceived anything of consequence, or cannot remember what he perceived, or is incapable of communicating what he perceives and remembers, or is psychologically or morally incapable of differentiating fact from fantasy, is "incompetent" to testify. Competence is a residual category. It was once much broader and excluded whole categories of evidence, such as "civilly dead"

---

[69] See chapter 6, below.

[70] In the language of evidence law, these highly reliable forms of evidence are "self-authenticating."

[71] *Federal Rules of Evidence*, Rules 901 and 902.

felons and spouses of the accused. It now excludes certain kinds of evidence because they are likely to be unreliable, such as the testimony of *very* young children and persons in psychotic states. The broad tendency of the law of evidence has been to eliminate total incompetencies to testify and permit, instead, forms of impeachment that allow the juror to weigh the troubling aspect of the witness's testimony like any other "impeaching" fact. Competency rules also exclude certain kinds of evidence for "structural" reasons: the judge's potential testimony in the case over which he presides and usually the trial lawyer's testimony in the case he tries.[72] The prohibition on the testimony of jurors to impeach the verdict is sui generis.

Finally, there is the rule against hearsay, which excludes out-of-court statements offered for the truth of the matter asserted. There is a wonderful scholasticism surrounding the definition of hearsay that has its interests but is not germane to my purposes here. The most fundamental purpose of the hearsay rule is to protect cross-examination, "the greatest legal engine ever invented for the discovery of truth." The notion is that only if the person whose perceptions are being reported is the same person who is reporting the perceptions can the cross-examiner properly explore (1) important weaknesses in perception, memory, and clarity of expression that may infect the testimony even of sincere witnesses, and (2) biases, interests, prejudice, and character failings that cast doubt on the witness's credibility.

The broad drift of the law of evidence has been to admit more and more hearsay evidence, and for the constitutional jurisprudence surrounding the analogous Confrontation Clause to follow the lead of evidence law. There have always been dozens of defined exceptions to the hearsay rule. Many jurisdictions also now have "catch-all" exceptions for hearsay that simply seems "reliable." Recall too that out-of-court statements are inadmissible only if offered for the truth of the matter asserted. This raises what we now know to be issues of multiple relevancies. Out-of-court statements can be offered for purposes other than the truth of what was asserted, and, once admitted, are usually considered for all purposes. The deferential principles of relevancy law that allow those other purposes to be logically quite weak and the ability of advocates to tailor actual theories in order to render desirable evidence logically relevant together reduce the actual bite of the hearsay rule. In the trial court the first words that well up in the mind of the proponent of evidence in the face of a hearsay objection is, "Your Honor, the evidence is not being offered for the truth of the matter asserted, but rather. . . ." It is, frankly, unusual, although not unheard of, for a lawyer to be unable to finish the

[72] This is also embedded in an ethical rule. See *Model Rules*, Rule 3.7.

sentence in a way that at least forces the trial judge to weigh probative value against prejudicial effect under the liberal standard of contemporary evidence law.

The best evidence rule, the requirement of authentication, most of the law of competence, and the hearsay rule all serve to ensure that evidence upon which a juror may decide a case is *reliable*. At a level below the rhetoric of judicial opinions, reliability is really a form of relevance. Evidence that is utterly unreliable is really irrelevant: it *really* does not render a fact that is of consequence to the litigation any more or less probable than it would be without the evidence. The Received View suggests that all these rules contribute to the factual accuracy of the value-free narrative on which the juror must then perform the task of legal categorization. Indeed, they can be understood quite well, almost exhaustively, from the perspective of the Received View.

I will argue below that the structure of the evidence rules is of a piece with what the contemporary trial has become. For now, I wish simply to point out that there is a largely "internal" dialectic of evidence law that has led to a system of the law of evidence as a small set of overlapping rules which only somewhat limit the evidence that a juror may see. The dialectic runs something like this.[73]

1. Given the adversary system, and the strong motives both parties have in presenting the most powerful (i.e., the most relevant) evidence, there seems to be no reason for the imposition of categorical exclusionary rules on the evidence presented at trial. A regime of truly free proof, limited only by rules of procedure and decorum, should prevail. There is no bright line between "reliable" and "unreliable" evidence that would justify total exclusion of evidence deemed unreliable. That kind of either-or deprives the jury, necessarily engaged in a subtle and holistic determination, of *all* of the probative value of a piece of evidence because it does not have *enough* probative value.[74] It is far better, so the argument goes, for the court to rely on the devices of the adversary trial, such as cross-examination, compulsory process to obtain contradicting evidence, and closing argument to point out to the jury the very same weakness that would, in a categorical scheme, lead to total exclusion. It is better for the trial to

---

[73] See Burns, "Bright Lines and Hard Edges," 843.

[74] I have referred to this problem elsewhere as an "epistemological notch." A "notch" in public benefits law is a feature of some legal requirements that unjustifiably condition eligibility for significant government benefits, say Medicaid eligibility, on the individual's falling above or below a specified dollar level. For example, a person earning $299 per month may be eligible for free health care worth $200 per month but lose all health care benefits if he earns his 300th dollar. Notches are pervasive and destructive features of certain kinds of categorical schemes. Robert P. Burns, "Rawls and the Principles of Welfare Law," *Northwestern University Law Review* 83 (1989): 184, 236–38.

include each bit of evidence and allow the jury to accord it whatever weight it deserves in light of the full context of the other evidence and after the critical analysis provided by the trial itself. Furthermore, any scheme that allows the judge to "micromanage" the trial gives an unfair or unperceptive judge the ability to shade the evidence in favor of one party or another, imposing her own unreflective prejudices on the process of proof and intruding upon the jury's democratizing functions.[75]

2. On the other hand, there are severe problems with this open system of free proof: in fact, the very problems that the Received View understands the law of evidence to address. The evidence that a competent, interested advocate may present may be the most powerful evidence, but its persuasive power may stem from its invoking political or moral norms other than those embedded in the instructions. This power may derive from passion or emotion. The Rule of Law requires the trial judge to aggressively patrol the evidence for materiality, and the jury must be kept from basing its decisions on evidence that is unreliable. There are situations where the devices of the adversary trial are inadequate to assess properly the reliability of evidence. Obtaining contradictory evidence in the short time frames of the trial may not be possible. Better to exclude this sort of evidence completely through the use of our familiar exclusionary rules of evidence.

3. Well, the dialectic continues, perhaps certain kinds of evidence ought to be kept from the jury, but the judicial determination to exclude should be highly contextual. Factors suggesting the exclusion of evidence in one case will not be sufficiently present in another to justify the epistemological costs of exclusion. Courts will often make evidentiary determinations before the parties have presented all the evidence and without full appreciation of the importance of evidence to the party's theory of the case. The contextual judgment of a wise judge should determine whether the factors mentioned at the second stage of our dialectic warrant exclusion. The *only* codified limitation on the introduction of evidence should be an injunction directed to the trial judge to exclude evidence whose prejudicial effects substantially outweigh its probative value. Any general categorical evidence rules will necessarily be overgeneralized.

4. At the fourth stage of our dialectic, some of our earlier concerns about judicial tyranny reassert themselves. Will trial judges actually make these contextual, and therefore effectively unreviewable, individual determinations wisely? What about the procedural side of the Rule of Law, requiring that similar cases be similarly decided?[76] Surely, there must be some recurring situations that it is possible to capture with general rules

---

[75] Abramson, *We, the Jury.*
[76] Rawls, *A Theory of Justice*, 235–43.

which serve to constrain judicial discretion. To the extent that it is necessary to contextualize broad rules, one might rely on the standard methods of common law adjudication[77] to identify binding considerations dictating admission or exclusion in light of the purposes of the rules as a whole.

5. To this call for the development of a comprehensive scheme of evidence law articulated through the common law method, the next stage of our dialectic brings a powerful objection. Evidence law addresses every possible event that could find its way into a criminal or civil courtroom from the booming, buzzing confusion of the world. Further, the law of evidence has to be sufficiently simple for advocates and judges to retrieve and apply in the second or so within which most evidentiary decisions take place in the trial courtroom. An enormously complex and refined set of "hard law" rules and exceptions, and exceptions to exceptions, necessarily enforced by reversal, seems unworkable even with the most perspicuous categories and the wisest judges.

6. We thus arrive at contemporary evidence law—a small set of overlapping evidentiary rules that function like guidelines for the trial judge and alert the appellate court to give a hard look for fundamental unfairness when one of the guidelines is violated. This rejects the ideal advanced at stage 5: a set of binding general rules qualified by those specific facts of prior cases whose inclusion or not in the stated authoritative rule is developed in light of that rule's purposes. We have instead contextualized judgments, like those described at stage 2 of our dialectic, *somewhat* structured for the trial court by general rules that alert the trial judge to problematic evidence. In short, there would be broad rules and individual facts, and little in between. And that, I believe, is where we are.

Conclusion

The rules of ethics as they apply to the trial require energetic partisanship, limited by a respect for brute fact. In relatively rare situations, even the latter gives way to the general nature of rules thought important to the control of state power. The complexity of the law of evidence is the result of a history in which both political and epistemological interests were at play. Given recent attempts at rationalization, it is now like an old city, "a maze of little streets and squares, of old and new houses, and of houses with additions from various periods; and this surrounded by a multitude of new boroughs with straight regular streets and regular houses."[78]

[77] Edward Levi, *An Introduction to Legal Reasoning* (Chicago: University of Chicago Press, 1948).

[78] Ludwig Wittgenstein, *Philosophical Investigations*, trans. G.E.M. Anscombe (New York: Macmillan, 1968), par. 18 (describing the nature of language).

Evidence law does force testimony into a relatively chaste narrative account of perceptual judgments of past events. It will turn out that this provides the matter not for the imprint of legal norms but for *reinterpretation*. It creates a sharp tension with the fully characterized narrative of opening statement. Doctrines of materiality and relevancy serve in practice to keep the trial focused on matters worth contesting and qualify, though only qualify, the continuity of the moral and the legal realms. The trial cannot present to the jury a humanly meaningful, or even comprehensible, account of events while confining that account to those details which are normatively significant *only* to the norms embedded in the instructions. The contemporary trial does not embody a legal positivist vision. In many different sorts of ways, the law of evidence reflects moral and political, rather than purely epistemological, judgments.

The drift of the law of evidence has thus been toward admissibility. In the main, it provides a small number of commonplaces for a rhetoric in which lawyers may argue the *practical fairness* of redirecting the inquiry at trial this way or that, while honoring a very small number of basic principles. It is only the political concern, with a deep constitutional pedigree, about the judge's exercise of discretion that limits the development toward admissibility, or "free proof." And it is still the case that it is almost always the *exclusion* of evidence that creates real unfairness at trial.

IV

An Interpretation from One Trial

Introduction

The trial makes possible different levels of normative judgment. Some are closely connected to factual accuracy, though not in the way that the Received View suggests. Other levels of judgment recognize that the trial is a public event, and that its task is not only to do justice but to preserve the conditions for the doing of justice. Thus the key task in most trials is to identify what is most *important* about the case and thus to determine what form of social ordering is appropriate, both of which require "metalevel" judgments.

I want now to show somewhat more concretely *how* these metalevel issues may be posed by simple, and relatively short, opening statements. The best way to do this is through the reproduction of two short openings, with a detailed commentary on the appeals encoded in their simple narratives. Concretely, of course, this approach illustrates the specific metalevel conflict between the encoded appeals that the advocates implicitly agreed should form "the issue," each for his own purposes and anticipating his opponent's theory. In this particular case, the basic tension was between a legalistic or bureaucratic ordering, on the one hand, and a more contextualized form of individual moral evaluation, strongly influenced by a psychiatric understanding of human compulsions. For a number of reasons, the lawyers chose to exclude other possible understandings of the issues as relatively weaker than the ones actually chosen.

What follows is an edited version of two opening statements in a murder case tried quite some years ago,[1] along with my own commentary, written shortly after the trial. The commentary tries to articulate precisely the significance of the major features of each of the opening statements in the full context of the trial. What was apparent to me at the time was the ways in which these competing narratives were actually arguments made across a number of levels. The openings said in the language of storytelling that the most important issues in the case were not narrowly factual at all. Rather, those issues forced the judge to decide what *kind* of

---

[1] The quoted material is exactly as spoken in court, except for names, dates, and other identifying material. Some ellipses are omitted for ease of reading.

event had occurred and, in a mutually determining manner, what form of social ordering was appropriate to the case. These pragmatic "meta-issues" were presented to the court in the language of fact-finding but actually required a decision that was truthful to the situation in a much richer way.

The Preliminary Circling

The trial began some eighteen months after Priscilla's death. It was held in one of the big old courtrooms in the county courts building of this small, now faded, industrial city: a room with fifty-foot ceilings, by-now-dirty oak paneling from the floor on up, easily able to hold three hundred people, useful for the administrative status-calls each morning and for the occasional case that drew significant public attention.

Judge John Anthony Ferraro presided. He was a man in his late fifties and wore black glasses. He seemed to many lawyers who had "grown up Catholic" like one of the more benign pastors from thirty or forty years ago. He was one of the relatively few judges with both the respect of the prosecutors and a reputation for fairness in the defense bar. Although not eloquent, he seemed to get it right.

The defense team had already told the court that they would be seeking a bench trial. Even after thousands of cases, Ferraro seemed agitated when he told Debra, the defendant, about the applicable sentences: "I cannot give you probation, periodic imprisonment, or conditional discharge, mandatory minimum sentence of 20 years, maximum sentence of 40 years in the penitentiary. Under certain circumstances, that penalty could be enhanced to 80 years." It was as if he were saying, "The law limits what I can do in these very serious cases and allows me to impose extremely severe punishments; you understand that, don't you?" Almost pleading: you understand how important this is, don't you? The judge was required to ascertain on the record that the defendant had "knowingly and volun-tarily" waived her jury right. But, again, there seemed to be something more personal happening: rather than the formulaic "making the record," Judge Ferraro told Debra that if she waived her jury right, "you place the fact-finding process in my hands. We call that a bench trial, and the Court, myself, will be solely responsible for deciding whether or not the state has proven you guilty." There seemed to be in his words an attempt to estab-lish a bond with her: that the relationship between judge and defendant was a human bond in which he acknowledged a human responsibility. In effect: "I am not seeking this awful power. . . ."

Then back to the workaday language, the bureaucratic "disposing" of cases. The prosecutor, Brian Kelly, sought to amend his list of witnesses to include all witnesses on the defense list, thus to deprive the defense of a procedural argument against his calling an additional witness. Granted. Motion to exclude witnesses. Granted. Then Kelly:

> Can I give you our schedule? Dr. Levy [the chief medical examiner] is supposed to be here sometime before 2:00 o'clock, okay? Come up to our office and come down here, so he's going to be a witness we'll be calling. We understand there's a doctor which may be called this afternoon from counsel. I have a district attorney who will be called as a witness who is finishing up a trial this morning and should be available after the lunch hour also, but I do have some police we can call possibly this morning, whenever.

What was he saying? "We're in this together, you and I, Judge: the processing and disposing of this one of hundreds of cases here in the city. Subject to all forms of constraint: scheduling, vacations, inadequate expert support systems. Don't forget all that, Judge: that's what we're doing here, disposing of a case, one of hundreds we can barely handle. Let's not forget the context. The context is bureaucratic and political: inadequate resources and scheduling headaches." Again:

> STATE: I think I told counsel Dr. Shapiro, although he's going to be here about 3:00 or 4:00 o'clock today, won't be back until Friday morning, so there's some problem with him, and I think that Dr. Pope, who is a defense witness, will be leaving fairly early today, but he's also available either tomorrow morning or Friday morning.
>
> DEFENSE: Well your honor, we are hoping to get Dr. Pope on before he leaves for the day today, and it's possible we'll finish. When does Dr. Pope leave?
>
> STATE: There's no way we'll get to Dr. Pope today. He will be back Friday morning. He suggested approximately 11:00 o'clock. I talked to Dr Pope with that in mind, since this is going to be a long day and I knew there was other stuff going. Dr. Pope is available for you too Friday morning, if you want, so you've got some flexibility if you want to call him this afternoon, but otherwise, he's available Friday.
>
> DEFENSE: Our logistical problem, we have a Dr. Freed and a Dr. Peterson and we really need to get both of them on this afternoon.
>
> STATE: We'll accommodate that. I expect the cross examination to be fairly long of those expert witnesses.

The judge became less and less interested as these matters consumed more time. Most of the managing and maneuvering and negotiating, begging and threatening and bluffing, that took thirty or so people away from the valued rhythms of their lives and brought them to one place at more or less one time wasn't apparent. That's the way the judge wanted it. We were about to step into an ideal world, a sacred space, a world constructed only by language, a language that had to be sufficient for the grave and often final purposes that were pursued there. Judges and lawyers had to be managers, too, had to organize the performance that was to occur, logistics and all, but that was not their highest calling. The judge wanted to leave the managerial world behind and enter the world of dramatic and moral substance. The prosecutor insisted on telling him that there were scheduling problems, "housekeeping matters," as lawyers put it. That was another real world, but the judge seemed tired of hearing about it.

The State's Opening

The state ("The People") then began its opening statement:

> Your Honor, the defendant in this case is charged with the offense of murder, the murder being committed back on November 9 of 1978 at 455 North Wagner in the City of Rockfield. Your Honor knows where Wagner is, somewhere near or within a few blocks of Central Avenue. That would be the Wilson Park neighborhood.
>
> The evidence will show that on that day, Priscilla Smith, November 9, Priscilla Smith was alive, and, in fact, Debra Miller was her babysitter. The evidence will show that the baby had been staying with Debra and her family, her family being her uncle, Mr. Ripkin. I believe the evidence will show that on that day, Debra Miller was at that address for the purpose of baby-sitting for Mary Taylor's children, those being young children.
>
> The evidence will show that on November 9 of 1978, the police responded to a call, and when they got to 455 North Wagner, they came in and they did note Debra Miller alone, the only, when I say alone, I mean the only adult in the apartment, and they did go to the two rooms in the apartment, being the bedrooms. The evidence will show when the officer came in, the two children who are not the subject of this case were in one of the bedrooms, in the bedroom in fact, that had the uncovered floor.

The state's opening sounded like an indictment, a kind of incantation: all those iterations of "being" this and "being" that. The form of language pulls the events out of ordinary description and says, implicitly, that this *legal* proceeding is where this situation belongs, its natural home. The *speaking* of this form of language says this is the right language, the appropriate language in which this sort of event should be understood, because this isn't an ordinary kind of event. It's literally "legally cognizable." And legally is the way it should be understood. Legal categories, concepts, and procedures are adequate to this event; they exhaust its reality.

The prosecutor knew that the defense had withdrawn its pretrial motions to suppress the defendant's statement as fruit of an illegal arrest and search. Thus it wasn't necessary for reasons of legal sufficiency to include a step in the narrative that showed the police entry into the apartment to have been proper. The story was being told strictly to conform to the requirements of the criminal code.

> The officer went to the other bedroom and found Priscilla Smith not breathing. He rushed her to Memorial Hospital, a few blocks away, where she was pronounced dead.
>
> The evidence will show that she had numerous injuries to her face and had numerous injuries to her skull, her skull being fractured.

Again the language of indictment. The story is being told from the perspective of the actors, how things unfolded to them. The prosecutor is deliberately forgoing a rhetorical possibility that opening statement affords him, that of telling what we have called the ultimate story, that is, the God's-eye narrative of what really occurred, what the evidence *shows*, not what the evidence will be.

Instead, he's just explaining how the events presented themselves to real-world actors who would have significance here only as witnesses. And so he is summarizing the various witnesses' testimony for the court. This approach provides some natural suspense, and it allows the judge to think he is drawing his own conclusions. Its disadvantages are a loss in coherence and the limitations it places on the narrator's ability freely to sequence details that were discovered by different actors at different times in one narrative form.

This choice was rhetorically significant. The audience for an opening statement is beset by a "blessed rage for order." A judge or a jury will hear over days, weeks, or months an enormous range of testimony from a large number of perspectives. In all trials, their responsibility will be to understand one or more human actions. Though what may ultimately be at issue about those human actions will differ from trial to trial, a human action can be understood only in narrative form.[2] The trier of fact will inevitably attempt to understand and organize this material in a narrative form.

If one party presents a reasonably complete narrative to the jury in opening, a narrative into which it can weave the evidence it later hears, and the other party merely recites the evidence, the trier of fact may begin early to interpret that evidence in light of the more comprehensive story. Indeed, the advantage the wealthy criminal defendant may have in some parts of the country is in great measure linked to the inability of the over-

[2] See chapter 6, below.

worked prosecutor to do much more than interview his witnesses and then tell the court or the jury, from his all-too-recent recollection, what he expects them to say.

The legalistic "numerous," to describe the child's injuries also responded to a difficulty with the state's proof. Real events are definite; daydreams are not. If you describe events in the world reliably, you do so definitely. A person who makes a definite statement is thought to be either reliable or a liar. If you can exclude the latter possibility, credibility is much enhanced. Vague descriptions, by contrast, do not provide an organizing framework.

On the other hand, the prosecutor here knew that some of these "numerous" injuries posed a problem for him. It had emerged that there was good reason to think that some of them had been inflicted by someone other than the defendant. Perhaps the prosecutor decided to blur the real fact for tactical reasons, hoping the defense would not "make an issue of it." Perhaps, and worse, he hadn't developed a theory to explain their presence, hoping that they would be just an unexplained detail, an anomaly we could ignore.

> Your Honor, further, the evidence will show that the defendant was brought initially to the 2nd precinct and then subsequently to the 4th precinct to determine what had happened to the child.

These details seemed extraneous. Facts that are not connected to the point of a story detract from the credibility of a story.[3] There was no defense motion to suppress the confession. They added nothing, save perhaps to begin to paint a picture of a scared sixteen-year-old being dragged from station to station, provoking sympathy and undermining the credibility of any statement she may have made.

There was, however, another message encoded in this description. The prosecutor was not a bad storyteller. He was describing the standard bureaucratic steps, the familiar places and events of the criminal justice system. This case was processed, disposed of, and closed as was appropriate for his kind of case. The prosecutor was saying to the court, in effect, "This proceeding is simply the last step in the processing and disposing of this sort of case."

An effective opening statement will portray the meaning, the human significance, of the events that the trial concerns. The most effective openings will say to the judge or juror, "You must condemn (or excuse) this action." To do otherwise would say that the convictions around which you weave your identity are false, and so your life is literally without significance or meaning. One of the convictions of a judge who sits in an

---

[3] Bennett and Feldman, *Reconstructing Reality in the Courtroom*, 41–65.

urban criminal court is that social order is an important value. Among the modes of social ordering that surround him are bureaucratic ones. As one commentator put it much more concretely, "The public regards criminals and the police as garbage and garbage collectors, respectively." There is tremendous pressure on such a judge to resort to bureaucratic modes of ordering in the disposition of criminal cases. The state's opening here gently and respectfully sought to put the judge in his place—that is, his place in the larger bureaucratic system.

> At that time, Debra told the police both on the scene and when they got to the 4th precinct that the baby just had trouble breathing and that she tried to call her uncle to see what to do, and she in fact tried to revive her.
> She was confronted with the obvious inconsistencies due to the severe injuries and she blurted out to the police that she had in fact killed Priscilla.

Though there had been no motion to suppress Debra's statement, Mr. Kelly still thought it was important to protect the voluntariness of the statement. He knew that all the mental health professionals who examined Debra agreed that she was mentally ill. She had also been sixteen at the time Priscilla died. Though the statement was admissible,[4] the prosecution had some reason to be concerned about its reliability. The prosecutor thus tries to make the confession a suppressed truth bursting out under the pressure of a guilty conscience. No suggestion of the kind of police coercion that could distort the truth.

The defense team, by the way, had quite a different version of what had occurred at the police station that night. The police threatened the defendant with the death penalty (for which her youth made her ineligible) if she didn't confess. They threatened the mother of the other children for whom Debra was baby-sitting as well, saying that her children would be taken from her unless Debra admitted injuring the child: "If it was an accident or just a burst of temper, no problem. . . ." Though you could find patches of language in appellate cases condemning this sort of verbal behavior, those little bits of coercion were nothing to shock the conscience, and, of course, it would be completely denied by all the police. The 4th precinct was notorious.

The defense would choose not to introduce any evidence of police coercion. They chose not to "make an issue of it." Such evidence would set up a credibility dispute with a number of officers who would all quite

---

[4] *Colorado v. Connelly*, 479 U.S. 157 (1986). The police reports indicated that Debra was given her Miranda warnings only *after* she admitted killing the child. So the state was committed to the position that Debra was not "under arrest" until after the admission. Otherwise, the admission would have been given in the course of a custodial interrogation without the required warnings.

adeptly swear that Debra was lying.[5] Even if she were not, the suspicion that she was might infect the court's judgment. Many judges were half-conscious of what the police did, but allowing truly awful crimes to go unpunished was a greater evil. And the police knew the judges wouldn't find coercion in serious cases because that would release dangerous people against whom a statement was the most reliable evidence. That there was no coercion in murder cases was a "pragmatic truth" or a "political truth"[6]—a desired result transformed into a historical fact. To make too much of it would be to place yourself outside the political-moral consensus from which cases like these were decided. So the events in the stationhouse would never see the light of day.

> The evidence will show that she told the police that she took the baby, lifted it up to chest level and threw it to the wood floor, causing the injuries to the head for no apparent reason. The evidence will show that she died as a result of this, and you will hear from Dr. Levy [the county medical examiner] about those injuries.

Here's the crux of it. The "lifted it up to chest level and threw it to the wood floor" is the description from which the prosecution seeks the crucial inference of intent to cause death or great bodily harm or at least knowledge that death or great bodily harm was very probable.[7] It was, of course, a matter of common sense that one could draw an inference about knowledge or intent from the circumstances of a killing. Absent a confession, in fact, there was no other way.

---

[5] Cloud, "The Dirty Little Secret."

[6] Binder and Bergman, *Fact Investigation*, 141–43.

[7] For reasons I will not describe here, a rigorous application of the definition of murder in the criminal codes was all but impossible. State legislatures, intent on looking ever tougher on crime, had tinkered with what had been at least coherent categories until they literally made no sense at all in crucial applications. It turned out, however, that the trial was fought out with the use of much simpler categories. Murder was simply "intentional killing." Involuntary manslaughter was "unintentional killing." It seemed to me then, as it seems now, that this simple distinction was good enough. Of course, you could set up gradations of categories and call each a different crime: killing with intent to kill, killing with intent to do great bodily harm, killing with the knowledge that great bodily harm was highly probable, killing with the knowledge that great bodily harm was probable, killing with the knowledge that great bodily harm was possible, killing while consciously disregarding the high probability of great bodily harm, killing while consciously disregarding what a reasonable person would have considered. . . . But at a point soon after the basic distinction, the intelligent assessment of the case and the degree of culpability of the defendant would be distorted by attention to categories that did not cut at the moral joints of the situation. Very broad categories with room for individualized decisions to be made within them seemed the best course. The only contrary argument, it seems, results from an unnecessary assignment of widely disproportionate penalties to the two categories.

But there was more contained in this opening, yet another implicit message. This was a bench trial. The prosecutor knew that the judge had studied a hundred appellate cases upholding murder convictions in which the appellate court invoked the formula that "intent or knowledge may ordinarily be inferred from the circumstances surrounding the killing." By his description of the events, he was bringing this case within that formula, or "codified inference," an inference which had the authoritativeness that those appellate cases gave it. Strictly speaking, those appellate cases held only that a trial court's finding of intent based on circumstantial evidence would not be reversed. But the prosecutor was trying to nudge that over to a rule implicitly providing that intent or knowledge *must* be inferred from the circumstances. The state's rhetoric would try to push a complex question of fact into a legally required "codified inference" of murder.

There was another such inference based on an appellate rule that appeared throughout the case: "Intent to cause death or great bodily harm or knowledge that death or great bodily harm was very probable may (will? should?) be inferred from the fact of instances of previous abuse." This was true even if, and perhaps even especially when, those previous instances of abuse had produced *neither* death nor great bodily harm, and the actions that caused death or great bodily harm in the case before the court were virtually the same as the actions that had previously caused a much lower level of harm. The appellate cases that enshrined this inference didn't even entertain the plausible contrary inference: that a repetition of abusive behavior which had not previously resulted in death or great bodily harm more probably occurred without any "conscious awareness" that *this time* the results would be different, or an intent that they be different.

Again, this "codified inference" was not an empirical generalization about states of mind at all. It was something quite different: a moral judgment transformed into a factual generalization. "Persons who consistently abuse children are monsters, while losing control in a single instance is a lesser evil" had been translated into a factual generalization about intent and knowledge, two "mental states" that were matters of "ultimate fact" with specific and serious legal consequences.

". . . for no apparent reason."

That was why the "legalization" of this event was so important, why the goal of the prosecutor's opening was to draw the judge into treating the case bureaucratically or legalistically. The story that the prosecution was telling lacked a key element of a plausible narrative about a human action and so a key factor in the moral judgment of a human action. It lacked motive. This would turn out to be the key battleground for the trial. The state continually reminded the judge that motive was not an "element" of the crime of murder. And this was true. The state was required to prove "intent" or "knowledge," but there was no legal requirement that the state specify a motive and prove its existence beyond a reasonable doubt. Otherwise, as the prosecutor would urge later in the trial, someone who just walks down the street and shoots people for no reason could not be guilty of murder.

Well, someone who *just* walks down the street and shoots people completely without motive may well have failed to perform a human act. Motives could, of course, be quite varied: from vindicating my absolute freedom, as with Raskolnikov in *Crime and Punishment*, to Orwell's account of the simple savor of power over others, the ever recurring joy of my boot in your face. But an act *completely* without motive may not be a human act at all, for it resists understanding through and representation in complete narrative structure, which requires scene, actor, act, agency, and motive or purpose.[8]

In defending the indifference of the law to motive, the prosecutor was telling the court implicitly that the criminal law could not be absolutely assimilated to the moral law. We *must* find people who just walk down the street and kill people guilty of murder; otherwise this city would not be safe. The criminal law is not so delicate an instrument that it can concern itself with matters so subtle as human motive. Even if you fail to discharge your bureaucratic or legal responsibilities, Your Honor, remember the limited purpose of our inquiry today.

The Received View of opening statement is quite simple. Counsel may preview the evidence that he expects to present. If he is more ambitious, or more accomplished, he may share with the jury his version of what happened, the factual conclusions that should be drawn from all particular bits of evidence presented. The jury will be provided the legal norms to "apply" to its factual conclusions later. The opening is, at best, a value-free account of what occurred.

But this simple opening sought to do much more. It certainly did present a "factual theory of the case." But more important was the prosecutor's implicit invocation of bureaucratic processing and specifically legal modes of understanding this situation. He was urging upon the court, in the guise of a simple narrative, the modes of social ordering appropriate for this situation. "What happened?" was inextricably intertwined with "What is to be done?"

---

[8] Kenneth Burke, *A Grammar of Motives* (Berkeley and Los Angeles: University of California Press), 127–320.

The Defense's Opening

The evidence presented by the state and by Debra Miller will largely overlap. There may be a few disputes of facts, but that's not what this case is about. There will be no dispute that on November 9, 1978, one child killed another, that a sixteen year old girl, Debra Miller, twice threw a ten-month old girl, Priscilla Smith, to the floor, and Priscilla died soon afterwards.

This was something that happened between children. Something truly awful, dreadful, but between children. The defense was focusing the inquiry and setting the theme. The defendant was a "child," a word that had an enormous "semantic range." What happened here happened between two children. "Child" was not a word that appeared in the criminal code. There were certain consequences that flowed from a defendant's being under one age or another, but there were no "children" in the code.

Simply by using this word, defense counsel was placing the event in other webs of meaning that stretched far beyond the code. The judge would remember his own childhood, with something between pity and gratitude. He would remember his own grown children. That they had been at times thoughtless, at times cruel, did not make them hateful. He would remember the scores of stories read aloud to him in schools and churches, that *he* had read aloud to his children, that he had pondered alone. They contained complex and delicate understandings of what it was and what it should be to have a childhood. In a sentence, this complex body of memory, experience, and meaning was now "before the court."

Counsel was conceding in his narrative that Debra "threw" the child to the floor. In fact, the evidence on that point was somewhat more favorable to the defense.[9] Why describe the events in anything other than the most favorable terms that the evidence may support? Because counsel didn't want the court's determination of the precise sequence of physical actions to be important, to be a resolution of a significant *issue* in the case. Of course, he knew it would become an issue, a question in the judge's mind. But the implicit concession in the opening claimed that it really didn't much matter. It said, "Our case does not stand or fall on your acceptance of a version of the sequence of events where you may believe that they have the better of the argument. We don't want to be on the other side of your best judgment: you might start to think that we are

---

[9] The defendant had admitted only "pushing" the child off the bed. The prosecution's forensic evidence cast doubt on that account but could not exclude the possibility completely.

generally trying to push you where your own best judgment does not want to go." Otherwise, we will almost certainly hear this reproach in the state's closing argument: "Remember what the defense promised to establish in her opening. Well, what the *evidence* has established is quite different. . . ." To contest a fact is to concede that it is *important*. To break a promise (even an implicit one) is to invite distrust.

As with the prosecution, so with the defense: even in the way in which the basic story was being told, there was a second-level argument about the significance, the human meaning, of a dreadful event. There was also an argument about what was important specifically for the decision that the court had to make. Defense counsel was moving more slowly than had the prosecutor toward a dispositional argument, an argument about what was to be done, because he wanted the court to *understand* what had happened here. Such an understanding would preclude any of the bureaucratic or legalistic resolutions implicitly urged by the state.

> Everyone will agree that Debra was that night mentally ill. She was in fact the victim of numerous instances of abuse in her own home during her very young years and the victim herself of a chaotic, confusing, abusive and unstable environment.

The defense was presenting another theme for the first time. The environment is the actor here, not merely the setting, and *both* Debra and Priscilla were the victims of that environment. The judge would, in fact, come to accept that characterization, probably by the end of opening statement, and that acceptance would be crucial to the eventual disposition of the case.

Once again, the notion of "common victimization" was nowhere to be found in the code. The code did recognize a small range of defenses: self-defense, necessity, compulsion, entrapment. None of those applied here. The defense's ability simply to tell a *fully characterized story* was pulling the event "outside" the categories provided by the code, and urging different categories and judgments on the court. The full narrative of opening statement gave counsel the ability to draw on any moral norms that his story could invoke.

The full narrative of opening could also move the trier of fact to reconceptualize the basic structure of the principal action in the case.[10] The code was built around a model of an Agent performing an Act against a

---

[10] Bennett and Feldman, *Reconstructing Reality in the Courtroom*, 62. The authors argue that every trial revolves around a central human action. Following Burke, they argue that understanding that action involves an interpretation of the varied relationships of scene, act, agent, agency, and purpose to each other.

Victim within a Scene. The story being told was urging an interpretation of the case in which a Scene caused an "Act" against common Victims.[11]

This notion of "common victimization" was not simply imposed on the data. It had emerged from long and difficult pretrial investigation. Both Priscilla and Debra were victims of abuse. Important evidence would show that Priscilla was the victim of recent abuse by unknown persons. Because it was unknown and faceless, it constituted an ominous and malignant background, literally able to act. The weight of the evidence suggested that the same background had victimized Debra. Finally, there was evidence of an unusually, perhaps significantly, close bond between the girls, so that they were, in some ways, one. The structure of the action could be understood as a Dark Background victimizing both girls, and victimizing each through the other. This could never be argued explicitly. It was too ominous, too "mythical" or irrational. But it could be "shown."[12]

The judge was a traditional moralist—probably the only kind of moralist[13]—and believed firmly in individual responsibility; but he understood that in the real world such responsibility could be diminished, that a person, perhaps especially a young girl, could be so victimized and under such immediate stress that she is but the tool of what would otherwise be merely the scene of her action.

> There will be some disagreement as to the precise diagnosis and, of course, on the ultimate issue that this case presents for your judgment: whether or not there is reasonable doubt that during those few moments, Debra had the conscious objective or purpose of killing Priscilla or doing her great bodily harm or whether she was consciously aware that her conduct would create a strong probability of death or great bodily harm.

Again the defense is attempting, through the way in which the story is told, to tell the court what the *real* issue is. The most important decision was, again, what *not* to engage. The "some disagreement" on the "precise" diagnosis suggests that the way in which psychiatrists may categorize Debra's mental illness is not the most important thing in this case.

Now, this was not quite the innocuous proposition it purported to be. Appellate cases had carved out a sharp line between "personality disor-

---

[11] Such a reconceptualization comes with a powerful philosophical pedigree. See Burke, *A Grammar of Motives*, 127–70.

[12] Narrators "may lack the language and concepts to focus what their style and choice of details is nonetheless constantly showing[.]" Hubert L. Dreyfus, *Being-in-the-World: A Commentary on Heidegger's "Being and Time"* (Cambridge: MIT Press, 1991), 13–14. There does, in fact, exist a psychiatric category for this kind of relationship.

[13] John Austin, "A Pleas for Excuses," *Proceedings of the Aristotelian Society* 1 (1956).

ders," on the one hand, and "psychotic disorders," on the other. Personality disorders were "not mental diseases or defects," in the crude Victorian phrase of the criminal law, and thus could not form the basis of an insanity defense. This judge-made rule had taken a psychiatric distinction drawn for therapeutic purposes and used it to erect an absolute *legal* prerequisite to the insanity defense. This was of less than paramount importance to the defense, however, because the preferred outcome was not a not-guilty-by-reason-of-insanity verdict but a conviction for involuntary manslaughter. The casual treatment of the question of diagnosis told the court, "There are no practically significant distinctions among the psychiatric categorizations." Of course, the evidence would have to bear that out.

And counsel's "of course" tries to suggest that this issue is not even a real one, or won't be. The prosecution *must* disagree on this: that's its role.

> The evidence will show that the more considered psychiatric opinion will be that at the time of the killing, Debra was engaged in what could only be called a psychotic act, without conscious objective or purpose, or conscious awareness of any consequences.

From the defense standpoint, there were a few salient pieces of evidence of the events. In her written statement given to the police, Debra had claimed that her mind had gone "blank" at the time of the killing, and that she had thrown Priscilla to the floor "for reason or reasons she could not explain." The police report had noticed that her motive was "unknown." In the opening statement, those bits of relatively "hard" evidence (because not readily deniable by their authors) would be joined to a psychiatric diagnosis in a fairly loose[14] way to suggest a "factual" understanding of the defendant's state of mind in the theory-laden factual language of psychiatry. Again, "psychotic" is not a term that can be found in the criminal code.

Why had those details been included in the reports and in a statement drafted by the prosecution? After all, those documents were drafted with a strong and experienced eye toward the trial of this case. The police and prosecutor would surely know that those phrases might be the basis of a defense theory later. Why should the police and prosecutor literally create this evidence? In this particular case, it was hard to say. Perhaps it was professional ethics, again, loosely described. They simply could not omit such a salient and obviously important aspect of what the defendant told them. Perhaps it was some more general exigency to present a minimally coherent story or, without such a story, to note its absence. The

---

[14] Though not especially "looser" than the use of the term "psychotic" by psychiatrists themselves. See *Psychiatric Dictionary*, 5th ed. (Oxford: Oxford University Press, 1981), 509–10.

police and the prosecutor simply had to report a story that contained a motive, or, failing that, inform the reader of their unsuccessful attempt to establish one.

There will be a large measure of agreement as to the underlying facts, the evidentiary facts, of what occurred on November 9. Debra was at that time 16 years old. Debra had lived with Priscilla since Priscilla's birth. Debra cared for Priscilla, took care of her, not only day care, but all the time, day and night. The baby's mother paid Debra's uncle, one George Ripkin, for Debra's work. Debra even brought Priscilla along when she went to baby-sit for others, as she was doing the night of Priscilla's death.

Again the narrative is woven around two of the themes. First, the child's mother paid Ripkin, not Debra. There was a hint of exploitation, of victimization, in that relationship. And again, Priscilla was always with Debra. They were inseparable. Priscilla was an aspect of Debra—violence against Priscilla was really directed against herself. Then the fuller statement of the theme and elaboration of the facts that supported it:

When Debra brought Priscilla to that apartment, Priscilla had already been injured, injured by someone else.

The undisputed forensic evidence will be that Priscilla had been bitten many times on her legs and on her arms and on her face by at least two people, at least one of whom was an adult and neither of whom was Debra Miller and that Priscilla was herself a victim of the same chaotic, unstable, and abusive household that Debra had been the victim of for the 16 years before that day.

Only now that the broader narrative structure was laid out did defense counsel turn to the specifics of what had occurred. These might seem to be the hard facts, the specifics from which conclusions about, and interpretations and evaluations of, the larger story would proceed. Good, solid, empiricist, inductivist logic. Nothing so simple would turn out to be true.

In a sequence of events I'll say more about in a moment, Debra was left alone to take care of Priscilla and the two boys. She fixed some milk for them and brought them into the bedroom where she got up onto a bed with them. First Priscilla fell off the bed and Debra picked her up. Then it happened. Without any conscious objective or conscious awareness of what she was doing and utterly without motive—no crying, no disobedience, no interruption or anything else that would provide a scrap of a motive—Debra pushed or threw Priscilla down onto that floor.

The legally crucial moment. Told quickly, as it happened. Try to eliminate the obvious reasons why a "normal" adult might injure a child in a flash of uncontrolled anger or irritation. We condemn such a failure of control, morally and so legally. To call this an "act" is merely to confess a failure of language.

Opening statement should present what the evidence will *show*, not what the evidence will *be*. There is, however, an exception: where the story urged on the trier of fact is intrinsically implausible, discontinuous with the standards of common sense that form the web of belief in which we catch the world, reinforcements are necessary. A motiveless human act is such an implausible fact. Thus quickly bring up the strong evidence of that otherwise implausible account:

> The police, of course, looked for a motive, but they could only say that the motive was unknown, that the reasons were unknown. The state's attorney, after his interrogation, could only say that it was for reasons that Debra could not explain. Debra could only say in her statement that her mind went blank. She had thrown the young child to the floor, then picked her up and told her how sorry she was, and then they lay in bed together, the two of them, for a short time. Debra then pushed Priscilla off the bed again.
>
> When Debra saw Priscilla getting pale, she was snapped back into reality, began giving CPR, breathing air into her lungs. A bruise began to appear on the young girl's head, and Debra ran and got an ice pack and placed it on her head. She kept up the CPR, interrupting it only to call her uncle, for help. She couldn't get through because the woman who answered the phone couldn't understand what Debra was talking about. Debra slammed down the phone and began screaming for help.

Chaos, physical and emotional. Debra was not a moral monster, a sadist: she was begging for forgiveness in the middle of this explosion. She didn't even understand that she was *hurting* someone until the physical signs of injury began to appear. Then "snapped back into reality." This piece of narrative (for which, of course, there was no direct evidence) solved a specific problem with the defense theory of the case.

Another of those codified inferences found in scores of appellate cases ran like this: action exhibiting rational, means-end thinking soon after a homicide is strong proof of intent or knowledge and of sanity. Debra had, in fact, engaged in (ineffectual, to be sure) cardiopulmonary resuscitation soon after Priscilla's death. The story the defense told sought to neutralize what might be a damaging inference supported by the weight of law transformed into fact. The rhetorical task was to remove that inference and substitute for the factual inference a potentially competing evaluation not of the behavior but of the person of the Defendant. The real Debra, the Debra in touch with reality, is decent. The pragmatic message: with proper precautions, she could be safely released. . . .

"Screaming for help" makes this same moral argument and a factual one as well. It illustrates a lack of "conscious objective" or intent in what Debra had done. A second after the event, Debra wants to help Priscilla. "Screaming and crying" was a possibility—that would have portrayed Debra as a child herself, a major defense theme. There probably was some element of truth in both descriptions.[15] But you only get to describe it once. After all, a determinate picture carries its own warrant of credibility.

> She took Priscilla to the bathtub and splashed cold water on her and continued to breathe air into Priscilla's lungs, stopping only to call the police but by that time somebody had heard the screams and called the police and they walked into the apartment.

Same factual theory and theme. The CPR is a "problem" for the diminished capacity defense because it seems to show rational, goal-oriented behavior. The defense's putting it in this narrative context allows the court to see through the overgeneralized formula lurking in the legal doctrine.

Notice how the story being told is filled with inferences, conclusions, and evaluations. No witness would be permitted to testify in this fashion. Opening statement provides the lawyers the opportunity to tell the story freely, and so, paradoxically, to tell it concretely. What is concrete is not a set of "sense-data," abstracted from experience and reported to the court. The concrete includes answers to all the questions about these events that would be asked, including questions about their proper interpretation and evaluation. In opening statement those answers are transformed into a narrative built up from inferences and evaluative themes rooted in common experience and ordinary morality.

It is hard to overemphasize the importance of the availability of what might be called "free narrative" in the opening statement for the American trial; it is essential for an understanding of what American law is. First, the permission a lawyer has to tell the story freely invites the jury to use the full range of its powers of inquiry in deciding what the event under consideration was. It vastly increases the range of what it *possibly* was. (The power to put questions, which is intelligence or insight, is just the power to entertain possibilities.) And it prevents the legal system from rigidly defining what factual conclusions are to be drawn from certain kinds of data. It makes any "codified inference" approved by appellate courts even hundreds of times only a single possibility, not an authoritative (and overgeneralized) definition (*de* + *finis*, delimitation) of what is real. It keeps the legal world in touch with the full range of human intelli-

---

[15] See Stuart Hampshire, *Thought and Action* (New York: Viking Press, 1960), 20–27, on the "inexhaustibility of description."

gence as it plays in the world of factual truth and falsehood. It keeps the legal world from ossifying.

Second, it keeps the trial, and so the law, in intimate touch with the full range of moral evaluation. As Shaftesbury put it, "historical truth is itself a part of moral truth. To be judge in one, requires a judgment in the other."[16] The opening narratives in this case, in particular the defense narrative, employed a whole range of words—"child" and "victim," for example—that carried serious moral weight though they appear nowhere in the criminal code. Those descriptive-evaluative terms could provide the norms through which the judge or juror decides the case. As we will see at greater length below, this is what the lord chief justice meant when he said that the juries "resolve both law and fact complicatively, and not the fact by itself."[17]

Finally, the adversary system gives each party the right to tell the story his or her own way. Each side can appeal to those aspects of common sense and invoke those modes of social ordering in the light of which his position is likely to receive the most sympathetic hearing. An attorney is not permitted to argue that his client should prevail based on norms other than those embedded in the jury instructions, but that is of far less consequence than his ability to tell his client's story unencumbered by officially approved logic and officially approved morality.

> Now, Debra told several inconsistent stories to the police over the course of the day. Finally, around four in the morning, she told the police that she had thrown Priscilla to the floor. The police wanted to know why, but Debra could not explain what caused her to do this and the police could only note, "unknown reason, unknown motive." The state's attorney later that morning could do no better: "Reason or reasons, she could not explain."

The prosecution would rely on the inconsistent statements, some of which are exculpatory, to "demonstrate" (1) awareness of the distinction between right and wrong and (2) strategic behavior soon after the killing, the ability rationally to order means and ends—two other broad principles embedded in the case law. The defense thus had to contextualize and reinterpret those inconsistencies in the confusion and chaos of the night of the killing, and to anticipate the explanation that they were the result of a "fluid sense of reality," about which the psychiatrists would soon speak. The constitutive rules of the trial allow exactly this kind of contextualization and reinterpretation. If "every fact has two faces," the trial would allow the trier of fact to look on both of them.

---

[16] Lord Shaftesbury, *Characteristics*, vol. 1 (Indianapolis: Bobbs-Merrill, 1964), 97.

[17] Chief Justice Vaughn of the Court of Common Pleas in *Bushell's Case*, 6 How. St., Tr. 999, 1015.

Again, the refrain of the absence of motive. Behavior truly without motive is an affront to common sense and so must be supported by especially strong evidence. Hence the reliance upon the admissions of the police and the state's attorney.[18] More broadly, motiveless behavior would become more plausible when placed in the full story of Debra's life and in the psychiatric story of her condition. And so the conclusion:

> The evidence will show this was an act of madness, that it can't be understood in the language of intention, conscious objective or purpose, or of knowledge, a conscious awareness that certain consequences in the real world will follow, or motive, doing one thing in order to accomplish something else.

Here counsel is bridging between the commonsense world and that of psychiatry. "Madness" is not a word that comes easily to the lips of trained psychiatrists. Again, the message is that precise diagnosis is not important. What is important is the inapplicability of the definitional terms of the murder statute. The implicit argument of the story is that this event is simply not one of those to which the usual paradigm of human action, in which intentions and awareness of consequences are important elements, applies. The implicit argument of the opening is not that the prosecution could not prove this particular element. It's that the whole "language" of intentions and knowledge doesn't apply here.

> What Debra could not explain in the language of sane human beings—motives, reasons, intentions—Dr. Daniel Freed, adolescent psychiatrist, and Dr. Peterson, a clinical psychologist with a large experience with adolescents, will explain.
>
> You will learn that in December of last year, Dr. Freed supervised a twenty day inpatient psychiatric evaluation of Debra. After those twenty days, he judged that additional interviews were necessary and conducted another six interviews early this year. He was, with great resistance from Debra, able to unearth the source of her psychopathology.

Again, the psychological analysis is not just grafted onto the case. The absence of motive, which we know of from unimpeachable sources, requires some sort of explanation. And there is such an explanation. It was not manufactured: Debra resisted telling her doctor about it. That will be

---

[18] The police are technically not able to make admissions against the state in criminal cases. In some jurisdictions, the state's attorney may make such admissions. By contrast, anything the defendant says "can and will be used" against him in a court of law. How can the distinction be justified? Well, perhaps by a normative judgment that no mere agent should be able to bind the sovereign people. Or perhaps by a merely strategic one: an instance where the fact-finding devices of the trial are skewed simply to produce a higher number of convictions, one of those inevitably overgeneralized counterbalances to the defendant's constitutional advantages.

a theme throughout the trial: even the state's psychiatrists will note that she seemed eager to present herself as *less* sick than she really was.

Counsel then recounted in strong language details I will omit here about Debra's home environment. There were often several children in the apartment and Debra was required to perform the very demanding and strenuous work of caring for those young children. The picture is one of chaos and exploitation of Dickensian proportions. Debra grew up in a context well out of the ordinary. That is her story.

> By her early adolescent years, she was engaging in classic self-destructive behavior. She was being physically abused in the house during the same period of time. By the time of Priscilla's death she had dropped out of school to engage in this work of caring for children.

Counsel then described the psychiatric interviews, highlighting her resistance to the notion that she was sick. She exhibited a tenuous and fluid sense of reality, a profound instability of mood, a fragile and unstable identity, and a deep, deep rage with which she was not in conscious contact.

His diagnosis: borderline personality disorder. The most important characteristics are intense anger, and lack of control of that anger, and the propensity to transient psychotic function. Function where she was literally out of touch with reality.

> Those psychotic episodes were tornadoes spun off the storm of her underlying mental illness. Dr. Freed concluded finally that prior to the night she killed Priscilla, Debra had been functioning in a stressful, unstructured environment, that the events of that night were particularly disorienting.
>
> She wanted to please everybody, and she couldn't please everybody because the people wanted her to do different things and contradictory things. That on that evening she was the victim of a transient psychotic episode that allowed her rage to burst through the weak and torn membrane of her personality. That the rage was directed at the child who was the object of Debra's own special care and attention, almost a part of herself.

The focus of the trial is Debra's own history, environment, and sickness. It is a startling account, especially for a decent, conservative, compassionate Catholic gentleman like Judge Ferraro. It "says" more than simply "an abusive background," an abstraction that can easily disappear into the perceived needs of bureaucratic processing. A moment's irrational rage can be genuinely understood only as part of two larger stories. One story is simply biography; the other is psychiatry, although with a deliberate softening of the importance of the more rigorously defined psychiatric categories.

The story does not ignore the legal categories for those of psychiatry and what might be called "narrative morality." Recall that bit of appellate elaboration of the insanity defense which excluded personality disorders from the range of "mental diseases or defects" that could serve as the basis for the insanity defense. Though the thrust of the case was toward the involuntary verdict, the defense team wanted to hedge the bet just a little. It was just arguable, though nothing more, that a very short psychotic episode spawned by a severe personality disorder might serve as the "mental disease or defect" on which the cases insisted for an insanity defense. The defense wanted to keep that possibility in the case, since it was unclear how the evidence would finally play out.

Conclusion

The opening statements in the case from which the above was taken consume less than fifteen pages of double-spaced transcript. Yet they brought an enormous range of considerations into play. They invoked fundamentally different ways of understanding a situation where there were relatively few factual disputes, and sought to persuade the judge to resolve this deeply problematic situation through contrasting forms of social ordering. The battle was over "what this case is about." By deciding what to make an issue and what potential controversies to avoid, they were offering different notions of the relative importance of significant social norms to the very specific context of this case. They showed respect even for those norms that they claimed *not* to be most relevant to this case. Both were strong interpretations, with deep bases in the evidence, and animated by important moral and social values.

V

The Trial's Most Basic Features and Some Observed Consequences

> People need to be reminded more than they need to be informed.
> *(Dr. Johnson)*

> The aspects of things that are most important for us are hidden because of their simplicity and familiarity. (One is unable to notice something—because it is always before one's eyes.) . . . [W]e fail to be struck by what, once seen, is most striking and most powerful.
> *(Wittgenstein)*

> "All there is to thinking," he said, "is seeing something noticeable which makes you see something you weren't noticing which makes you see something that isn't even visible."
> *(Norman Maclean)*

WE HAVE SEEN that the Received View is beset with anomalies which cast doubt on its understanding of the trial. I have reviewed the practices and constitutive rules that make the trial what it is. I have interpreted a relatively simple trial performance and found it to put into play levels of questions well beyond the "issues of fact" envisioned by the Received View. In this chapter, I begin the task of constructing a more adequate understanding of the contemporary trial, one that both is more accurate and can hold its ground normatively. I begin in a phenomenological or descriptive idiom (a radical empiricism) to draw attention to aspects of the American trial almost too basic to be noticed. Then I review the most consistent and reliable of the social science findings about the trial and show how they are consistent with what we know about the trial's practices, rules, and basic aspects. Eventually I will offer an account of the real significance of the trial's elements and an alternative model of decision making at trial that is more adequate to the trial's practices and constitutive rules, its most basic aspects, and the empirical work.

Having already examined the practices and rules out of which the trial is built, its elements, I want now to provide a thick description of aspects of the trial itself—what those elements help create. This descriptive task is an important counterweight to some forms of social scientific investigation of the trial because the latter naturally "see the method of science before their eyes, and are irresistibly tempted to ask and answer questions in the way science does."[1] Excessive confidence in causal explanation under general laws or model building can stem from a "craving for generality"[2] that is unhelpful in attempts to understand forms of human language, of which the trial is a particularly complex example.[3] Ultimately both perspectives, those seeking causal explanation and those relying on thick description, are necessary. As Pitkin puts it with regard to the full understanding of any form of public action: "[I]t is a mistake to choose between these perspectives at all. We need to see at both levels, to be both hedgehogs and foxes simultaneously. In the same way, we need the 'sociological, or political imagination' to see action from both the perspective of choice and the perspective of causation."[4] Pitkin is, of course, alluding to Isaiah Berlin's division of thinkers into foxes, who know "many things," and hedgehogs, who know "one big thing." In this section, I will imitate the foxes.

Features of the Trial Too Basic to Be Noticed and Preliminary Notes on Their Significance

The Elevation of the Concrete, the Factual, and the Multiple

I have provided an illustration of how opening statements can put into play broad issues well beyond what the Received View understands as "issues of fact." I want now to remind the reader of aspects of the trial event that occur after opening statements which are so basic and familiar that their significance can easily be lost. I take another step here toward the concreteness of what the trial is, beyond its constitutive practices and rules. This is a task of simple description: the features of the trial that I

---

[1] Ludwig Wittgenstein, *The Blue and Brown Books* (New York: Harper and Row, 1965), 18. See John W. Danford, *Wittgenstein and Political Philosophy: A Reexamination of the Foundations of Social Science* (Chicago: University of Chicago Press, 1978), 80–83; Hanna Pitkin, *Wittgenstein and Justice* (Berkeley and Los Angeles: University of California Press, 1972), 241–86.

[2] Wittgenstein, *Blue and Brown Books*, 17.

[3] "I want to say here that it can never be our job to reduce anything to anything, or to *explain* anything. Philosophy really *is* 'purely descriptive.' " Ibid., 18.

[4] Pitkin, *Wittgenstein and Justice*, 286.

recount here are far more important than the more arcane points of evidence or professional responsibility law that occupy many legal scholars. Indeed, that law is most often a more or less adequate attempt to prop up these more basic features and will be fundamentally misunderstood outside their context.

Though I claim here that groups of these features do function together to create yet more general aspects of the trial, which I identify, I do not argue that these more general effects exhaust the significance of the features I describe. There is an element of sheer multiplicity in the trial's characteristics—they have developed historically over many years for many reasons. To understand the trial is, in part, to gain some imagination for these basic features and their contribution to the multiplicity of perspectives and values at play in the trial.

First, there are a number of basic features of the trial that elevate the importance of the *concrete and specific features* of the case and draw the mind away from easy generalizations. For example, the rules that control witness examination and opening statement force the conversation that occurs in the trial courtroom, and thus the attention of the juror, into a focus on the past. A problematic situation that cries out for present resolution is refocused into a rigorous, perhaps obsessive, concern with exactly what occurred in the past, the one thing no one can change. Moreover, once the evidentiary stage of the trial begins, a trial lawyer can make a general point only by eliciting a specific fact. Every universal must be embedded in a particular: "No ideas but in things!"[5] In particular, witnesses are limited to the "representational"[6] function of language; they may say only what they perceived on an earlier occasion. They may not make promises other than to tell the truth in this very limited sense[7] (e.g., promise not to do it again). They may not usually make predictions. They may not advise the jury on what it ought to do. They may speak only of what they perceived on some earlier occasion, and that only in the lan-

---

[5] William Carlos Williams, *Paterson* (New York: New Directions, 1951), 14.

[6] Richard K. Fenn, *Liturgies and Trials: The Secularization of Religious Language* (Oxford: Blackwell, 1982), 126.

[7] *How* limited is the point Sandburg makes:

"Do you solemnly swear before the everliving God that the testimony you are about to give in this cause shall be the truth, the whole truth, and nothing but the truth?"

"No, I don't. I can tell you what I saw and what I heard and I'll swear to that by the everliving God but the more I study about it the more sure I am that nobody but the everliving God knows the whole truth and if you summoned Christ as a witness in this case what he would tell you would burn your insides with the pity and the mystery of it."

Carl Sandburg, *The People, Yes* (New York: Harcourt Brace, 1936), 193.

guage of perception. This "speech situation" that focuses on the past constitutes, in large part, the reality to which the jury must respond. The witnesses' bringing the past through language into the light of the present forces the audience to consider the meaning of the events recounted and, in the context of the trial, to act in response to that meaning.[8]

This is in marked contrast to the language characteristic of other forums into which problematic situations may be brought, and thus to other "modes of social ordering."[9] In mediation, for example, discussion of the past is usually viewed as a kind of preliminary "venting," sometimes necessary before the parties can get on with the serious business of reconstituting their relationship for the future. Since Thucydides and Aristotle,[10] it has been understood that the feature of a problematic situation which defines it as political is the focus on the future course of action advantageous to the parties deliberating. Some understandings of the "political" give primacy of place to the importance of reconstituting the relationships among parties who occupy distinct and irreducible positions and perspectives in a forward-looking way. Despite important differences, bureaucratic modes of social ordering, at least in their pure forms, are similar to political modes in their focus on the future, involving the exercise of power through technical knowledge to achieve efficient outcomes.[11] The sustained focus of the trial on the past is quite extraordinary and in marked contrast to other and distinctively modern modes of social ordering.

---

[8] Mostly the past is allowed to fade into oblivion, largely without regret. To bring the past into the light of the present and to act in response to its unchangeable present meaning can occasion the shipwrecks (and perhaps the redemptions) of tragedy. Sophocles' Oedipus plays are the classical example. This is part of what Chesterton meant when he likened the trial to the "wild terrors" of tragedy. See chapter 6, below.

[9] Lon Fuller, "Mediation: Its Forms and Functions," *Southern California Law Review* 44 (1971): 305.

[10] In the debate concerning the fate of the city of Mytilene, Thucydides has the Athenian statesman Diodotus distinguish sharply between debates in the law courts designed to achieve justice and truly political deliberation aimed at public expediency. Thucydides, *History of the Pelopenesian War*, trans. Rex Warner (New York: Penguin Books, 1954), 219–21. Likewise Aristotle distinguishes between forensic rhetoric, the discourse of the law courts, and deliberative rhetoric, the discourse of public policy, in precisely these terms. Larry Arnhart, *Aristotle on Political Reasoning: A Commentary on the "Rhetoric"* (De Kalb: Northern Illinois University Press, 1981), 48–50. Aristotle notes that *narrative*, the form of direct examination, has little place in purely political debate. Aristotle, *Rhetoric* 1414a, trans. John Henry Frese (Cambridge: Harvard University Press, 1926). It is the prominence of the narrative of direct examination that limits the political nature of the trial.

[11] MacIntyre, *After Virtue*, 79–87. Utilitarianism is the corresponding normative theory for purely bureaucratic modes of social ordering. The practical incompatibility of bureau-

Furthermore, lawyers have a right to the presence of virtually all witnesses and answers to all proper questions. Again, this is something dramatically discontinuous with ordinary conversations and even most public interchanges. The trial is a forum where every consideration not protected by a specific rule may be urged and virtually every privacy invaded. We have seen how the ethos of the profession encourages this invasiveness, a kind of intrusive brazenness that has not done much for the public estimation of attorneys. The lawyer's right (and obligation) to call upon all the power of the state to force the answer to a question relevant to the assertion of a right is so familiar that its significance can be missed. As Arendt has noted, in the modern world "factual truth, if it happens to be opposed to a given group's profit or pleasure, is greeted with greater hostility than ever before."[12] Even where facts are publicly known, the "same public that knows them can successfully, and often spontaneously, taboo their public discussion, and treat them as though they were what they are not—secrets."[13] And so "it is not difficult to imagine what the fate of factual truth would be if power interests, national or social, had the last say in these matters." The ethos of the profession and the rules of the trial guarantee that unpopular truths can find their way into a forum where real power can be exercised.

At the heart of the trial lies the testimony of a succession of witnesses through time. If time is "the moving likeness of eternity,"[14] each account of every episode recounted by the witnesses becomes the *only* and, for an instant, the privileged lens through which *all of the evidence* is viewed. Although the opening statements usually provide, by contrast, two unified and comprehensive perspectives from which the evidence may be viewed, the actual progress of the trial presents to the juror an enormous range of evidentiary details, any one of which may provide the juror with the factual or normative key to the entire trial. Trial lawyers are often surprised by the details that jurors find crucial. This feature of oral presentation of the evidence available to the jury only in succession would be absent if the jury were provided only a written account of

---

cracy with respect for moral rights corresponds to utilitarianism's incompatibility with a rights-based or desert-based moral philosophy. Rawls, *A Theory of Justice*, passim.

[12] Arendt, "Truth and Politics," 236.

[13] Ibid. Arendt goes on to observe that public discussion of uncomfortable *facts* seems to be more offensive to ideologically driven tyrannies than even the expression of disfavored philosophies: "Even in Hitler's Germany and Stalin's Russia it was more dangerous to talk about concentration and extermination camps whose existence was no secret, than to hold and to utter 'heretical' views on anti-Semitism, racism, and Communism." Ibid.

[14] Plato, *Timaeus* 37d, trans. Francis Cornford (New York: Bobbs-Merrill, n.d.), 98.

witness statements and depositions. The succession of witness testimony multiplies the serious perspectives from which the juror may see the evidence.[15]

Finally, it is extraordinary—shocking, really—that in a "common law" system the jury has before it no precedent whatsoever when it makes its decision. "The law" comes to it in the form of a few legal categories, only some of which are even defined.[16] Appellate courts spend much of their time debating, refining, and sometimes altering these formulas. This refinement often does involve the courts' distinguishing earlier cases "on their facts," identifying those factual aspects of earlier cases that explain and justify differing results. This process takes place most clearly (and abstractly) when the issue comes to the court of appeals from a decision on a motion to dismiss, where the factual allegations in the complaint are assumed true, or on those summary judgment cases where it is fairly clear that there are no real disputes of fact and the only dispute is over the correct result as a "matter of law." As I mentioned in the first chapter, common law systems draw the facts of earlier cases more intimately up into the law than do Continental systems, since the former understand the law as a never completely determined tension among announced facts, results, and rationales in which the rationales can, with relative ease, be considered mere dictum. This process allows, although it surely does not compel,[17] the development of a complex and refined body of law in which different patterns of fact are joined to results in a manner that can in some sense be called "consistent."

The jury sees almost none of this. Instead the jury is provided with a statutory formula or judicially created definition, "a rulelike pronouncement of higher authority, the facts . . . stripped to their shadows."[18] It sees only the minuscule portion of the discussion in the earlier cases that has found its way into the instructions, and so cannot engage in the process of legal interpretation distinctive to common law systems. On the one hand, the jury has before it two extraordinarily detailed factual narratives, presented witness by witness, and including every fact each attorney believes significant. On the other hand, the jury hears only the most for-

---

[15] We will see that this feature is linked to the nature of the "reflective judgment" which the jury exercises. See chapter 7, below.

[16] Notoriously, many courts refuse to define "proof beyond a reasonable doubt."

[17] Appellate courts can surrender the discipline of common law development and allow conflicting precedent to develop without concern about consistency and reconciliation. They, too, can begin to decide cases "on their facts" with only a nod toward legal reasoning.

[18] The reader will recall that this is Damaska's phrase for what the Continental judge looks for in a precedent!

mulaic statement of "the law." It cannot be surprising, then, that the key to an understanding of jury verdicts lurks in the so-called factual portion of the case, and not in the instructions.

Devices That Intensify the Struggle over the Meaning of Events

Second, there are basic features of the trial that serve to intensify the *meaning* or *significance* of the events being recounted. The American trial, especially the jury trial, occurs over a relatively compressed period of time. This is in stark contrast to the Continental model,[19] where the trial literally evolves over a much longer period of time and ends only when the judge has determined that further investigation is not warranted. The Anglo-American compression has a number of effects. It elevates the opportunity for and necessity of thematic unities, the theory and theme of the case. Temporal compression also fosters more "holistic" approaches to the evidence by removing the obstacles that fading memory may pose to a grasp of the vastness of the varying implications of the evidence. It allows for the "showing" of things that cannot easily be said. And it fosters the tacit grasp of "the cumulations of probabilities . . . too fine to avail separately, too subtle and circuitous to be convertible into syllogisms."[20]

Furthermore, the parties have considerable control over "what to make an issue of" or "what this trial is about." This is true, as we have seen, both in the initial framing of the case and, as the case proceeds, in decisions about which portions of the opponent's evidence to challenge. These are among the most important decisions a trial lawyer makes. Almost as important as the initial cut into the evidence, the inspired simplification that is the theory of the case, are the numerous decisions a lawyer makes as the trial proceeds, about which gambits to accept, which feints to engage, and which issues to join. The back-and-forth of direct and cross and then, on a larger scale, the shape of the defense case and of rebuttal and surrebuttal tend to narrow the dispute to a small number of "factual" issues. The issues chosen inevitably provide the ever-narrowing end of the telescope through which all the rest of the evidence will be viewed as the trial comes to an end, a process that elevates their importance. Each side will want his endgame to be played on the most favorable factual and normative terrain. Neither side may fail to engage an issue, however unfa-

---

[19] Damaska, *The Faces of Justice and State Authority.*

[20] John Henry Newman, *An Essay in Aid of a Grammar of Assent* (London: Longmans, Green & Co., 1930), 288.

vorable, where its silence will be deafening. In the trial courtroom, what is most talked about often becomes what is most important; the oral medium takes on a life of its own, heightening the reality of its subjects, and obscuring that about which it is silent. As the trial comes to an end, each lawyer will want to be talking about his strongest evidence but also must be giving his best responses to his adversary's best evidence. These contrary considerations elevate the evidentiary pressure on just the right issues through which the rest of the evidence should be seen.

Aspects of the Trial That Suspend Judgment

Third, in contrast to the features that intensify the meaning or significance of the events being tried are a series of features that serve to postpone judgment, almost to force the jury to keep an open mind. For example, there exists a taut balance between opportunities to speak continuously and to dispute what has been said. In opening statement, each lawyer may speak for an extended period without interruption.[21] Next, the party with the burden of proof presents his evidence continuously, and the opposing party is usually forbidden to present any evidence[22] during the plaintiff's or prosecution's case in chief. The defendant then presents evidence continuously with similar limitations on the plaintiff. Rebuttal and sometimes surrebuttal follow, subject to similar restrictions. The juror may thus assess those qualities of a party's case that are characteristics of the *whole* case, its coherence and the importance of its themes, for example.

This is not, however, the whole story. The defendant may ask the juror in opening statement to keep an open mind until all the evidence is in. He may interrupt the direct examinations with objections that sometimes tell the juror, even where the evidence is finally deemed admissible, that it is unreliable. Most important, there is cross-examination. Cross-examination serves as a continual reminder, as we have seen, that there is another way of looking at the case, or that there is reason not fully to credit the testimony offered. It serves to keep the mind of the juror just open *enough*, so that he can appreciate the coherence of the proponent's case and yet still be open to evidence and argument to the contrary.

A related basic feature is embedded in the rules that prohibit jurors (1) from discussing the case until all the evidence is in and (2) from asking

---

[21] There are only a few grounds for objection to opening statement, notably the elusive prohibition on "arguing" the case, and objections are relatively rare. Underwood and Fortune, *Trial Ethics*, 310–16.

[22] The rule in most jurisdictions is that the cross-examiner may not offer evidence in the course of the cross-examination.

questions of the participants. These prohibitions impose a kind of passivity on the juror and assure that all the values immanent in the full range of the trial's linguistic performances have their effect before the inevitable narrowing and abstracting that comes with "taking a position," or the kind of commitment that often comes with asking a question in public.[23]

Finally, with the atrophy in America[24] of the British practice of the judge's commenting on the evidence, the trial contains *only* the competing narratives and deconstruction of those narratives. The juror is thus faced with a true "polyphony" of a sort usually achieved in dramatic or narrative art, where the author makes the best case for each of the perspectives represented in speech and action by the characters. The premise of the trial is analogous to that of such art, where no omniscient narrator exists to explicate the meaning of the action. In each case, the truth of the situation emerges or is "shown," if at all, from the tension of opposites. This is all the more true at trial because the stories told by the witnesses and the dramatic interaction of witnesses and lawyers are scripted not by a single author but by many authors, both witnesses and lawyers, who are in *actual* conflict. Thus, in a sense, the juror is the artist of the piece, though he is asked only for judgment and not for the rarer gift of expression.

The Courtroom Drama as Lens and Metaphor

Characteristics of the trial, then, force the mind downward toward the concrete, intensify the competition over the meaning of the events being tried, and cultivate the suspension of judgment until all the aspects of the situation are explored. Additionally, and perhaps most pervasively, the

---

[23] These last two features are sometimes thought to be likely candidates for reform efforts. See, e.g., Franklin Streier, *Reconstructing Justice: An Agenda for Trial Reform* (Westport, Conn.: Quorum Books, 1994), 236–42, 245. Obviously, I believe that they have positive functions.

[24] The version of Rule 105 of the *Federal Rules of Evidence* proposed to Congress by the Supreme Court would have provided:

> After the close of the evidence and arguments of counsel, the judge may fairly and impartially sum up the evidence and comment to the jury on the weight of the evidence and the credibility of the witnesses, if he also instructs the jury that they are to determine for themselves the weight of the evidence and the credit to be given to the witnesses and they are not bound by the judge's summation or comment.

As the Report of the House Committee on the Judiciary put it, this grant of "authority not granted to judges in most state courts" proved "highly controversial" and was not enacted. Jack Weinstein et al., eds., *Evidence: Rules, Statutes, and Case Supplement* (Westbury, N.Y.: The Foundation Press, 1993), 163.

trial is a powerful dramatic event where the performances of the participants can easily become the key to the jury's comprehension of and then
judgment about that situation. The trial itself thus becomes a kind of
metaphor for the underlying events in a way, I will argue in later chapters,
that does not distort but illuminates those events.

First, the juror must look through, and so at, the performances of the
lawyers and the witnesses at trial in order to "see" the past events on
which the principles of trial evidence focus the juror's attention. Although
there are sometimes truly neutral or "third party" witnesses, it is often
the case that the parties, parties in interest (such as the victim in a criminal
case), and those aligned with either are the most important witnesses in
the case. Testifying is a difficult performance fraught with dense moral
significance, and the juror must rely upon it in discharging his heavy duty
of judgment.[25] The most important norm governing testimony, of course,
is truthfulness. Truthfulness is not just one norm among others but is
fundamental and generative of other norms. A person who is not truthful
in the right way at the right time is likely to be otherwise flawed. A person
who is not truthful at trial offends the juror by trying to frustrate his
sworn task.

The trial puts the truthfulness of the participants of the real-world dispute and of their representatives at issue. This can be a subtle business.
Where one of the participants can be shown to have lied to the jury or
willfully shaded the testimony, the jury cannot but wonder about the general willfulness of that person, his willingness to submit to common
norms or, by contrast, his willingness to "make himself an exception."[26]
But it is more than simply lying or distorting testimony that the trial
exposes. The requirement that a witness on direct examination testify in
response to nonleading questions means that he must choose the words
in which to tell his story. Telling the story of a past event is a moral enterprise that reveals a great deal about the storyteller. To do it perfectly, to tell
a story as it happened, may well require "a purity of soul, an unmirrored,
unreflected innocence of heart."[27] It certainly requires him to make one
choice after another among the infinite possibilities for characterizing any
event, choices that cannot but reveal a great deal of who the witness is
and to which our tacit abilities of assessment and recognition are highly
attuned. And, as we have seen, on cross-examination a witness can be

[25] On the centrality and irreducibility of testimony as a source of human knowledge, see
Coady, *Testimony.*

[26] See Arendt, *The Life of the Mind,* 188. Arendt argues that the moral agent's willingness
or unwillingness to make himself an exception to a universal rule that he himself must at
least implicitly affirm is at the core of Kantian ethics.

[27] Hannah Arendt, *Eichmann in Jerusalem: A Report on the Banality of Evil,* rev. ed.
(New York: Viking, 1964), 229.

asked to describe and interpret events in revealing ways, something from which the witness cannot be protected.[28]

The lawyers, too, must achieve a kind of truthfulness.[29] A failure on their part can also undermine a case. This kind of truthfulness has, no doubt, more artifice about it than that of the witness. For lawyers, there is no pretense of telling the truth, the whole truth, and nothing but the truth; perhaps "fairness" is a better word than "truthfulness" for the ideal that animates their performance. A lawyer's speech must take into account the public norms that shape the proceeding, including the sometimes odd "grammar" imposed by the law of evidence, the legal norms embedded in the instructions, and the moral and political sensibilities of the jury. Yet it must not appear strained or willful in its account of the people and events that the jury will consider. The ability to speak this way is a further refinement of the lawyer's insight, the "inspired cut into the evidence" by which he or she chooses a theory and theme. A theory that cannot coherently be "performed" is unlikely to be persuasive.

Most obvious of all, the trial is spoken. The jury hears most of the important evidence (1) through the testimony of witnesses (2) with whom they do not converse, (3) whom they can *see*, (4) but from a distance larger than that typical of ordinary conversation[30]—certainly greater than "touching distance."

Here again we have a tension of opposites. The "aural" medium involves the listener in the inner life of the speaker in a way that sight alone cannot do. "Sound always tends to socialize,"[31] and "[v]oice is inherently relational."[32] McLuhan noticed long ago that "the world of sound is essentially a unified field of instant relationships."[33] The kind of selflessness

---

[28] For example, I recall the cross-examination of a plaintiff in a race discrimination case that involved, in part, the distribution of racist cartoons in a workplace. The defense attorney asked the plaintiff a series a questions about which pieces of literature were "racist" or offensive and which were not and why, a line of questioning cleverly designed to reveal any oversensitivity or willfulness. It required the plaintiff to make extremely fine distinctions among the writings, a task that he, in fact, performed superbly, but in a context where a misstep could have changed the case.

[29] I have tried to address this issue at greater length in Burns, "A Lawyer's Truth." White explores the nature of this truthfulness in his "reply" to Socrates in "The Ethics of Argument."

[30] On the relationship of physical proximity to styles of oral communication, see Edward T. Hall, *The Hidden Dimension* (Garden City, N.Y.: Doubleday, 1966), 72.

[31] Walter J. Ong, *Rhetoric, Romance and Technology: Studies in the Interaction of Expression and Culture* (Ithaca: Cornell University Press, 1971), 284.

[32] Elizabeth Bernstein and Carol Gilligan, "Unfairness and Not Listening: Converging Themes in Emma Willard Girls' Development," in *Making Connections: The Relational Worlds of Adolescent Girls at Emma Willard School* (Troy, N.Y.: Emma Willard School, 1989), 20.

[33] Marshall McLuhan, *Understanding Media: The Extensions of Man* (New York: McGraw-Hill, 1964), 241.

implicit in oral conversation has been described this way:[34] "Consider what it is to listen and understand someone speaking to us. In a certain sense we have to become the other person; or rather, we let him become part of us for a brief second. We suspend our own identities, after which we come back to ourselves and accept or reject what he has said."[35] Listening to witnesses, including party-witnesses, makes the trial an intersubjective experience in a way that reading written transcripts could not. The medium makes it difficult for the jury to objectivize the case, to treat it simply as a stereotype of a certain kind of controversy.

Similarly, oral communication also makes it virtually impossible to separate the content of the spoken communication from an assessment of its source:

> An "objective" assessment of spoken words alone is difficult. Spoken words are carried by a personal voice; they are mouthed by a personal presence from which they cannot be readily detached. In such a context, objective "meaning" merges with subjective "opinion." Because of the physical closeness of most aural relationships and the resultant difficulty in achieving objectivity in such a context, persons in aural contact tend to develop more of a feeling for one another and may be better able to empathetically appreciate each other's position. Even in extreme cases, "addressing . . . and listening to one's enemy, experientially reveals that one's enemy is truly human."[36]

Trial lawyers know that how a witness performs in the dense interpersonal field which the trial creates is often more important than what the witness has to say. The trial heightens our already refined sensibilities for perceiving this always implicit form of character evidence.

On the other hand, the physical setting of the trial and the procedural rules foster the critical process by putting limits on the identification with the witnesses and parties. We typically feel the inclination to respond to the human voice, an urge that the rules of the trial frustrate. Witnesses and lawyers speak from distances well beyond those typical of ordinary conversation and physical contact. The American artist Maurice Grosser expressed his need to paint a model from some distance this way:

[34] Bernard Hibbits, "Making Sense of Metaphors: Visuality, Aurality and the Reconfiguration of American Legal Discourse," *Cardozo Law Review* 16 (1994): 229, 344. He quotes James M. O'Fallon and Cheyney C. Ryan, "Finding a Voice, Giving an Ear: Reflections on Masters/Slaves, Men/Women," *Georgia Law Review* 24 (1990): 883, 896–97: "[L]istening . . . unlike sight, involves a turning toward the Other. An epistemology of listening compels us toward dialogue rather than detachment."

[35] Hibbits, "Making Sense of Metaphors," 344, quoting psychologist Julian Jaynes, *The Origin of Consciousness in the Breakdown of the Bicameral Mind* (Boston: Houghton Mifflin, 1976), 96.

[36] Hibbits, "Making Sense of Metaphors," 344, quoting Robert J. Lipkin, "Kibitzers, Fuzzies, and Apes without Tails: Pragmatism and the Art of Conversation in Legal Theory," *Tulane Law Review* 66 (1991): 69, 109.

[A]t touching distance, the sitter's personality is too strong. The influence of the model on the painter is too powerful, too disturbing to the artist's necessary detachment, touching distance being not the position of visual rendition, but of motor reaction or some physical expression of sentiment. . . ."[37]

Physical distance beyond touching distance and ordinary conversation distance emphasizes the inevitability that a judging person is, at least in part, a spectator.[38] The physical semiotic of the trial thus embodies what Beiner has called the two moments of good judgment: sympathy and detachment.[39]

My own experience suggests that the distance from which the witnesses and lawyers must address the judge and jury reduces the level of particularity that is communicable. This is in part what supports Louis Nizer's "rule of probability," the canon of trial practice that improbable conduct should be rejected as untrue regardless of any intensely personal conviction that it occurred.[40] The physical distances seem to impose a kind of limit to the degree to which a speaker can appeal to considerations that have not achieved a fairly broad level of acceptance in the society, that pose too much of a challenge to common sense. It may be that the physical distances remind the hearer of his relative ignorance of who the speaker is—that he is, however convincing, in most ways a stranger—thus reducing the range of issues on which the speaker can say implicitly, "I know this is hard to believe, but just trust me." The effect of these distances explains, in part, the trial lawyers' hard-won saying, "If it sounds bad in your office, it will only sound worse in the courtroom."

Finally, it has frequently been noted that the trial has some of the characteristics of a *dramatic* performance. All the trial's actions, whether of witnesses, lawyers, or judges, are public performances. As such, they have the capacity to mediate between the general norms that a jury brings to the decision of the case and the highly particular factual context on which the trial focuses. There is a kind of paradox here: performances can be exquisitely sensitive to public norms but can, at the same time, be ex-

---

[37] Hall, *The Hidden Dimension*, 72.

[38] Beiner, *Political Judgment*, 158–62. Merleau-Ponty called vision a "dissecting" sense. "Vision is that sense which places the world at greatest remove." Evelyn F. Keller and Christine R. Grontworki, "The Mind's Eye," in *Discovering Reality: Feminist Perspectives on Epistemology, Metaphysics, Methodology, and the Philosophy of Science*, ed. Sandra Harding and Merrill B. Hintikka (Dordrecht: D. Reidel, 1983), 207, 213. Walter Ong observed that "[l]ooking at another person has normally the effect of reducing him to a surface, a non-interior, and thus to the status of a thing." Walter J. Ong, *The Presence of the Word: Some Prolegomena for Cultural and Religious History* (New Haven: Yale University Press, 1967): 8. All cited in Hibbits, "Making Sense of Metaphors."

[39] Beiner, *Political Judgment*, 102.

[40] Nizer, *My Life in Court*, 12.

tremely attentive to the particular details of the individual case.[41] Performance can integrate what on a conceptual level appear as so many contrary considerations.

Even testifying accurately, is, as we have seen, performance. The attorneys' task is to render a performance which interprets the entire case in light of the most compelling norms that surround it. What Steiner has said of all dramatic performance applies, in different ways, to each of these performances:

> An interpreter is a decipherer and a communicator of meanings. . . . He is, in essence, an executant, one who "acts out" the material before him so as to give it intelligible life. . . . [I]nterpretation is understanding in action; it is the immediacy of translation. Such understanding is simultaneously analytical and critical . . . an act of penetrative response which makes sense sensible. . . . The true hermeneutic of drama is staging. . . .[42]

The performances of the trial activate the jury's capacity to hear whether the case "rings true." The performance of the meaning of the case, its theory and theme, relates it more directly to the central convictions of the jury's life world. It places the case in the rich tangle of norms that is common sense and moves the case further from the vision embodied in the Received View: "Live presentation . . . may give more urgent reality to the particular acts that establish distance between a given case and general rule or that expose a given case to competing rules. Performance of cases, by thus contributing to indeterminacy, helps to bring about the conditions for creative resolution."[43]

Of course, the trial cannot be the "imitation of an action"[44] in exactly the same sense as is a play: past events are seldom literally reenacted under a willed suspension of disbelief. By contrast, the trial proceeds by different sorts of narratives that are oriented, in different ways, toward an actual past event. Nonetheless, important continuities exist that make the dramatic analogy irresistible.[45] Witnesses and lawyers tell stories that are internally "dramatic." Lawyers interact with each other and with witnesses in ways that create the interpersonal tensions associated with drama.

---

[41] Bernard J. Hibbits, "'Coming to Our Sense': Communication and Legal Expression in Performance Cultures," *Emory Law Review* 41 (1992): 874, 957.

[42] Steiner, *Real Presences*, 7–9.

[43] Ball, *The Promise of American Law*, 61.

[44] Aristotle, *Poetics* 1450a, trans. S. H. Butcher as *Aristotle's Theory of Poetry and Fine Art* (Dover Publications, 1951), 27.

[45] See Ball, *The Promise of American Law*, 42–63. Ball's treatment is acute and deeply humane. He concludes that the theatrical nature of the trial proceeding serves to communicate nonverbal information, redirect aggression, encourage impartiality, and induce creativity in judgment. Ibid., 58–62.

Those tensions function positively to reveal, in ways that are only partially articulated, what is at issue in the case.[46] The trial does not just reenact but is itself a set of actions and judgments with enormous consequences[47]—an (in-court) drama about a (real-world) drama.

The dramatic form provides the specific kind of "metaphoric substitution" that occurs in the courtroom, "a tacit comparison in which presentation of selected fact and law is substituted for the events themselves and the prior law."[48] The dramatic form of the trial deepens the general tension between involvement and distance distinctive to the trial as oral communication[49] and reflects a feature of the trial that is close to my central argument. It allows for some sympathetic identification with those aspects of common sense invoked in different ways by each lawyer, while distancing the audience from each vision, in order to allow some limited transcendence of commonsense judgment. It thus achieves something akin to what Brecht called drama's "alienation effect," achieved in the theater through

---

[46] As Chiaromonte put it:

In the theatre, the main thing is the drama, the conflict of individual situations, of idea and passions—*the clash of characters who are left, so to speak, on their own*. If this is so, then the fictional elements . . . lose all importance.

Chiaromonte, "On Pirandello's 'Clothing the Naked,' " *New York Review of Books*, February 20, 1975, at 31. Ball comments:

At its best, the representation of a case is a coincidence of reality and illusion, not in the sense of perjury, but in the sense of theatrical metaphor—the reenactment of relevant and material elements for reflection and judgment. Although elusive, this paradoxical interplay of reality and illusion does seem to correspond with the deeper truth of the way we experience life, which is to say that it is a strength, and not a weakness or fault, in the playhouse and the courtroom.

For Ball's deliberately provocative "illusion," I would substitute, "those beliefs which enable us to act."

[47] " 'There is something at stake'—the essence of play is contained in that phrase." J. Huizinga, *Homo Ludens*, at 49, quoted in Ball, *The Promise of American Law*, 166 n. 107.

[48] Ibid., 51.

[49] Trials occupy a complex position on the orality-literacy span. If one reflects on the characteristics that Walter Ong has identified as distinctive to primarily oral culture, one can easily see them in the language and structure of the trial. Ong tells us that oral style is "additive" (and. . . . and. . . . and) rather than complexly subordinating. Oral discourse tends to resort to repeated formulas, to be close to the human life world, to be "agonistically toned," and to be situational rather than abstract. Trial rhetoric has those characteristics. On the other hand, the tightness of the organization of the narrative structures presented by the participants in a contemporary trial would probably not be possible in a preliterate culture. See Walter Ong, *Orality and Literacy* (London and New York: Methuen & Co., 1982), 36–57, 147.

devices which subtly remind the audience that it is, after all, an audience, and that the actors are playing roles.[50]

This same attitude of limited identification with attorney or parties while observing them and forming judgments about them is the attitude appropriately developed in judge and jury as audience. The courtroom equivalent to alienation may arise from the way attorneys present their cases, from comments by the judge, from bench conferences, and the like, all of which may remind the judge or jury that a decision about the action must be reached.

In a sense more profound than that of Brecht's "alienation effect" and its courtroom equivalents, the distancing necessary to good judgment lies in the very nature of drama and the dramatic. . . .[51]

Ball argues that what Eric Bentley has said of theater is true of trials as well: "the little ritual of performance, given just a modicum of competence, can lend to the events represented another dimension, a more urgent reality."[52] The "urgency" of the trial drama leads to another of its principal features, that it persuades not logically but "histrionically."[53] It engages more of the person than merely his or her intellect, something that broadens rather than contracts the audience's understanding, as Aristotle understood:

Emotions can sometimes mislead and distort judgment; Aristotle is aware of this. But they can also . . . give us access to a truer and deeper level of ourselves, to values and commitments that have been concealed by defensive ambition or rationalization.

But even this is, so far, too Platonic a line to take: for it suggests that emotion is valuable only as an instrumental means to a purely intellectual state. We know, however, that for Aristotle appropriate responses . . . can, like good intellectual responses, help to constitute the refined "perception" which is the best sort of human judgment.[54]

This form of perception is especially appropriate to the jury, given the fundamentally practical task it faces: it is the frame of mind suited to deft action. By contrast, the importance of this dramatic form is missed when "the courtroom is thought of as a laboratory or a research library, with the mistaken consequence that methods employed in the courtroom are

[50] Ball, *The Promise of American Law*, 60.

[51] Ibid.

[52] Ibid., 58, quoting Eric Bentley, *The Theatre of Commitment and Other Essays on Drama in Our Society* (New York: Atheneum, 1967), 207.

[53] Fergusson, *The Idea of a Theater*, 236–40.

[54] Martha C. Nussbaum, *The Fragility of Goodness: Luck and Ethics in Greek Tragedy and Philosophy* (Cambridge: Cambridge University Press, 1986), 390.

urged to approximate the 'methods of historians or physicians or geologists' rather than those of playwrights, actors and directors, and may be described as the making of metaphor."[55]

Trial lawyers understand that the metaphors they propose—what they want the case to be understood *as* ("This is a case about . . .")—are not necessarily to be found in the words of the various trial languages: they are to be found "in performance or by imagining a performance."[56] The "enactment" of the trial provides the material for a dramatic sensibility on the jury's part, a "primitive and direct" awareness "before predication," as Aristotle put it, of the actions and performances displayed before it.[57] Because "[w]e do actually in some sense perceive the shifting life of the psyche directly, before all predication," our dramatic sensibility "perceives and discriminates actions."[58] The trial requires that all the evidence come before the jury in the form of performances which, in this "primitive" but profound way, ring true or false.

G. K. Chesterton, in his reflection on his own jury service, expressed this sensibility most acutely:

> All the time that the eye took in these light appearances and the brain passed these light criticisms, there was in the heart a barbaric pity and fear which men have never been able to utter from the beginning, but which is the power behind half the poems of the world. The mood cannot even adequately be suggested, except faintly by this statement that tragedy is the highest expression of the infinite value of human life. Never had I stood so close to pain; and never so far away from pessimism. Ordinarily, I should never have spoken about these dark emotions at all, for speech about them is too difficult. . . .[59]

In a sense akin to the action of tragedy, the trial addresses the "misery of human nature and destiny with the health of the soul in view."[60]

Pity and fear are "modes of . . . being outside of oneself, which testify to the power of what is taking place before us."[61] Dramatizations serve to "extricate their subject matter from that which is considered to be inessential to it and simultaneously reveal that which is most signifi-

---

[55] Ball, *The Promise of American Law*, 49, quoting Fergusson, *The Idea of a Theater*.

[56] Ibid. It is precisely by imagining such a performance that trial lawyers seek to make the inspired cut into the materials around which everything else is organized. See chapter 2, above.

[57] Fergusson, *The Idea of the Theater*, 239.

[58] Ibid., 16. Fergusson offers the example of the good teacher's provoking the histrionic sensibility to "reveal directly to the student the peculiar focus of psychic being, the kind of concentration, which their discipline requires." Ibid., 238.

[59] G. K. Chesterton, *Tremendous Trifles* (London: Methuen, 1920), 64–65.

[60] Fergusson, *The Idea of the Theater*, at 232.

[61] Gadamer, *Truth and Method*, 117.

cant."[62] In the end, what is most significant is an aspect of those events, now fatefully and unchangeably determinate, that the juror can recognize, with distress and apprehension,[63] in their heightened truth as part of his world.

What Emerges Most Clearly from the Empirical Studies

I turn now to the empirical studies of the trial, most often the jury trial, and identify the points that emerge most clearly from them. They confirm the effects of the practices, rules, and basic aspects of the trial that we have already examined, and further demonstrate the partial nature of the Received View. There is surely room for argument about the particular points I consider the most important, and I will necessarily omit provocative results of studies that are unconfirmed or difficult to interpret. The normative import of these studies is open to debate. Were an empirical jury study to discover something truly surprising (which has, I believe, never occurred), one might find it difficult to claim that such a hitherto undiscovered aspect of the trial, about which its framers were unaware, was the result of a considered judgment of justice. It might more likely suggest a target for reform. I believe, however, that the jury studies have generally performed the very useful function of confirming the intuitions of thoughtful participants in the American trial system. As such, they provide material important for a normative theory of the trial and fruitful hints as to the limitations of the Received View.

Jury study research is of quite different sorts, including survey research on actual juries,[64] participant-observer ethnological studies of trials or trial transcripts,[65] and simulated jury studies conducted under a large range of conditions more or less abridged from those that prevail in actual trials and with greater or lesser degrees of rigor.[66] As the more sophisti-

---

[62] Georgia Warnke, *Gadamer: Hermeneutics, Tradition and Reason* (Stanford: Stanford University Press, 1987), 58.

[63] Gadamer argues that the traditional "pity and fear" are too subjective and psychological.

[64] The classic work remains Harry Kalven, Jr., and Hans Zeisel, *The American Jury* (Boston: Little Brown, 1966). There has been no comparable work of similar scale. For a fascinating account of the reception of that work in the legal community, see Valerie P. Hans and Neil Vidmar, "The American Jury at Twenty-Five Years," *Law and Social Inquiry* 16 (1991): 323. The authors call for a replication of the study to determine the effects of social and institutional changes since the original work. Ibid., 347–51.

[65] See, e.g., Amsterdam and Hertz, "An Analysis of Closing Arguments to a Jury,", 55.

[66] See, e.g., Reid Hastie, ed., *Inside the Juror: The Psychology of Juror Decision Making* (Cambridge: Cambridge University Press, 1993); Hastie, Penrod, and Pennington, *Inside the Jury*.

cated investigators are themselves aware, each form of study has its own marked limitations.[67] Questionnaires are limited by the self-selection and perceptions of those who choose to respond; ethnomethodological studies have been criticized for failing to produce falsifiable or reliably general hypotheses; and the more "rigorous" simulated studies often take place under "laboratory" conditions so far removed from those of actual trials that, to use considerable understatement, "literal extrapolation" to actual trials "would be imprudent."[68]

Leaving this work out of account, however, would be foolish, especially where there appears to be a convergence of findings, and especially where investigators using different methods seem to reach analogous conclusions. An adequate normative theory of the trial gives normative weight to the actual practices that make up the trial. Its "justification is a matter of the mutual support of many considerations, of everything fitting together into one coherent view."[69] Both the legal developments surveyed in the first chapter and the relatively secure results of empirical studies have to be taken into account.

This is not to say that such an integrated understanding is simple. Difficult methodological issues may prevent the integration of methods of social science research that explicitly seek to create a "scientific image" of the jury by discovering quantifiable relationships between certain bits of "jury behavior" and independent variables of one sort or another. Precisely what those independent variables are makes a great deal of difference, as does the interpretation of the relationship between those independent variables and the dependent variables (jury "behaviors") they "explain." Where the independent variables and the postulated relationship are such that no normative account can be given of that same relationship, difficulties of integration into a normative account are probably insurmountable. These are cases where the independent variables cannot serve as *reasons or justifications* within a recognizably normative perspective for the results that form the dependent variables in the "scientific" account. For example, if social scientists could isolate the variable of the defendant's race and demonstrate its causal effect on verdicts, they would have identified an aspect of jury decision making ripe for reform, not a defensible situated ideal. To invoke once again a distinction important within the philosophy of science, certain independent variables affecting jury behavior may provide a behavioral or causal explanation of an intellectual practice (whether a science or a trial) but not a rational reconstruc-

---

[67] See Finkel, *Commonsense Justice*, 58–62, for an account of the strengths and weaknesses of the experimental method.

[68] Hans and Vidmar, "The American Jury at Twenty-Five Years," 339–40.

[69] Rawls, *A Theory of Justice*, 579.

tion of the *validity* of the practice's results.[70] By contrast, where such a distinctively normative account can be given, methodological problems are delicate, but not insurmountable. In fact, it turns out that most often the independent variables are capable of a normative redescription, and the notion of social scientific "explanation" invoked by the investigators is, to say the least, not fundamentally incompatible with a normative appreciation of the relationship between the "causal factor" and the behavior "caused." *This*, not the mere quantity of the independent variables that frustrates "cross-tabulation," is what is really "flattering to law."[71]

When social scientific research produces the kind of qualified generalizations that seem most in keeping with its capacities,[72] it can shed important light on the questions I am asking here, about what the trial has become. It is in fact indispensable to "thinking what we do," in Arendt's phrase, in the trial, and at least as important as the more traditional study of the constitutive normative rules of the trial. This is not to say that issues for judgment do not remain even after the best descriptive work: part of a practice can become decadent and no longer deserve normative status. To use Hegelian language, it no longer expresses the ethical substance, the moral ideals embedded in the actual institutions of the society, that underlies the practice.[73] It should be reformed, not followed.

The Importance of the Evidence

We saw in the last section that the devices of the trial drive the mind of the juror downward, toward the specific details of the case. The empirical literature reflects the importance of the evidence. First, jurors are deeply engaged with the evidence, and their verdicts emerge from that engagement. Negatively, this means that attempts to predict juror decision making from general characteristics like race, gender, age, or nationality fail.[74]

---

[70] See Richard J. Bernstein, *Beyond Objectivism and Relativism: Science, Hermeneutics, and Praxis* (Philadelphia: University of Pennsylvania Press, 1983), 61–66. The fact that normative elements loom larger in the trial than in empirical science does not itself preclude such a reconstruction. Indeed, my entire effort here is such an attempt.

[71] Kalven and Zeisel, *The American Jury*, 91.

[72] MacIntyre, *After Virtue*, 88–108.

[73] On the importance, once again, of *situated* ideals, ideals that are actually implicit in current practices but stretch beyond their current level of realization, see Taylor, *Hegel*, 537–71.

[74] See, e.g., Abramson, *We, the Jury*, 143–78; Valerie P. Hans and Neil Vidmar, *Judging the Jury* (New York: Plenum Press, 1986), 76–77. For a philosophically sophisticated review of the major book-length jury studies, see Marianne Constable, "What Books about Juries Reveal about Social Science and the Law," *Law and Social Inquiry* 16 (1991): 353–72. ("The studies claim that attempts to connect demographic states, abilities, aptitudes, tem-

This engagement with the evidence has several salient characteristics. Juries do not often decide cases in the teeth of the law or directly and consciously exercise their power of nullification of positive law,[75] though it does sometimes occur. This agreement between jury verdicts and (what judges believe to be) the legally correct result stems more from the fact that the norms embedded in the legal categories are usually not far distant from those that a cross-sectional jury might apply to decide a case even in the absence of instructions, rather than from the jury's mechanical or even conscious application of those instructions.[76] In a democratic society, a major discrepancy between legal rules and public mores should not occur too often nor last too long. In fact, jury comprehension of instructions, for reasons obvious to anyone who has ever listened to them, is quite low.[77] Where the jury decides a case differently from the way in which a judge would decide it,[78] this usually occurs because what the

---

peraments, and personalities of juror to verdict had met with 'limited success' . . . and they argue that cases are decided by the evidence. . . . 'different issues, different defendants, different contexts, different evidence should and did make for different verdicts' " (quoting Rita Simon, *The Jury: Its Role in American Society* [Lexington, Mass.: D. C. Heath & Co., 1980]: 146). Perhaps the best recent survey of all the social science literature is Reid Hastie, introduction to *Inside the Juror*, 3.

[75] The power of nullification is a legally recognized authority in only two states, Indiana and Maryland. In the federal system, jury nullification has been rejected since 1895, and jurors now receive an instruction telling them that their obligation is to decide the case in conformity with the law whether they agree with the law or not. *Sparf and Hansen v. United States*, 156 U.S. 51, 64–106 (1895).

[76] Kalven and Zeisel, *The American Jury*, 495–96.

[77] See, e.g., R. Charrow and V. Charrow, "Making Legal Language Understandable: A Psycholinguistic Study of Jury Instructions," *Columbia Law Review* 79 (1979): 1306–74. There is some evidence that instructions can be made more comprehensible and thus, the proponents argue, more important in the trial. Hans and Vidmar, *Judging the Jury*, 121. Simulated studies have suggested that making what might appear, to an academic criminal lawyer, key changes in the definition of the insanity defense makes little difference in outcomes. Ibid., 193.

[78] There are methodological problems about determining how a judge "would have" decided a case. Kalven and Zeisel asked the judges in their sample to tell them how they would have decided the case, and to do so based on notes made before the jury returned its verdict. As they realized, of course, the judge was aware that he or she was not actually deciding the case, and this absence of real responsibility might well have changed the result. Kalven and Zeisel, *The American Jury*, 53–54. It would be theoretically possible to conduct an experiment in which one deceived juries in what were actually bench trials into believing that they were deciding the case in order to solve these methodological problems. But the ethical problems are, it seems to me, insurmountable. First there is the deception in an important matter of public concern. Then there is the need to impose the experiment on often unwilling defendants and prosecutors or risk the danger of a prejudiced sample. Who would want to do that? And so we have, at a metalevel, a case where we would sacrifice factual (here social scientific) truth to ethical values. Just as we do in the trial itself! See generally "Forbidden Knowledge" (symposium) in *The Monist* 97 (1996).

social scientists blandly call "values" have influenced the very fact-finding process itself, not usually because the jury has found the same "facts" as the judge and then consciously applied different norms, an act that looks more like nullification.[79] As Kalven and Zeisel tell us, the jury's "war with the law is thus both modest and subtle."[80]

Moreover, the most reliable predictor of a jury verdict is the first ballot, a finding that was made by Kalven and Zeisel and consistently replicated in the other studies. Thus it appears that jury deliberation is not the most important determinant of results, which poses a bit of a problem for proponents of the jury as the embodiment of the "deliberative ideal."[81] This conclusion underlines the centrality of what we have called the engagement of the individual juror with the evidence and reemphasizes that the central focus of further investigation should be the way in which the evidence is presented to the jury in the first place.

Finally, the social scientific study of actual juries that attempts to explain behavior by isolating causal factors (the method of "cross-tabulation") quickly runs aground on the need for enormously large samples. This failure is "flattering to the law"[82] in that "[t]he variety of circumstances that affect the verdicts in criminal cases turn out, as a trial lawyer would suspect, to be so great as to hobble the use of cross-tabulation."[83] The significance of this failure is important. It means that sensitive empirical investigators observe such a large number of *potentially determinative*

---

[79] Kalven and Zeisel found that in four out of five cases where the judge and jury disagreed, "evidence problems" were at the core of their disagreement. Indeed, in 43 percent of cases, the judge thought that *only* "evidence problems" separated them. *The American Jury*, 111–14.

[80] Ibid., 495. Kalven called it "the jury's polite war with the law," in Harry Kalven, "The Jury, the Law and the Personal Injury Damage Award," *Ohio State Law Journal* 19 (1958): 158. Again there is a methodological problem. Kalven and Zeisel seem to assume either (1) that the judge can engage in value-free fact-finding to which he or she can then apply the legal norms (the Received View) or (2) that the judge can apply precisely the legally defined norms in the process of fact-finding. In the absence of evidence of either of the foregoing, a jury's "war with the law" may be more a "war with the judge." If the latter's fact-finding has become routinized or bureaucratic, there is no reason to call the jury's differences from the judge a war with the law at all. For a thoughtful argument that a jury's construal of the law's requirements at odds with its fair meaning should be viewed as nullification, but also as consistent with the Rule of Law, see Darryl K. Brown, "Jury Nullification within the Rule of Law," *Minnesota Law Review* 81 (1997): 1149.

[81] Hans and Vidmar, "The American Jury at Twenty-Five Years," 343; Hans and Vidmar, *Judging the Jury*, 110; Abramson, *We, the Jury*, 198–99. Abramson argues plausibly that deliberation is nonetheless important, and that we must safeguard the quality of deliberation. I agree that the performance of juries during deliberation is important and worthy of serious attention. My focus is, of course, on the trial itself, largely because Abramson has already so ably explored the deliberative process.

[82] Kalven and Zeisel, *The American Jury*, 91.

[83] Ibid.

factors that it becomes literally impossible for them to isolate individual independent variables using the usual social scientific methods. Even the notion "potentially determinative factors" itself somewhat understates the problem, since it necessarily relies on a researcher's own judgment that a limited (though still enormous) subset of a yet larger number of factors may *plausibly* motivate jurors (and so "cause the verdict") in a given case, a judgment that inevitably contains both empirical and normative elements. It shows that the more rigorous social scientific methods necessarily have a limited, though important, role in contributing to understanding of the trial. Rather, the vastness of possible factual inferences, the range and variety of the kinds of "inputs" produced by the trial, *and* the complexity, subtlety, pervasiveness, and tacit nature[84] of the normative judgments that constitute jurors' life worlds create empirical shoals on which any exhaustive empirical investigation will founder. This is a major methodological consideration that drives empirical investigators to create the controllable abstractness of laboratory conditions, increasingly unlike those that prevail in real trials.

The Multiple Sources of Jury Norms

We have begun to see how the practices, rules, and basic aspects of the trial provide the jury with moral sources reaching wider and deeper than legal formulas. Those sources include the norms implicit in narrative and in the dense personal interactions at trial, intensified by devices we have just examined. In fact, the social science literature suggests in different ways that trials are decided in modes that are inconsistent with the methods proposed by the Received View. Kalven and Zeisel documented at length that the considerations which "explain" jury behavior do not fall along the fault lines of legal categories but usually derive from aspects of the case that do not fit nicely within the legal categories that find their way into the jury instructions.[85] To refer back to figure 1, the crucial step where the jury "fairly" characterizes its purely factual conclusions seems not to be an important factor in actual decision making.

The investigators agree that a jury's approach to the evidence is "equitable" rather than "rule-oriented."[86] Among other things, this means that the jury will find some things important that the law judges irrelevant,

---

[84] See Jürgen Habermas, *Between Facts and Norms: Contributions to a Discourse Theory of Law and Democracy*, trans. William Rehg (Cambridge: MIT Press, 1996), 21–23.

[85] Kalven and Zeisel, *The American Jury*, 76.

[86] Ibid., 495.

and may deem unimportant facts the law suggests to be crucial.[87] As Kalven and Zeisel put it, "while the jury is often moved to leniency by adding a distinction the law does not make, it is at times moved to be more severe than the judge because it wishes to override a distinction the law does make."[88] Put somewhat more abstractly, this suggests that the jury does not organize the evidence for itself as so many logical trains aimed precisely at the norms and distinctions embedded in the instructions.[89] Rather, the jury makes many factual distinctions important to a whole range of evaluations subtly connected with various *levels* of moral and political judgment. If the juror is a moralist, it is in the mode of novelist, not the moral philosopher who tries to derive all judgments from a single first principle.[90]

Specifically, though the law of evidence sometimes provides that evidence may be considered for only one purpose but not for another, juries cannot but consider all evidence for all purposes.[91] They may not distin-

---

[87] For example, the jury may consider it important that the defendant was seriously injured at the time of the crime, or that the victim is not enthusiastic about prosecuting, or that the defendant's behavior is rarely prosecuted, or would not be illegal across the river in the next state, or that the defendant was not represented by counsel. Ibid., 270, 293, 305, and 319. More specifically, it can be important that a defendant was suffering horrendous personal tragedies during the time he (even "knowingly") failed to file an income tax return, or that the defendant used a toy gun rather than a real gun in an armed robbery (even if the law makes the distinction irrelevant). Ibid., 293 and 338.

[88] Ibid., 494.

[89] Perhaps the most rigorous attempt to analyze evidence in these terms was Dean Wigmore's "charting" system. See John Henry Wigmore, "The Problem of Proof," *Illinois Law Journal* 8 (1913).

[90] See Nussbaum, *The Fragility of Goodness*, 12–14. The structure of the trial moves the judges in the same direction, though they may sometimes "remember" that they are, after all, legal technicians and ought to proceed in another way. As Louis Nizer put it:

Although jurors are extraordinarily right in their conclusion, it is usually based upon common sense "instincts" about right and wrong, and not on sophisticated evaluations of complicated testimony. On the other hand, a Judge, trying a case without a jury, may believe that his decision is based on refined weighing of the evidence; but . . . he, too, has an over-all, almost compulsive "feeling" about who is right and who is wrong and then supports this conclusion with legal technology. Because Judges, sometimes, consciously reject this layman's approach of who is right or wrong and restrict themselves to precise legal weights, they come out wrong more often than the juries.

Nizer, *My Life in Court*, 359. Nizer's judgment is consistent with Judge Hutcheson's classic realist statement of the importance of intuition in bench trials. Hutcheson, "The Judgment Intuitive: The Function of the Hunch in Judicial Decision," *Cornell Law Journal* 14 (1929): 274.

[91] See *Federal Rules of Evidence*, Rule 105 (authorizing the judge to instruct the jury to consider evidence for one purpose but not for another). D. W. Broeder, "The University of

guish among (1) what is likely to have occurred, (2) whether this witness, particularly this party-witness, is to be believed, and (3) what kind of a person this party is.[92] In another idiom, they tend to elide the issues of factual accuracy and witness credibility, on the one hand, and corrective and distributive justice, on the other.[93] It is likely that jury acquittals result not so much from any pro-defendant sensibility as from their specific way of understanding the evidence, which can broadly be called "equitable" rather than "rule-oriented" or "legalistic."[94]

It does happen that juries disagree with judges for what, with some naïveté, might be called "purely" factual reasons, perhaps because they resolve credibility issues differently or have a different operational notion of the burden of proof.[95] Other juries may disagree with the determination that the judge would have made because of simple disagreement on "values." Most often, however, juries differ from judges because judgments about the evidence are strongly influenced by evaluative considerations: "In the world of jury behavior, fact-finding and value judgments are subtly intertwined."[96] As Lord Devlin put it, "I do not mean that they [the jury] often deliberately disregard the law. But if they think it is too stringent, they sometimes take a very merciful view of the facts."[97] This is Kalven and Zeisel's central thesis, the "liberation hypothesis." It is not that juries often deliberately and consciously disregard the instructions as given. Rather, "[d]isagreement arises because doubts about the evidence free the jury to follow sentiment."[98]

Narrative structure is a key factor in the outcome of trials, in ways that social scientists are struggling to identify and measure. If cases are decided, thankfully, through an intense engagement of the trier of fact with the evidence, then that evidence is encountered as a battle between com-

---

Chicago Jury Project," *Nebraska Law Review* 38 1958): 748; see generally Hans and Vidmar, *Judging the Jury*, 124–26.

[92] Hans and Vidmar, *Judging the Jury*, 131.

[93] Aristotle, *Nicomachean Ethics* 1129a–1138b. Corrective justice involves restoring an individual to his legally defined expectations, regardless of his moral worth, while distributive justice aims at achieving a distribution according to individual virtue.

[94] Hans and Vidmar, *Judging the Jury*, 134, 154; Kalven and Zeisel, *The American Jury*, 87. "Greater" here means ultimately "greater than the number of acquittals the trial judges would have issued, if they can be believed."

[95] Ibid., 166.

[96] Ibid., 164.

[97] Patrick Devlin, *The Enforcement of Morals* (London: Oxford University Press, 1959), quoted in Kalven and Zeisel, *The American Jury*, 165 n. 4.

[98] Kalven and Zeisel, *The American Jury*, 166. Another judge, whom Kalven and Zeisel quote, referred to a jury "hunt for doubt." Ibid., 165. My own judgment is that the "liberation hypothesis," though helpful, is insufficiently radical. It represents a judge's post hoc understanding, within the framework provided by the Received View, of a jury determination reached in quite a different manner. See chapter 6, below.

peting narratives.[99] The narrative structure of the trial provides the "systematic means of storing, bringing up to date, rearranging, comparing, testing and interpreting available information about social behavior" and so answers the question of "how jurors actually organize and analyze the vast amounts of information involved in making a legal judgment."[100] The jury seems to organize and remember evidence in narrative form, rather than as logically tied to specific legally defined issues.[101] If we are to understand what the jury actually does, we must grasp the ways in which the narrative proposed by one litigant is deemed superior to that proposed by the other. For example, mock jurors find a case presented in narrative form more compelling than one presented as a simple sequential preview of available evidence.[102] The acceptance of a story and the reaching of a verdict seem to be the same human act.[103] In other words, those of the language of empirical social science, the story selected "determines" or "causes" the verdict rendered.[104] Some potential jurors may be inclined simply to seize upon an attractive story and disregard competing evidence, while others have the capacity to entertain several stories and weigh the evidence for and against each one. The devices of the trial are, in ways we are now in a position to understand, designed to encourage the latter process.[105]

The "scientific description of the mind of the juror" finds him, in the rather mechanical language of experimental psychology, "a sense-making information processor who strives to create a meaningful summary of the evidence available that explains what happened in the events depicted through witnesses, exhibits, and arguments at trial."[106] Our "sense-mak-

---

[99] The seminal work is Bennett and Feldman, *Reconstructing Reality in the Courtroom*.

[100] Ibid., 5; Kalven and Zeisel, *The American Jury*, 6–7.

[101] Nancy Pennington and Reid Hastie, "A Cognitive Model of Juror Decision Making: The Story Model," *Cardozo Law Review* 13 (1992): 519, 535.

[102] Ibid., 542. This is consistent with the traditional advice given to young trial lawyers about the most effective way to present opening statement, as a richly characterized story which the advocate promises that the evidence will *show*, not a mere catalog of what the evidence will *be*.

[103] Ibid., 519.

[104] Nancy Pennington and Reid Hastie, "The Story Model for Juror Decision Making," in Hastie, Penrod, and Pennington, *Inside the Juror*, 193. There are, as usual in the context of causality, very subtle philosophical issues here. For example, to say that the trial is over when a jury "accepts" one story over another does not entail that characteristics of the story accepted formed the sufficient conditions of its acceptance.

[105] Deanna Kuhn, Michael Weinstock, and Robin Flaton, "How Well Do Jurors Reason? Competence Dimensions of Individual Variation in a Juror Reasoning Task," *Psychological Science* 5 (1994): 289–96.

[106] Pennington and Hastie, "A Cognitive Model of Jury Decision Making," 519. To call a juror a "sense-making processor" is, at *very* best, paradoxical. Processors do not recognize meaning. On the inability of information-processing models to account for judgments of

ing processor" depends on the interpretation of behavior through narrative to create that meaningful summary. The meaning we bestow on social action stems from the interrelations determined to exist among Burke's "pentad of social action elements . . . scene, act, agent, agency and purpose"[107] that we saw at work in the opening statements recounted in the last chapter. More concretely, "the meaning and, therefore, the interest and importance of social activity depends on who does it, for what reasons, through what means, in what context, and with what sort of prologue and denouement."[108] The connections among these elements are of different sorts, and some of these connections cannot plausibly be called "logical" or "empirical."[109] Rather, these stories "have the capacity to *create* clear interpretations for social behavior—interpretations that might not have been obvious outside the story context."[110] Stories solve the problem of information overload by allowing a continuing reintegration of new information and reorganization of that information according to the changes in meaning that the new information allows or requires.[111] They allow integration of the disjointed perspectives from which the witnesses testify; they function specifically to represent some central social action; they allow the listener to evaluate their plausibility; and they otherwise serve "powerful analytical functions."[112]

Jurors implicitly apply certain criteria to determine the acceptability of one story rather than another and to fix their level of confidence in their decision. One investigator identifies these criteria as "coverage" and "coherence." The "uniqueness" of the story will also contribute to juror confidence in its correctness.[113] "Coverage" is the capacity of a story to account for the evidence. "Uniqueness" is the absence of a plausible competing story. "Coherence" comprises a number of distinct criteria:

---

meaning—central, in my view, to the trial—see Bruner, *Acts of Meaning*, 2–11. The "cognitive revolution" in psychology, originally focused on the perception of meaning, has been largely redirected, *mis*directed in Bruner's view, by information-processing models of human intelligence. The "scientific description of the mind of the juror" is thus in large part an artifact of the notion of "cognitive science" that informs it.

[107] Bennett and Feldman, *Reconstructing Reality in the Courtroom*, 62. See Burke, *A Grammar of Motives*.

[108] Bennett and Feldman, *Reconstructing Reality in the Courtroom*, 7.

[109] Ibid., 50–59. This, of course, presents a serious problem for the Received View, which requires the jury to build up a value-free account of "what happened" out of purely empirical generalizations and operations that can be called "logical."

[110] Ibid., 7 (emphasis added).

[111] Ibid., 8. See Anderson and Twining, *Analysis of Evidence*, 31–34, for a delightful exercise designed to show how additional bits of information require the reinterpretation of the *significance* of earlier evidence.

[112] Bennett and Feldman, *Reconstructing Reality in the Courtroom*, 8–9, 18.

[113] Pennington and Hastie, "A Cognitive Model of Juror Decision Making," 527.

(1) consistency, the absence of internal contradictions, either with other episodes in the narrative or with evidence claimed true; (2) plausibility, the congruence between the episodes of the story and the commonsense knowledge of the audience as to "how it goes" in the world; and (3) completeness, the presence of all the parts of a well-formed story.[114] Some investigators assume that the jury first accepts the story and only then consults the instructions to determine "goodness of fit"—that is, which of the applicable legal categories the already accepted story naturally falls under.[115] Others find evidence of jurors' "cycling" back and forth between not-quite-accepted narratives and verdict categories, with the acceptability of the former somewhat dependent on the nature of the latter.[116]

The experimental psychologists agree with the sociologists[117] that the internal structures of the stories told in the court can be decisive. Consistency, plausibility, and completeness may, in a given case, be more important than the quantity of evidence in support of one or another of the competing narratives.[118] Additionally, what appear to be purely rhetorical matters are of some significance. A witness's use of "strong" language, language that projects confidence and command, increases the likelihood of his being believed.[119] The "ways in which stories represent the incidents in legal disputes produce often radical transformations of 'reality' that are hard to reconcile with commonsense understandings about objectiv-

---

[114] Ibid., 528.

[115] Pennington and Hastie, "The Story Model for Juror Decision Making," 199–201.

[116] Ibid., at 201–2. If this were true, it would present a problem for the Received View, which requires the factual account to be settled *before* the decision-maker turns to the instructions for the applicable norms, and might upset the research design of some of the jury studies, since it suggests a circular relationship between what the verdict categories are and what is found to "have happened"—that is, between perceived consequences and a version of historical fact. The model presented in chapter 7, below, is consistent with the legal moment in decision making and also with the cycling phenomenon.

[117] Bennett and Feldman, *Reconstructing Reality in the Courtroom*.

[118] Ibid., 80. Of course, the quantity or "weight" of the evidence cannot be evaluated in abstraction from qualitative factors. In an experiment in which undergraduates were exposed to well-constructed stories that were in fact false, most believed them to be true. Ibid. In other such experiments, by increasing the number of "structural ambiguities," the investigators decreased the believability of the story. "Direct extrapolation" to the trial context would be "unwise," however, since the stories told by the advocates in opening statements are always already structured by the quality of the anticipated admissible evidence. This is a major characteristic of actual trial narratives to which many empirical investigators do not advert.

[119] William O'Barr, *Linguistic Evidence: Language, Power, and Strategy in the Courtroom* (New York: Academic Press, 1982); see also John M. Conley and William M. O'Barr, *Rules versus Relationships: The Ethnography of Legal Discourse* (Chicago: University of Chicago Press, 1990). This does not show that someone who uses "strong" language who is *shown* to be lying or stretching the truth will be credible.

ity."[120] We have seen that we must judge stories "according to a dual standard of 'Did it happen this way?' and 'Could it have happened this way?' " Not surprising, then, is empirical investigators' finding that "the teller and the interpreter" of a story have some measure of control over its key symbols, and that, consistent with our account of pretrial lawyering practices, in "no case can empirical standards alone produce a completely adequate judgment."[121]

Furthermore, "there are cases in which the structural characteristics are far and away the critical elements in determining the truth of a story."[122] As Bennett and Feldman put it: "Although it is doubtful that completely undocumented stories will be believed in many instances, it is quite possible that adequately documented but poorly structured accounts will be rejected because they do not withstand careful scrutiny within a story framework. Similarly, a well-constructed story may sway judgments even when evidence is in short supply."[123] In sum:

> [T]he way in which a story is told will have considerable bearing on its perceived credibility regardless of the actual truth status of the story. This means that the symbols chosen, the structural elements (scene, act, agent, agency, and purpose) that are defined and left undefined, and the amount of detail provided to facilitate connections between story symbols, will all have a significant bearing on audience judgments about stories—judgments based on the overall completeness, consistency and adequacy (in other words, the degree of ambiguity) of story connections.[124]

These structural elements are especially important in cases that depend on circumstantial evidence, or where the direct evidence has credibility problems that must be resolved through circumstantial evidence—that is, in precisely those cases that are most likely to go to trial.[125]

The studies also note what might be called a "political dimension" to the jury's work, something wholly inconsistent with the Received View. The jury has always been understood in political terms. The Founding Fathers embedded the civil jury in the Bill of Rights with the expectation that juries would act in "political" ways, different from the expected per-

---

[120] Bennett and Feldman, *Reconstructing Reality in the Courtroom*, 33.

[121] Ibid. On some of the limitations of the notion of "truth" employed by empirical investigators, see Marianne Constable, *The Law of the Other: The Mixed Jury and Changing Conceptions of Citizenship, Law, and Knowledge* (Chicago: University of Chicago Press, 1994), 28–66.

[122] Ibid.

[123] Ibid., 67.

[124] Ibid., 89.

[125] Ibid., 88–90.

formances of judges.[126] Tocqueville deemed the criminal trial "above all, a political institution."[127] Lord Justice Devlin called the criminal jury "a little parliament . . . more than an instrument of justice and more than one wheel of the Constitution: it is the lamp that shows that freedom lives."[128] The United States Supreme Court has spoken of the jury's institutional purpose as "to prevent oppression."[129] Moreover, praise for the jury has often been in explicitly political terms.[130] The empirical investigators find that this political self-consciousness on the part of the jury is very much alive, and that juries will use their authority to counter what they take to be abuses of political power.[131]

The Quality of Trial Judgments

We have seen how the practices, rules, and basic aspects of the trial intensify the contest over the meaning of the underlying events and operate to postpone jury judgment until the full presentation of both cases. Is there any social scientific evidence on the elusive issue of quality of judgment at trial?

The work of juries is generally highly regarded by those in a position to know. Jurors usually regard their service as important and meaningful and recognize the elevation of their capacity for factual and moral reasoning that their encounter with the trial brings.[132] Moreover, in the large majority of situations the judge and the jury reach the same conclusion, and their disagreements are not related to the complexity of the case. Thus it appears that juries understand the evidence as often as does the judge— or, put more slyly, do not misunderstand it more often. Kalven and Zeisel referred to their findings as a "stunning refutation of the hypothesis that the jury does not understand."[133] This conclusion is consistent with simulated studies which suggest that juries have admirable powers of collective

---

[126] Charles W. Wolfram, "The Constitutional History of the Seventh Amendment," *Minnesota Law Review* 57 (1973): 639, 653.

[127] Tocqueville, *Democracy in America*, 1:293.

[128] Patrick Devlin, *Trial by Jury* (London: Stevens & Sons, 1956), 164.

[129] *Duncan v. Louisiana*, 391 U.S. 145, 155 (1968).

[130] Abramson, *We, the Jury*, 88–90.

[131] See, e.g., Hans and Vidmar, *Judging the Jury*, 18 (sensitivity to entrapment issues); Kalven and Zeisel, *The American Jury*, 237 (acquittals granted to punish police for misconduct).

[132] J. Tapp, M. Gunnar, and D. Keating, "Socialization: Three Ages, Three Rule Systems," in *Social Psychology*, ed. D. Perlman and P. Cozby (New York: Holt, Rinehart, and Winston, 1983).

[133] Kalven and Zeisel, *The American Jury*, 157.

memory for the evidence presented.[134] In sum, juries are "competent."[135] Perhaps the leading contemporary empirical investigators of the jury conclude in their study, "Because jury performance of the fact-finding task is so remarkably competent, few innovations are needed to improve performance."[136] Social scientists speculate that the various devices of the trial may thus be well suited to counter the more significant limitations of human reasoning about matters of fact.[137]

The empirical work, then, paints a picture of the actual operation of the trial that is striking and consistent with our phenomenological study of its basic features. Juries bring an elevated intelligence to their work. Their results cannot be predicted by demographic factors, or any small number of independent factual variables in the cases before them. Legal rules play a limited role, and the values implicit in the language practices of the trial loom large. Juries understand the public or political dimension of their work. Deliberation is much less important than the encounter of the individual juror with the trial itself, which is intense and searching. The trial *is* the thing.

[134] Hastie, Penrod, and Pennington, *Inside the Jury*, 80–81.

[135] Hans and Vidmar, *Judging the Jury*, summarizes the empirical work and notes the high level of consensus from different perspectives even among those inclined to be skeptical.

[136] Hastie, Penrod, and Pennington, *Inside the Jury*, 230.

[137] Kuhn, Weinstock, and Flaton, "How Well Do Jurors Reason?" 289–96. The research report indicated that some simulated jurors adopted a "satisficing" style of reasoning that accepted one story quickly and ignored disturbing counterevidence, while others employed a "theory-evidence" style that entertained conflicting stories and assessed them in light of the evidence. The study was based on interviews with 152 subjects who listened to a twenty-five-minute audiotaped abridgment of a mock trial, obviously a presentation far removed from trial conditions. The finding that some subjects did not adequately focus on the evidence was widely reported as casting doubt on jury competence. See "Study Finds Jurors Often Hear Evidence with Closed Minds," *New York Times*, November 29, 1994. However, the authors themselves noted that "the jury process was designed to remedy defects of just this sort." Kuhn, Weinstock, and Flaton, "How Well Do Jurors Reason?" 295. In the latter observation they seem to refer to the process of deliberation, though I would suggest that an actual trial, something far beyond a twenty-five-minute audiotape, is itself likely to draw the jury toward higher modes of reasoning about the facts.

VI

Thinking What We Do

> They do not understand that it is by being at
> variance with itself that it coheres with itself:
> a backward-stretching harmony, as of a bow
> or a lyre. . . . One must realize that conflict is
> common to all, *and justice is strife*, and all things
> come to pass according to strife and necessity.
> (*Heraclitus*)

Introduction

I began by recounting the Received View of the trial, an understanding with deep roots in our allegiance to the Rule of Law and one that seems to explain some of the most striking and distinctive features of the actual conduct of American trials. We saw that even the trial's legal infrastructure, where we ought to see a high level of consistency with the Received View, presented significant anomalies. This led us to a more searching description of the actual linguistic practices that constitute the trial, largely written from the perspective of the lawyers who perform those practices. I then turned to an account of the most important of the vast web of rules—evidentiary, ethical, and procedural—that structure and limit those practices. I recounted a number of its concrete features too easily overlooked and reviewed the most important social science findings concerning the trial.

I have thus left a sizable offering at Wittgenstein's altar: we have done a lot of looking.[1] It is time that we move to a more theoretical idiom, all the while trying to ensure that our ideas remain "in things." This chapter

---

[1] "[D]on't think, but look!" Ludwig Wittgenstein, *Philosophical Investigations*, trans. Elizabeth Anscombe (New York: Macmillan, 1953), 31. Wittgenstein's advice is especially pertinent when inherited concepts prove a distorting mirror of actual practices. The law surely is a "continuing and collective process of conversation and judgment." Patterson, "Law's Pragmatism," 983, quoting James Boyd White, *When Words Lose Their Meaning* (Chicago: University of Chicago Press, 1984), 264. But the "conversation" that takes place in the trial itself proceeds under constraining rules and conventions which dramatically affect the nature of *this particular* conversation. In this chapter, I increase my focus on the *significance* of those constraints.

is devoted to that specifically interpretive task. Although I will be relying on different bodies of learning, themselves of considerable internal interest,[2] I will fix my sights on "the things themselves." I will be focusing on the meaning or significance of the practices and rules we have examined, and my language will become more philosophical. What does it add up to? Can we "think what we are doing?"[3] What has the trial become for us?

The "meaning of a practice is an *internal* phenomenon. It is within the practice, and by virtue of the acts of the participants in the practice, that the practice has meaning."[4] When we come to focus on the jury's tasks, we have to recall that "action is, on the whole, an unreflective reaction to the meaningfulness of the situation in which one is engrossed,"[5] and it is the meaning of the particularly engrossing practices of the trial that I will be exploring. If almost all cases are decided through "the discipline of the evidence,"[6] we must appreciate the intense and distinctive experience that jurors share just before rendering their decisions, something which has received too little attention even from thoughtful students of the American trial.[7]

---

[2] Sometimes the internal disciplinary development of a field and the understanding that field can bring to bear on the trial are closely intertwined. For example, much of the burgeoning field of jury research was carried out within the "cognitive revolution" in psychology and served to connect up a field that was in some danger of becoming aridly scholastic ("one little paper responding to another") with study of an important public institution, and so, in the language of an earlier era, to establish "relevance."

[3] Robert P. Burns, "Hannah Arendt's Constitutional Thought," in *Amor Mundi: Explorations in the Life and Thought of Hannah Arendt*, ed. James Bernauer (Boston: Martinus Nijhoff, 1987), 157.

[4] Patterson, "Law's Pragmatism," 966.

[5] Ibid., 979. That general principle is, as we have seen, amply supported by the social science literature on the trial. This principle has perhaps the greatest power when the situation is so consciously structured as a world apart:

> The arena, the card table, the magic circle, the temple, the stage, the screen, the tennis court, the court of justice, etc., are all in form and function play-grounds, i.e., forbidden sports, isolated, hedged round, hallowed, within which special rules obtain. All are temporary worlds within the ordinary world, dedicated to the performance of an act apart.
>
> Inside the play-ground an absolute and peculiar order reigns. Here we come across another, very positive feature of play: it creates order, *is* order. Into an imperfect world and into the confusion of life it brings a temporary, a limited perfection. Play demands order absolute and supreme. The least deviation from it "spoils the game", robs it of its character and makes it worthless.

Johan Huizinga, *Homo Ludens: A Study of the Play Element in Culture* (Boston: Beacon Press, 1950), 10.

[6] Abramson, *We the Jury*, 162. I have argued elsewhere that the major limitation of Abramson's fine book is an absence of any treatment of the trial itself. Robert P. Burns, "The History and Philosophy of the American Jury," *California Law Review* 83 (1995): 1477.

[7] Ibid., 1491.

This chapter continues my focus on the "objective" side of the trial event. I discuss the significance of open narrative[8] at the beginning of trial and of the simple fact that the jury almost immediately faces two competing narratives in a context where an "either-or" choice must be made. I discuss the sense in which consistency with commonsense "factual" generalizations, ordinary morality, and what I will call public identity make one narrative initially more or less plausible. I then explore the significance of the simple fact that the trial does not end after opening statement.[9] In the next chapter I will draw together many of the observations made in this and in the previous chapter into a more complex model of trial decision making than that which the Received View envisions.[10] That model shows how the linguistic practices of the trial establish a set of demanding tensions. Generating these tensions is the task of the varied set of linguistic performances, the "consciously structured hybrid of languages," that impose the discipline of the evidence. These performances provide the meaningful situation to which jury decision making is a largely unreflective reaction. I further explain how the various judgments the jury makes are related to each other—which are independent, which dependent, and which mutually determining. The resulting structure is complex and shows how the decision a jury makes inevitably involves determinations among incommensurable values, which are themselves the basic principles of forms of life that exist in tension in the broader society. We can then appreciate the ways in which the "objective" side of the trial is not neutral among the multiple perspectives the jury may take and the forms of life that they reflect.

Is there any reason to believe that a jury can, in some meaningful sense, actually do what the trial's languages seem to demand? Answering that question requires us, in the latter half of chapter 7, to look at the "subjective" side of the trial event, the cognitive operations the trial requires. We can no longer simply repeat the comforting truisms of the Received View, on the one hand, nor should we rely on usually cynical and always oversimplified notions of "emotional" decision making, on the other.[11] This brings us to the last questions that naturally arise. To what extent can it be said that the various rule-bound linguistic practices of the trial reveal or "show" the truth? To put it with a deliberate theoretical innocence, in what way can a jury's verdict be valid? Having

[8] By open narrative, I mean a form of storytelling that need not be structured by the norms embedded in the jury instructions.

[9] In the jury studies, very many of the "stimuli" presented to the subjects are short stories that are *not* followed by the presentation of evidence.

[10] See figure 2, below.

[11] Even Kalven and Zeisel fell prey to this uncritical notion of decision based on "sentiment." *The American Jury*, 105–17.

answered that question, I step, for the first time, "outside" the trial to conclude with a short account of the importance of the trial within American institutions.

The General Significance of the Narrative Structure of the Trial

I have stressed the distinctiveness and multiplicity of the trial's languages, including the differences among kinds of narrative, factors that have been almost universally ignored. However, I deem it worthwhile to begin by recounting the general significance of the centrality of narrative in the trial.

Narrative Organizes Vast Amounts of Information in Complex Ways

First, narrative structure allows the jury to "actually organize and analyze the vast amount of information involved in making a legal judgment."[12] "Stories are systematic means of storing, bringing up to date, rearranging, comparing, testing, and interpreting available information about social behavior. As witnesses deliver testimony bearing on alleged illegal behavior, a juror operates much like someone reading a detective novel or watching a mystery movie replete with multiple points of view, subplots, time lapses, missing information and ambiguous clues."[13] This is consistent with the findings of cognitive psychologists[14] that "what does not get structured narratively suffers loss in memory,"[15] and with the weight of social science findings as to what actually occurs at trial.[16] Even at the stage of the trial when no evidence has yet been offered for or against a story, standards of relative plausibility or "objectivity" apply: "uniform structural and interpretive characteristics of stories that enable diverse individuals to hear cases in fairly uniform ways."[17] These "structural rela-

[12] Bennett and Feldman, *Reconstructing Reality in the Courtroom*, 5.

[13] Ibid. Bennett and Feldman's account seems to suggest that the final understanding of the trial is itself a narrative, what I call the "screenplay of past events." It seems to me that their focus on *general* narrative structure and relative inattention to the differences among the trial's linguistic structures mislead them. The jury's final grasp is not a determinate picture of past events.

[14] Jean Mandler, *Stories, Scripts, and Scenes: Aspects of Schema Theory* (Hillsdale, N.J.: Lawrence Erlbaum Associates, 1984).

[15] Bruner, *Acts of Meaning*, 56.

[16] See chapter 5, above.

[17] Bennett and Feldman, *Reconstructing Reality in the Courtroom*, 22–32.

tions among symbols in the story," over which, as we have seen, the parties have significant control, have their own internal criteria of plausibility that largely define "objectivity."[18] It is through narrative that we remember, and the internal characteristics of a given narrative contribute significantly to its concrete plausibility.

Narrative Forms Are "Natural" Modes of Understanding Events

Narrative structure is such a natural mode of understanding that it appears to be an innate schema for the organization and interpretation of experience:

> Is it unreasonable to suppose that there is some human "readiness" for narrative that is responsible for conserving and elaborating . . . tradition in the first place—whether, in Kantian terms, as an "art hidden in the human soul," whether as a feature of our language capacity, whether even as a psychological capacity like, say, our readiness to convert the world of visual input into figure and ground? . . . I mean a readiness or predisposition to organize experience into a narrative form, into plot structures and the rest. . . . It seems to me that such a view is irresistible.[19]

It would be a dismal fate if narrative were both inevitable *and* illusory, a kind of consoling fiction, added on after the fact.[20] (I argue against such a view in chapter 8.) The trial assumes that narrative is at least a reliable starting point for the comprehension of human action, that there is at least some truth in the notion that "stories are lived before they are told"—that is, that narrative is in some way congruent with the actual structure of experience. Insofar as it can distort such experience, the trial's assumption is that its other devices—cross-examination and argument—can correct those distortions.

---

[18] Bennett and Feldman rely on these considerations to approach a kind of coherence theory of truth for the trial: the importance of the internal features of the stories told at trial seems to overwhelm the importance of the evidence. Once again, this imbalance stems from their relative inattention to the trial's constitutive rules and to *all* the linguistic practices available at trial.

[19] Bruner, *Acts of Meaning*, 47.

[20] Karl Vaihinger, *The Philosophy of the "As If"*, 2d ed. (New York: Barnes & Noble, 1966) is the locus classicus. Vaihinger pushed to an extreme the Kantian notion that our modes of organizing experience can never reveal the "things in themselves." This "Kantian" notion of narrative structure is probably associated most closely in literary studies with Frank Kermode's *The Sense of an Ending: Studies in the Theory of Fiction* (London: Oxford University Press, 1966). On the debates surrounding narrative in historiography, see Joyce Appleby, Lynn Hunt, and Margaret Jacob, *Telling the Truth about History* (New York: W. W. Norton, 1994), 228–31, 262–66.

Narrative Structure Requires Judgments of Relative Importance That Assign a Meaning to an Event

It is impossible to tell a story without making judgments about the importance of events, which in turn dictate which of an innumerable number of details will be omitted in the telling. That same simplification creates or actualizes the meaning of the story: "the judgment of importance, by getting rid of the accessory, creates continuity: that which actually took place is disconnected and torn by insignificance, the narrative is meaningful because of its continuity."[21] As Arendt insisted, "[n]o philosophy, no analysis, no aphorism, be it ever so profound, can compare in intensity and richness of meaning with a properly narrated story."[22] A well-told story can sometimes achieve "a transparent display of the inner truth of the event," which other devices cannot approach. "There are things that cannot be put into words. They *make themselves manifest*."[23] Good storytelling, then, can unveil "epiphanies of the ordinary," can "reveal meaning without committing the error of defining it" and bring about "consent and reconciliation with things as they really are. . . ."[24]

In the relatively unencumbered storytelling of opening statement, the hard edges of legal formalism are relaxed, and the full and particular *human* significance of events can enter the courtroom, limited only by the internal discipline of the story, providing an essential antidote to the bureaucratic ossification that always threatens any legal system.[25] There are few legal constraints on the meaning that an attorney may perceive in

---

[21] Maria Vallela Peit, "Thinking History: Methodology and Epistemology in Paul Ricoeur's Reflections on History from *History and Truth* to *Time and Narrative*," in *The Narrative Path: The Later Works of Paul Ricoeur*, ed. T. Peter Kemp and David Rasmussen (Cambridge: MIT Press, 1989), 35–36.

[22] Hannah Arendt, *Men in Dark Times* (New York: Harcourt Brace Jovanovich, 1955), 22.

[23] Ludwig Wittgenstein, *Tractatus Logico-Philosophicus* 6.522, trans. D. F. Pears and B. F. McGuinness (London: Routledge & Kegan Paul, 1961), 73. David Luban comments that Wittgenstein never abandoned this conviction even in his later period, and urges that "[w]e narrate stories in order to make manifest whatever unsayable meaning resides in them." *Legal Modernism*, 201.

[24] Arendt, *Men in Dark Times*, 104.

[25] Hannah Arendt puts it this way: "No doubt, wherever public life and its law of equality are completely victorious, wherever a civilization succeeds in eliminating or reducing to a minimum the dark background of difference, it will end in complete petrifaction, for having forgotten that man is only the master, not the creator of the world." *The Origins of Totalitarianism*, 302. No one who has not tried to persuade a bureaucratic adjudicator of a simple truth can, in my view, really understand Arendt's words. Kafka was himself an official in a system of "bureaucratic justice."

the events that have come to trial. Opening statement is a time when the "masks of the law"[26] least conceal all the reality of events that the ordinary language of a culture can reveal. Though the law may say "slaves are chattel"[27] or "Jews are subhuman," a story about their lives and actions will show otherwise. Though the law may fail to reflect the norms of a relevant community, the stories told at trial may invoke those norms in all their complexity. And, as we saw above, those narratives may suggest not only how events should be understood but also what is to be *done*. Bernard Jackson calls this the "narrativization of pragmatics,"[28] the capacity of what appears to be a factual narrative to encode a judgment about the action to be taken in response to the events described.

The Centrality of Narrative Means That the "Internal Morality"[29] of the Trial Is Highly Contextual

Trial narratives inevitably involve not only the assignment of meaning to a past event but that of a specifically *moral* meaning. It is the *kind* of moral judgment, however, that is significant. The forms both of opening statement and direct examination serve as bulwarks against abstract thinking in moral judgment. As Stuart Hampshire aptly put it, "An abstract morality places a prepared grid upon conduct and upon a person's activities and interests, and thereafter one only tends to see the pieces of his conduct and life as they are divided by lines on the grid."[30] Hampshire argues that the best way to understand the limitations of "abstract computational" morality in human affairs is to try to tell a story about the event to be evaluated. "If the story is well told, nothing that is relevant to the decision is left out and not much that is irrelevant to the decision is included in the story. . . . The theoretical interest in the story-telling is always in the selection of the circumstances . . . which ought to be included in the story if the complexity of the original moral problem was to be fully reproduced. . . . There are always dangers in circumscribing a lived-through situation and in converting it into a definite and

---

[26] John T. Noonan, Jr., *The Persons and Masks of the Law: Cardozo, Holmes, Jefferson, and Wythe as Makers of the Masks* (New York: Farrar, Straus and Giroux, 1975).

[27] The example is from Ball, *The Promise of American Law*, 26.

[28] Jackson, *Law, Fact, and Narrative Coherence*, 161–74.

[29] I adapt the phrase from Lon Fuller's notion of the "internal morality of law." Lon Fuller, *The Morality of Law* (New Haven: Yale University Press, 1964).

[30] Stuart Hampshire, "Public and Private Morality," in *Public and Private Morality* (Cambridge: Cambridge University Press, 1978), 39.

clearly stated problem."[31] Most generally, then, the prominence of narrative form ensures that all the subtlety embedded in the commonsense morality of the culture can find its way into the moral judgments made at trial.

Narrative Is Internally Related to Questions of Justice

Bennett and Feldman concluded that "[s]omething about story operations must correspond to the implicit criteria for doing justice."[32] This appears to be a general characteristic of the narrative form: "Stories tell us how each one finds or loses his just place in relation to others in the world. And the communication of the story is confirmed when justice has been recognized. Is there *any* story we tell in which justice is not at issue? It is almost as if we constitute a jury out of our listeners, so that it falls to them to judge the particular view of the case that we present in our story."[33] In the real world, "it is only when constituent beliefs in a folk psychology are violated that narratives are constructed. . . . When things 'are as they should be' the narratives of folk psychology are unnecessary."[34] The "negotiated meanings" that hold a culture together are constituted by narratives' capacity to recognize both common norms and exceptions to those norms. Narrative comprises interpretive methods that make deviation comprehensible in light of the common sense of the society.[35] In other words, stories are told when there has been a disruption of habitual patterns, where there is a problematic situation, and achieve the kind of coherence that comes from people's explaining deviation from authoritative norms by dipping into an inventory of commonsense beliefs about the motives and circumstances that lead to deviation.[36] This peacekeeping function may require "searching judicial trials" in cases where the level

[31] Ibid.

[32] Bennett and Feldman, *Reconstructing Reality in the Courtroom*, 64.

[33] Melvyn A. Hill, "The Fictions of Mankind and the Stories of Men," in *Hannah Arendt: The Recovery of the Public World*, ed. Melvyn A. Hill (New York: St. Martin's Press, 1979), 290.

[34] Bruner, *Acts of Meaning*, 39–40. Bruner uses the phrase "folk psychology" as roughly equivalent to the web of commonsense beliefs that constitute the life world.

[35] *Acts of Meaning*, 47. Hanna Pitkin calls speech about deviations from accepted norms "the center of gravity" of the moral life. *Wittgenstein and Justice*, 150. See below, concerning the relationship of the trial's narrative to the moral point of view. See also Austin, "A Plea for Excuses."

[36] "The function of the story is to find an intentional state that mitigates or at least makes comprehensible a deviation from a canonical cultural pattern." Bruner, *Acts of Meaning*, 49–50.

of "insane" deviance challenges the most important social norms.[37] Otherwise the offense would remain one of an "unbearable sequence of sheer happenings" and so a challenge to the experienced meaningfulness of the lives of the citizenry.[38]

Trial Narratives Place the Jury within the Structure of Commutative Justice and So Remind the Jury of Its Practical Task

The deep structure of narrative serves to remind the jurors that their task is a practical one. Story structure is built around a sequence of legitimate status quo, a disruption of that status quo, and its restoration.[39] That structure exactly parallels the demand of corrective (or "commutative")[40] justice—the restoration of legitimate expectations that have been thwarted by deviant behavior. The key point here is that this structure inevitably places the jury within the story as a key actor[41] and communicates to the jury that its task is a practical or moral one. The competition for the imagination of the jury that begins in opening statement rightly assumes that "the relations between imagination and the world of possibilities is a relation to an unreality that becomes real in the act of transforming the world . . . it is not simply a descriptive relationship to reality, but it is the 'reference' to reality that is creative and transforms it."[42] The structure of narrative tells the jury that it stands between past and future.

In sum, the centrality of narrative at trial allows the jury to organize vast amounts of information around a few invariant elements of a crucial human action. The story told is the result of a simplifying judgment of importance that inevitably assigns a meaning to the human action, a meaning rooted in a highly contextual concrete commonsense moral perspective.[43] In contradistinction to technical legal language it can "preserve and cherish a strong truth-bearing everyday language, not marred or cor-

---

[37] Ibid., 39–40. As we saw in chapter 4, the issue in such trials will be the appropriate interpretive scheme that both comprehends the deviance and implicitly tells us what is to be done.

[38] Arendt, *Men in Dark Times*, 104.

[39] Bruner, *Acts of Meaning*, 50.

[40] Aristotle, *Nicomachean Ethics*, chap. 5.

[41] See Amsterdam and Hertz, "An Analysis of Closing Arguments to a Jury," 55. Recall that Amsterdam's analysis of closing argument noted that one of the litigants (the criminal defendant) focused on the responsibility that the jury bore for its action in deciding the case, while the prosecution's rhetoric tended to "remove" the jury from its role as moral actor by "objectivizing" its findings.

[42] Peter Kemp, "Ethics and Narrativity," in *The Philosophy of Paul Ricoeur*, ed. Lewis E. Hahn (Chicago: Open Press Publishing, 1995), 374.

[43] This may or may not conform to the norms embedded in the instructions.

rupted by technical discourse or scientific codes; and thereby promote the clarified objective knowledge of man and society of which we are in need as citizens, and as moral agents."[44] Finally, the structure of narrative has a deep relationship to judgments of justice and deviant disruptions of a just social order that the jury is invited to remedy.

The Significance of Competing Narratives

I have been addressing the general significance of narrative at trial. However, at trial there is not one narrative; there are two that become rival suitors for the jury's imagination. This scheme of competing narratives has roots deep in personal history. Competing narratives summon up familiar aspects of jurors' ordinary extralegal experience. The rhetorical use of narrative is something they have learned themselves in the family drama, where we learn to master both the standards for approved behavior and the mitigating circumstances that justify or at least excuse deviations from those standards.[45]

The "two-story" scheme also reflects an aspect of ordinary moral experience, in which we often construct competing narratives:

> Every reflective person has had the experience of oscillating between two possible descriptions of his own conduct, where it is actual conduct or only envisaged conduct; one correct description mentions features of the conduct which make it morally questionable and regrettable. Two competing ways of life, between which a man chooses, explicitly or implicitly, may impose different descriptions on the same envisaged conduct, which may emerge as prohibited in virtue of the descriptions relevant to one way of life and as positively required within another way of life.[46]

---

[44] Iris Murdoch, *Metaphysics as a Guide to Morals* (New York: Penguin Press, 1992), 162.

[45] "To narrate in a way that puts our case convincingly requires not only language but a mastery of the canonical forms, for one must make one's actions seem an extension of the canonical, transformed by mitigating circumstances." Bruner, *Acts of Meaning*, 87. He notes that "[i]n the process of achieving these skills, the child learns to use some of the less attractive tools of the rhetorical trade—deceit, flattery, and the rest. But she also learns many of the useful forms of interpretation and thereby develops a more penetrating empathy." Ibid. The former should make the juror justly wary of the advocate; the latter makes it possible for her to understand the trial at all.

[46] Hampshire, "Public and Private Morality." As I explain at greater length below, the center of gravity of a given trial can be the "bare facts" that occurred (the O.J. criminal trial), that is, what movements would have been seen and sounds heard by the physically competent observer; the interpretation of what occurred (Was a question really an accusation? Was a walk toward the door flight?); an "ultimate fact" embedded in the instructions (intent); or an explicitly normative determination (what would a "reasonable man" have

Note that in Hampshire's account, there is no single "neutral" description of the conduct with which one might compare the rival interpretations in order to determine which is the more accurate. Despite the absence of a determinate representation of the conduct other than that provided by the two competing descriptions, we often seem able, in our ordinary moral experience, to determine that one description is superior. We say that one is "more powerful" or "fairer."

It will turn out that something like this capacity must be at work in the trial. For example, the opening statements in triable cases often talk past one another, in that they are enacting two quite different perspectives on the case, answering different questions, presenting different issues, and suggesting different modes of social ordering. These characteristics "make it difficult or, more likely, impossible for an individual to hold both theories in mind together and compare them point by point with each other"[47] and with external reality. The jury cannot decide between the distinct perspectives embedded in the competing narratives simply by comparing them to the evidence.

In addition, competition between narratives relativizes both narratives. The contrasting narratives of opening statement remind the jury both that the moral adequacy of any narrative to a lived situation depends on "the selection of the circumstances to be included in the story," and also of the "dangers in circumscribing a lived through situation and in converting it into a definite and clearly stated problem."[48] Consequently, the two-story structure of opening statement assures that the jury will not act on the basis of One Big Story authorized by a state official. A trial is significantly different from a historical narrative, more pluralistic or democratic: "Histories . . . insist on a homology between the sequence of their own telling, the form they impose to create coherent explanation in the form of a narrative on the one hand, and the sequence of *what* they tell on the other."[49] The trial's "consciously structured hybrid of lan-

---

done?). A case can become "triable" because of a conflict of interpretation at *any* of those levels. See, e.g., *Sioux City and P. Railroad Co. v. Stout*, 84 U.S. 657, 21 L.Ed. 745 (1873) (even where the "historical facts" are undisputed, there can exist a jury issue on whether those facts constitute due care on the one hand or negligence on the other, making a directed verdict inappropriate).

[47] Thomas S. Kuhn, "Objectivity, Value Judgment, and Theory Choice," in Thomas S. Kuhn, *The Essential Tension: Selected Studies in Scientific Tradition and Change* (Chicago: University of Chicago Press, 1977), 338. ("I simply assert the existence of significant limits to what the proponents of different theories can communicate to one another. The same limits make it difficult, or, more likely, impossible for an individual to hold both theories in mind together and compare them point by point with each other and with nature.")

[48] Ibid., 39.

[49] Bakhtin, *The Dialogic Imagination*, xxviii.

guages" dramatizes "the gaps that always exist between what is told and the telling of it."[50] This dramatization begins with the competing narratives in opening and continues throughout the trial, inviting the jury to look *through* the stories. It reflects a distinctively Anglo-American appreciation that the inability to agree on one story to be told is precisely what brings the parties to trial. The power to produce (or issue) an authoritative metanarrative would take from the parties what is most important about their day in court.[51] In the jury trial at least,[52] the American legal order never produces a metanarrative that resolves the differences between the opening statements or the theories of the case that are embedded in them.

Note that the competing narratives of opening statement relativize the moralizing impulse implicit in narrative. The very presentation of inconsistent narratives cannot but awaken suspicion that one or both of these constructions is a willful distortion of the moral point of view. At a higher level, this begins the process, intensified at later stages in the trial, that prepares the way for the minor miracle of an always tacit appreciation of the limitations of the morality implicit in the society's social system.[53] A story that seems adequate and consistent with common sense is shown to be partial, even by the standards of common sense. That process occurs over and over again as the trial progresses, and is an important source of the often perceived "elevation" of the common sense that the jury brings to the case. As Milner Ball has put it: "Aeschylus' and Herodotus' stories permitted even a recent enemy a place of equal dignity. So also does the drama of the courtroom elevate perspective when and if it works; judges and juries are led beyond prejudice, and the larger audience, the society as a whole, is enabled to look with equal eye upon offenders and offended, the feared and the abused, the powerful and the weak."[54] Eventually the jury has to decide that one case is superior to the other, a process that begins, though only begins, with opening statements. I turn now to the criteria by which that initial choice is made.

---

[50] Ibid., at xxix. And in *this* regard it is more like the novel, of which the author of the language in the text was speaking, or the drama. See chapter 5, above.

[51] John Thibaut and Laurens Walker, *Procedural Justice: A Psychological Analysis* (Hillsdale, N.J.: Lawrence Erlbaum Associates, 1975), 67–101. Thibaut and Walker focus on subjective satisfaction. I suggest that the satisfaction is well grounded.

[52] Judges sitting without juries are required to file "findings of fact and conclusions of law." *Federal Rules of Civil Procedure*, Rule 52. Even these are fairly schematic and are often written strategically to protect the judgment against reversal on appeal.

[53] Again to use Hegelian language, the trial can bring the perspective of "absolute spirit" (art, religion, and philosophy) in a limited way into the realm of "objective spirit," the implicit ethic of the institutions of a concrete society. See Charles Taylor, *Hegel and Modern Society* (Cambridge: Cambridge University Press, 1979), 89, 126.

[54] Ball, *The Promise of American Law*, 19.

The Normative Sources for Preliminary Theory
   Choice at Trial

The stories told in the opening statements are told within a context where
the jury is pressured to accept one or the other of them.[55] How can a
jury make a preliminary[56] determination of which opening statement is
superior, on either factual or normative grounds? The parties' theory-
theme complexes inevitably raise three distinct questions. With regard to
the bare historical facts embedded in the narrative, the jury will ask, "In
which way is this more likely to have happened?" Second, the jury will
ask, "Which understanding of those events invokes a 'more powerful
norm?' " Third, though not necessarily in sequence, the jury will ask,
"Which understanding of the events that have led up to the trial is more
consistent with our public identity?"[57] I address each of these questions
in the sections that follow.

Factual Plausibility

In deciding what is more likely to have happened, the jury is influenced
both by the internal coherence and completeness of the competing narrative and by its external factual plausibility.

INTERNAL COHERENCE AND COMPLETENESS

We have already seen the importance of the internal elements. Each of
the opening statements will identify the story elements and define their
relationships to each other.[58] "The inadequate development of setting,
character, means, or motive, as any literature student knows, render a
story's actions ambiguous. . . . In a trial it is grounds for reasonable

[55] This is another reason that the stories told at trial are different from those told in
literary works and in historical narratives. I continue in this section to inquire into the
meaning of the trial's linguistic practices by following the general interpretive principle that
one understands the meaning of such a practice by grasping the truth or validity of which
it is capable. See, e.g., Warnke, *Gadamer: Hermeneutics, Tradition, and Reason*, 7–8.

[56] There exists a lively debate in the social science literature as to the importance of opening statement. See William Lewis Burke, Ronald L. Poulson, and Michael Brondino, "Fact
or Fiction: The Effect of Opening Statement," *Journal of Contemporary Law* 18 (1992):
195. At one extreme, there exists the claim that most juries decide the case after opening
statement. That view has been vigorously debunked. Nonetheless opening appears to be a
very important aspect of the trial for reasons that should already have appeared.

[57] I could say "political" identity, but that word is much too likely to be confusing.

[58] Bennett and Feldman, *Reconstructing Reality in the Courtroom*, 10.

doubt."[59] "[T]he way a story is told will have considerable bearing on its perceived credibility regardless of the actual truth status of the story. This means that the symbols chosen, the structural elements (scene, act, agent, agency, and purpose) that are defined and left undefined, and the amount of detail provided to facilitate connections between story symbols, will all have a significant bearing on audience judgments about stories—judgments based on the overall completeness, consistency, and adequacy (in other words, the degree of ambiguity) of story connections."[60] As we saw implicitly in chapter 2, a story may be implausible simply because the relationships among the key story elements are indeterminate or ambiguous. This relative intolerance for ambiguity in the trial context is one of the distinctive features of storytelling at trial. It stems *both* from the implicit reference of the story to an actual determinate[61] event and also from one of the defining features of the legal context, that some decision between the theories must be made, rather than the possibilities implicit in the two stories dreamily entertained.[62]

"EXTERNAL" FACTUAL PLAUSIBILITY

We inevitably judge stories according to a dual standard; we ask not only, "Did it happen that way?" but also, "Could it have happened that way?"[63] A story may be weaker or stronger not because of its teller's failure to develop the relationships that define the latter question, but

---

[59] Ibid.

[60] Ibid. Bennett and Feldman stress the "remarkable margin of freedom available for the symbolization of the competing stories about the disputed action." Ibid., 89. That may be true *theoretically*, though the various forms of plausibility available, and the evidence that an advocate may present, can sharply curtail that "freedom."

[61] There are some challenging philosophical questions surrounding the notion that any real event must be a *determinate* event. Kant's distinction between an intuitive intellect (God) and our discursive intellect is helpful here. A discursive intellect must multiply abstractions in order to understand any particular event or thing. This is true for even the most "basic" perceptual judgments. To use Peirce's example, I do not even *see* patches of color, I see "an azalea." Thus even perceptual judgments are, so to speak, collapsed inferences. It is for this reason that medieval philosophers liked to say, "Individuum est ineffable" (pure individuality cannot be expressed in language). Putting aside this limiting case, an aspect of the individual event that multiplying ever more accurate predicates will never reach, the notion that past events are determinate, that "each thing is what it is and no other," serves important normative, Kant would say "regulative," purposes. Without such a notion, the goal of creating rules and procedures to achieve even *relatively greater* accuracy, or even "fairness," would dissolve into a purely sophistical notion of the trial. For there would be nothing, or at least nothing available to *us*, on which the understanding achieved by the practices of the trial could even converge.

[62] This is to say that the trial involves a moral question, not an aesthetic question. See Mark Taylor, *Journeys to Selfhood: Hegel and Kierkegaard* (Berkeley and Los Angeles: University of California Press, 1980), 201–16, 241–51.

[63] Bennett and Feldman, *Reconstructing Reality in the Courtroom*, 33.

because the relationships actually developed are inconsistent with the common sense of the jury. Common sense may be viewed, at this stage in our discussion, as a store of empirical generalizations concerning human behavior, the "web of belief" or "prejudgments" relatively implicit and usually uncriticized, that constitute the life world, the commonsense world in which we live. The generalizations that concern human actions, around which most trials revolve, are stored within "general frames of reference within which interpretations can be crystallized, tested and re-arranged," frames of reference that have a narrative structure.[64] The sto-ries told in opening statement necessarily invoke this web of belief; thus after opening statements, the jury's common sense seems to permit a pre-liminary judgment about which narrative is supported by the more univer-sally valid empirical generalizations.[65]

We thus have the notion that the initial plausibility of the opening state-ments can be determined by the degree of correspondence between them and a preexistent common sense (viewed as an inventory of factual gener-alizations with previously assigned probabilities); this notion breaks down quickly, however. Common sense rarely confronts the level of sys-tematically developed factual detail that it sees even in the opening state-ments, and certainly in the trial taken as a whole. In the adversary trial, those details have been developed so as to support two *competing* deter-minations of common sense. Each advocate, of course, relies on state-ments like, "Generally and for the most part, close relatives have affection for their kin." But each also continually says implicitly, ". . . but not where. . . ." As the factual development becomes ever more complex, the trier of fact is faced with a concrete situation well beyond, in its relevant specificity, anything his predetermined commonsense generalizations have been called upon to determine. He is likely to confront two factual narratives between which all previous commonsense generalizations of his culture do not conclusively adjudicate.

In short, even the issue of "factual"[66] plausibility requires of the trier of fact a genuine insight[67]—the intelligent grasp of intelligible structures

---

[64] Ibid., 22.

[65] It will turn out that this is not quite true. The reason is the structure of common sense. For the set of empirical generalizations that common sense, viewed abstractly, comprises, all have the structure "Generally, and for the most part. . . ." Lonergan, *Insight*, 173–80. Common sense assigns no "all other things being equal" numerical probabilities to those generalizations and contains no exhaustive set of exceptions and exceptions to exceptions (and so on) to those generalizations. The latter would, of course, be impossible and would, in any event, limit common sense's ability to address new situations.

[66] This notion of purely "factual" decision making is an abstraction from the jury's actual judgments, but a useful one.

[67] Peirce called these insights "abductions." See, e.g., Thomas Sebeok and Jean Umiker-Sebeok, " 'You Know My Method': A Juxtaposition of Charles S. Peirce and Sherlock Holmes," in *The Sign of Three: Dupin, Holmes, Peirce,* ed. Umberto Eco and Thomas

in the presentations before him. It is not just, as Kant reminds us, that there are no rules for the correct application of rules (in this case empirical generalizations); it's that there are no rules at all. In triable cases, the lawyers for both parties identify those aspects of the situation which suggest the relevance *and* the irrelevance of the most obvious commonsense generalizations that support or question the conclusions proposed. Each case requires of the jury genuine intelligence, the ultimate source of the insights *from* which generalizations (and the limits of their reach) emerge. The precise insight required of the jury by the evidence in any triable and well-tried case has literally never occurred before, and only a rigid conceptualism would say that it was for that reason arbitrary.[68] Just as the trial is the "law's self-criticism," the systematic presentation of factual details that test culturally transmitted empirical generalizations makes the trial the forum for the self-criticism of common sense as well.

The competing stories told in opening statements thus dramatize the gaps between the telling and what is told, and cultivate a higher level of jury self-consciousness about the indeterminately probabilistic commonsense principles that hold the stories together. This is, however, just the beginning.

Narrative and the Moral Point of View

The opening statements also compete to occupy the higher moral ground, to show that the party from whose perspective the opening is given is more worthy of individual praise and less worthy of blame,[69] a world that can be somewhat discontinuous with either factual accuracy or political sensibility. Placing real-world events in a narrative frame "is a demand . . . for moral meaning, a demand that sequences of events be assessed as to their significance as elements of a moral drama."[70] "Each narrativized

---

Sebeok (Bloomington: Indiana University Press, 1983), 11–54. Peirce was often at pains to understand how it could be that we are so accurate in these insights.

[68] Lonergan, *Insight*, 695. Conceptualism "places conception before understanding and things before their orders. . . ." Ibid.

[69] This is what Aristotle calls "forensic rhetoric." He notes that narrative is its preferred rhetorical form. Aristotle, *Rhetoric* 1414b.

[70] See Hayden White, "The Value of Narrativity in the Representation of Reality," in *On Narrative*, ed. W.J.T. Mitchell (Chicago: University of Chicago Press, 1981), 1. White argues that this narrative structure is a distortion of what he takes to be the incongruence between (1) real-world events and (2) their moral significance, on the one hand, and narrative structure, on the other. This argument raises what can only be called metaphysical questions. White's claims may be that trying to understand the moral significance of events through recounting them in narrative form is a distorting "aestheticizing" of their real moral significance, apparently available through some other (theoretical? intuitive?) means, or that his-

pattern of behavior is accompanied by some tacit social evaluation: that such behavior is good, bad, pleasing, unpleasing, etc. Social action is intelligible because we compare what we see with a stock of socially transmitted narrative models, each one of them accompanied by a particular social evaluation. The one which most resembles that which we observe renders our observation intelligible in a cognitive sense; it also provides an evaluation of it."[71] Narrative is "based on an experience of an *ethics already realized*" in a world in which, as Ricoeur puts it, "there is no action that does not give rise to approbation or reprobation, to however small a degree, as a function of a hierarchy of values for which goodness and wickedness are the poles."[72] The norms around which stories are told are not derived from an abstract morality of principle; they are those actually embedded in the forms of life of the community in which storyteller and listener find themselves.[73] "The world of recountable events" *is* an ethical world.[74] "[T]he strategy of persuasion undertaken by the narrator is aimed at imposing on the reader a vision of the world that is never ethically neutral, but that either implicitly or explicitly induces a new evaluation of the world and of the reader as well. In this sense, narrative already belongs to the ethical field in virtue of its claim—inseparable from its narration—to ethical justice."[75] The doubling of narratives in the opening

---

torical events have no moral significance (or at least none available to human beings). By the end of a trial, I argue, what is "left" is not a narrative structure that the jury accepts but something far less "aesthetically" configured, a truth beyond storytelling.

[71] Jackson, *Law, Fact, and Narrative Coherence*, 99.

[72] Kemp, "Ethics and Narrativity," 371, 376.

[73] The locus classicus is Hegel's distinction between *Moralitat* and *Sittlichkeit* in the *Philosophy of Right*. Perhaps the most thoroughgoing attempt to link narrative, the moral point of view, and legal authority is Hayden White's explicitly Hegelian account:

> Perhaps the growth and development of historical consciousness which is attended by a concomitant growth and development of narrative capability . . . has something to do with the extent to which the legal system functions as the subject of concern. . . . [I]t seems possible to conclude that every historical narrative has as its latent or manifest purpose the desire to *moralize* the events of which it treats. Where there is ambiguity or ambivalence regarding the status of the legal system, . . . the ground on which any closure of a story one might wish to tell about a past, whether it be a public or private past, is lacking. And this suggests that narrativity, certainly in factual storytelling and probably in fictional storytelling as well, is intimately related to, if not a function of, the impulse to moralize reality, that is, to identify it with the social system that is the source of any morality that we can imagine.

White, "The Value of Narrativity," 13–14.

[74] T. Peter Kemp, "Toward a Narrative Ethics: A Bridge between Ethics and the Narrative Reflections of Ricoeur," in *The Narrative Path: The Later Works of Paul Ricoeur*, ed. T. Peter Kemp and David Rasmussen (Cambridge: The MIT Press, 1989), 65.

[75] Paul Ricoeur, *Time and Narrative* (Chicago: University of Chicago Press, 1988), 249. Ricoeur is speaking of fictional narratives here, and so "it belongs to the reader, now an

statements then intensifies the exigency, always present when a story is told, "to take a position with respect to ethics or the vision of the good life which the work, at least implicitly, suggests."[76] If each opening statement is spun around a central norm—or "theme," as trial lawyers put it—then the jury is forced to begin making a comparative judgment about the relative importance of the norms that the two positions represent. This happens not abstractly but only at that level of concreteness that the narrator chooses, for rhetorical purposes, which most powerfully illustrates that norm.[77] The implicit ethics of narrative always requires that the story make a point about good and evil and, more fundamentally, reflect a vision of a good life, as opposed to a senseless life.[78] On the other hand, the trial is not simply a forum for judgments about the morality of individuals and actions. It is a public forum in which the jury engages in important public action. Such action reflects and redefines public identity, a topic to which I now turn.

Narrative as the Vehicle for Public Identity

"Communication between proponents of different theories is inevitably partial, . . . what each takes to be facts depends in part on the theory he espouses, and *an individual's transfer of allegiance from theory to theory is often better described as conversion than choice.*"[79] This principle prob-

---

agent, an initiator of action, to choose among the multiple proposals for ethical justice brought forth by reading." Kemp, "Ethics and Narrativity," 375. As I noted above, there exists a diminished range of ambiguity in the opening statement *both* because of its claim to recount a determinate past event and also because of the "legalistic" context. In his reply to Kemp, Ricoeur raises the yet more fundamental question of whether there exists a hierarchy of levels among narratives based on the relative power of the visions they embody. Ricoeur goes most of the way with that suggestion but maintains (with Kant and against Aristotle) that ultimately ethics is based not on historically conditioned stories and intuitive visions but on a principle, by which culturally and narratively embedded norms can be criticized. Donagan agrees. *A Theory of Morality*, 57–66 (the most adequate understanding of the moral point of view is Kant's statement of the categorical imperative). Recall that we are now speaking only about the narrative embodied in opening statements. I will argue shortly that the full trial's "hybrid of languages" does embody a principle of critique of the culturally conditioned norms embedded in the opening statements.

[76] Kemp, "Toward a Narrative Ethics," 65.

[77] See chapter 2, above (since the opening statement recounts what the evidence will *show*, not what the evidence will *be*, the lawyer *chooses* how much of the evidence to recount).

[78] Kemp, "Toward a Narrative Ethics," 75. Recall that the stories can draw the jury into them so that the moral point of the story emerges only when the jury *acts* to right a wrong.

[79] Kuhn, "Objectivity, Value Judgment, and Theory Choice," 338. Kuhn's view is obviously much more controversial in science than in law, where normative considerations have always been understood to be inevitable.

ably has the most force at trial insofar as the choice between theories requires a self-definition of public identity. The language of narrative has a "signaling" as well as a "labeling" function.[80] It seeks not only to achieve the more accurate account of the real-world event that has brought the case to trial, and fairly to pass moral judgment on the principal actors in that real-world drama (and so properly to "label" the event and the participants); it also seeks to "signal" to the jury that they will be defining their identities, deciding who they are, in their "choice" between opening statements. "By his manner of judging the person discloses to an extent also himself, what kind of person he is, and this disclosure . . . is involuntary."[81] Indeed, the coherence of the self is maintained by our being the storytellers of our own lives, and the jury, as we have seen, has been drawn into the stories told in opening statement in a way that makes the trial an important, sometimes a unique, event in this task of self-definition.

A juror's decision between competing narratives is, moreover, a definition of public identity. Because he is taking public action through public institutions, his judgment is inevitably determination, in a strong sense, of the nature of his community. This requires a device enabling him to assign the "meaning of what otherwise would remain an unbearable sequence of sheer happenings."[82]

> Storytelling offers us the means of reconciliation with reality. But, in effect, it also makes a common understanding of reality, and so, a world, possible for us in our plurality. In this respect storytelling must be understood not just as the primary form of thinking about experience, but also as the primary form of communicating with each other about experience. . . . *Stories tell us how each one finds or loses his just place in relation to others in the world. And the communication of the story is confirmed when justice has been recognized.* . . . In enabling us to appreciate the reality of what happens by means of storytelling, the imagination allows us to take the world to heart, and do justice to the fact that we share it others.[83]

By accepting "conversion" to one narrative over another, the juror locates himself in a public world. It is a judgment that "does justice to our sense of human plurality—of how men are likely to act and react in relation to each other."[84]

Tocqueville understood clearly the importance of the jury trial, which he always considered a "preeminently political institution," in the preser-

---

[80] Pitkin, *Wittgenstein and Justice*, 67–85.
[81] Beiner, *Political Judgment*, 18.
[82] Arendt, *Men in Dark Times*, 104.
[83] Hill, "The Fictions of Mankind and the Stories of Men," 289–90 (emphasis added).
[84] Ibid., 298.

vation of a vigorous public identity. His classic statement deserves extended quotation:

> The jury, and more especially the civil jury, serves to communicate the spirit of the judges to the minds of all the citizens; and this spirit with the habits which attend it, is the soundest preparation for free institutions. It imbues all classes with a respect for the thing judged and with the notion of right. If these two elements be removed, the love of independence becomes a mere destructive passion. It teaches men to practice equity; every man learns to judge his neighbor as he would himself be judged. . . . The jury teaches every man not to recoil before the responsibility of his own actions and impresses him with that manly confidence without which no political virtue can exist. It invests each citizen with a kind of magistracy; it makes them all feel the duties which they are bound to discharge towards society and the part which they take in its government. By obliging men to turn their attention to other affairs than their own, it rubs off that private selfishness which is the rust of society.[85]

It is, then, by engaging in the process of common judgment that one takes responsibility for and decisively shapes what the community is becoming.

And so openings are addressed not only to the empirical generalizations about how things happen "generally and for the most part" in the world. They are addressed to the "opinions"[86] or "folk psychology" of the jury. The latter is "not *just* a set of self-assuaging illusions, but the culture's beliefs and working hypotheses about what makes it possible and fulfilling for people to live together, even with great personal sacrifice."[87] They are "negotiated" public truths. Thus the act of judgment between competing narratives is an act of public allegiance to the opinions that constitute the identities of the jurors. An effective opening will suggest implicitly, therefore, that accepting the opponent's story would diminish the public identity of the juror, an identity that has often been achieved "with great personal sacrifice," and diminish, too, the way of life built around it.

This connection of the full narratives of the trial, where lawyers assign the meaning of the events, with the juror's public identity is one source of the "equitable, not rule-bound" style of decision making that the empirical investigators consistently find: "In deciding how to act well in a particular situation we draw upon an understanding of ourselves and our historical situation, *of who we are and what ends we desire, and this necessarily entails an activity of interpretation. What we are interpreting is ourselves, and the past and present social worlds that make us what we are.* . . . [W]e already possess a preunderstanding of our historical identity

---

[85] Tocqueville, *Democracy in America*, 1:295.
[86] See Hannah Arendt, *On Revolution* (New York: Penguin Books, 1963), 268–69.
[87] Bruner, *Acts of Meaning*, 32 (emphasis in original).

and social relationships. This we get from our past, from the cultural and linguistic traditions that compose our historical identity."[88] What lawyers begin to do for the jury, then, in the opening statements of a well-tried case is to begin the creation of the "hybrid of languages" that invite the jurors to begin "burrowing down into the depths of the particular, finding images and connections that will permit us to see it more truly, describe it more richly; by combing this burrowing with a horizontal drawing of connections, so that every horizontal link contributes to the depth of our view of the particular, and every new depth creates new horizontal links."[89] These links are both "factual" and normative, and the normative links involve moral judgment and political self-definition.

Of course, the trial does not end with opening statements. But even at this preliminary level the storytelling of opening statement has qualities distinct from those of stories told elsewhere. First, the teller must anticipate the story that will be told by the opponent. Second, the storyteller is limited by the ethical rule that forbids alluding to any matter for which there will not be admissible evidence.[90] Furthermore, the storyteller must be aware of the "performative" aspect of opening statement: it constitutes a promise that the evidence actually will show that the story is true. The storyteller knows that his opponent will be alert to point out to the jury when that promise has not been kept.[91] Put simply, the rules of ethics, and of evidence, and the adversary context of presentation all conspire to prevent the lawyer from simply telling the "most persuasive" story. Social science investigators sometimes ignore this fact and so exaggerate the importance of internal narrative structure at trial. Fourth, opening statement is akin in this regard to history:[92] it makes a claim about the past, a past that is inevitably determinate—after all, *something* happened, and what has happened has happened. Relatedly, the opening statement is made in an explicitly legal context, a context which demands that the jury make an either-or judgment. Opening statements thus have a lower level of "subjunctivity" than do stories told informally or in literary contexts. Although they sometimes leave one of the elements of the story (or a relationship between elements) indeterminate because of uncertainties about the weight of the evidence, the storyteller must insist on that level

---

[88] Beiner, *Political Judgment*, 19 (emphasis added).

[89] Nussbaum, *The Fragility of Goodness*, 69.

[90] And so the opening statement is implicitly limited by all the policies embedded in the rules of evidence.

[91] Arguing in closing that the opponent has not "kept his promise" is a standard rhetorical device in trial practice.

[92] Dewey, "Logical Method and the Law," draws the parallels (and the discontinuity stemming from the absence of disinterestedness) between the lawyer preparing his case and a historian at work on his analysis.

of factual and normative determinativeness which would justify a verdict in his favor and against his opponent. Indeterminateness or ambiguity is a much more dangerous quality in opening statement than in other storytelling contexts.[93]

The jury can begin to assess the empirical and moral adequacy of a party's opening statement, and so the strength of its theory and theme, by implicitly comparing the competing statements, comparing which details the lawyers include and omit, and, derivatively, what facts each lawyer cannot integrate into his "theme," his normative perspective on the case. When the jury makes a preliminary determination between opening statements, it is not simply deciding who is telling the prettier story. The concern that the trial awards the victory solely to the lawyer who is the "better storyteller" is, "given a modicum of competence," thus far misplaced. When the jury makes a preliminary determination between opening statements, it is choosing between two highly *constrained* accounts. These constraints pull the accounts toward each other, since they must anticipate each other's best factual and normative considerations; toward the evidence, since the performative element in opening statement is a promise about what the evidence will show; and toward the law, since the lawyers must always be concerned about the possibility of a directed verdict. This discipline, and the extreme cognitive tension it generates, are precisely what make the trial a "crucible." Even such constrained narratives do not, however, stand on their own. By far the larger part of a trial is consumed with the presentations of the evidence.

The Deepening of the Tensions: The Evidentiary Phase

The Moral Limitations of Free Narrative

Though "trials and their stories are the embodiment of the law's self-criticism,"[94] narrative itself has its limits and its dangers, both normative and empirical. The inevitable moralizing of events that narrative brings can both degenerate into moralism and tend to manifest all the limits that the prevailing ethos of the community contains.[95] A well-crafted narrative that is attentive to complete and unambiguous internal relations among story elements may in fact serve to "represent the moral order

---

[93] On the "subjunctivity" of literary narrative, see Jerome Bruner, *Actual Minds, Possible Worlds* (Cambridge: Harvard University Press, 1986), 29–37.

[94] Luban, *Legal Modernism*, 381.

[95] Donagan, *The Theory of Morality*, 140–41.

under the aspect of the aesthetic."[96] Part of our life world that provides the frames for trial narrative *does* consist of "a set of self-assuaging illusions."[97] Each of those well-constructed and complete stories told in opening is likely, then, to be inadequate in two ways. It will be inadequate to those aspects of social reality that the dominant belief system of the society obscures.[98] At a deeper level, it will likely be inadequate to what is dark and incomplete about the human condition and so hardest to look upon. This "renders narrative techniques that offer clarity and realism less useful"[99] even if our need for order[100] makes those techniques more *persuasive*. Finally,

> [N]arrative . . . can be "real" or "imaginary" without loss of its power as a story. That is to say the *sense* and the *reference* of a story bear an anomalous relationship to each other. The story's indifference to extralinguistic reality underlines the fact that it has a structure that is internal to discourse. In other words, the sequence of its sentences, rather than the truth or falsity of any of those sentences is what determines its overall configuration or plot.[101]

Thus in order for the trial to be fair to extralinguistic reality, it must rely on devices other than free narrative and must contain within itself methods of disrupting the distorting allure of storytelling concerned only about its own aesthetic configurations. Obviously cross-examination and argument perform these functions, but, perhaps even more important, so does the entire evidentiary phase. The trial, as it progresses, can create an almost unbearable tension between the narrative assimilation of a problematic situation to prevailing moral and political norms embedded in the opening statements and other demanding values. It is to the means by which such tension is created that I now turn.

---

[96] White, "The Value of Narrativity," 23. See Alan M. Dershowitz, "Life Is Not a Dramatic Narrative," in *Law's Stories: Narrative and Rhetoric in the Law*, ed. Peter Brooks and Paul Gewirtz (New Haven: Yale University Press, 1996), 99.

[97] Bruner, *Acts of Meaning*, 32.

[98] Donagan, *The Theory of Morality*, 140. The prophetic strain in the Judeo-Christian tradition, expressed, for example, in certain of the parables of Jesus, invokes the inadequacy of the ordinary story frames and the need for extraordinary, indeed shocking, linguistic forms. See, e.g., John Dominick Crossan, *In Parables: The Challenge of the Historical Jesus* (New York: Harper & Row, 1973).

[99] W. R. Johnson, *Darkness Visible: A Study of Vergil's Aeneid* (Berkeley and Los Angeles: University of California Press, 1976).

[100] Wallace Stevens wrote of our "rage for order." "The Idea of Order at Key West," in *The Palm at the End of the Mind*, ed. Holly Stevens (New York: Vintage Books, 1972), 97.

[101] Bruner, *Acts of Meaning*, 44 (emphasis in orginal). Plato was keenly aware of this discontinuity between narrative plausibility and truth, though there are hints, later developed by Aristotle, that the discontinuity may be bridged. See chapter 8, below.

The Essential Tension

Opening statements appeal to a variety of distinct perspectives, each of which is public in a way—empirical generalizations, commonsense morality, public identity, and, to the extent necessary to avoid a directed verdict, legality. Each attempts a coherent, statesmanlike integration of those public norms through the telling of a story that seems probable in the light cast by those same norms. By contrast, the evidentiary phase of the trial offers something quite different in two important ways, each roughly corresponding to one of the two most prominent features of trial testimony emphasized by the Received View: testimony in response to nonleading questions and testimony in the language of perception. First, witnesses who take the stand and testify in response to nonleading questions and so "in their own words" are unlikely to be public people, and even less likely to have learned to speak "diplomatically," so as to minimize offense to the range of moral, political, and legal values represented in any triable case. However well-prepared, witnesses inevitably reveal their personal perspectives and values. I have already discussed the importance of the witnesses' performance and its "truthfulness," together with the ways in which they are revealed and tested by the trial's devices. This, again, provides important, and largely tacit, information about who the real-world actors (now witnesses) are, and, inevitably, about how they are likely to have acted, and perhaps even about what they deserve. Here, though, I focus on the distinct kind of perspective on the facts to which the witnesses testify.

We remember events as a core interpreted pattern, a gestalt (it was "an accusation," "a threat," "an assault"), and those details that tend to support this central interpretation.[102] This does not at all imply that we remember inaccurately, but simply that accuracy depends on how "true" the witness's normative perspective is. The judgments witnesses make, and so their good-faith recollection of events, inevitably bring into the trial the individual moral judgments and the local knowledge of the witness, which may well be discontinuous with commonsense morality and particularly with the sense of public identity—the "political" perspective—the jury is likely to bring to the case.[103] Although witness preparation may sometimes soften those conflicts, and the form of direct examination keep them implicit, they will nonetheless put before the jury perspectives on the evidence distinct from those of commonsense moral-

---

[102] Bruner, *Acts of Meaning*, 58–59.

[103] For example, a jury strongly inclined to support vigorous law enforcement may be morally discomforted by the attitudes toward arrestees that police witnesses carrying out the jury's own program manifest.

ity, public identity, or law. In addition, because witnesses' stories, unlike opening statements, have not "taken account" of the other evidence in the case, they are likely not to fit perfectly into the sponsoring party's theory and theme. They are likely to be partial, to be told from one perspective. Yet they can be deep and powerful in ways that diplomatic and strategic stories tend not to be. As we saw, every value-laden description in such a story can be the prism through which the entire case is seen.

Second, testimony is usually given in the language of perception. Perceptions, as elaborated and tested by direct and cross, are somewhat resistant to the witness's expectations and values. We tend to see what we expect or want to see, but we can see that which surprises or deeply disappoints us. Here the contrast with opening is not with the personal moral perspective of the witness—public norms as against personal values—but between meaning and truth. The lawyer is not like a novelist, howsoever honest, who writes the dialogue of his characters. He is not like a historian, whose characters have sometimes not spoken on their own behalf, or whose statements can be deeply embedded in the paragraphs of the author's own interpretive narrative. Witnesses really are on their own. And in the adversary context each party will usually have an interest in presenting those accounts which do not fit well within the opponent's theory and theme.

At trial, the simple credibility of a witness, as well as the specific combination of unusual circumstances, can, just barely, overcome the general unlikeliness of the testimony. Testimony is, after all, a basic, irreducible source of human knowledge, and our reliance on it is "an absolutely fundamental epistemological attitude which is far more pervasive in ordinary life and specialized theory than we normally recognize."[104] We often base important decisions on testimony alone. The important point for us is that in triable cases *no* theory of the case can fully integrate the personal perspectives or perceptual testimony of the witnesses. They remain throughout as a challenge not only to lawyers' but also to jurors' desires for subsumption of particulars of the case under a few inevitably overgeneralized abstractions and scripts. Both the personal moral perspectives of witnesses and their reporting of "brutally elementary data"[105] justified only by their testimony to their perceptions stand in stark contrast to the crafted and diplomatic storytelling of opening statements.

The testimonial phase of the trial intensifies the tension between public meanings, on the one hand, and truth, on the other. Some evidence is

---

[104] Coady, *Testimony*, 262–63.

[105] Arendt, "Truth and Politics," 239. Arendt's essay concerns the tension between the political realm, based on the "opinion" that serves as the vehicle for what I have called public identity, and factual truth.

comparatively reliable and relatively impervious to reinterpretation. The evidentiary basis is not a homogeneous pudding awaiting only that structure which comes from "above," in the form either of normative or political importance or of commonsense probabilities, although those are powerful forces in the trial. The evidentiary basis is, as Henry James put it in another context, a "lumpy pudding." Some evidence can be so credible that it resists—sometimes just resists, sometimes overcomes—opinion, reinterpretation, and its own general factual implausibility.

How can this be? Only because accuracy itself connects up with deep values. The Received View properly emphasizes accuracy's relevance to the ideals embedded in the Rule of Law: predictability, stability, and fairness. Accuracy has central *moral* significance as well.[106] "What looks like mere accuracy at one end looks more like justice or courage or even love at the other."[107] Indeed, as Iris Murdoch has put it, morality itself involves "an exercise of justice and realism that is really *looking*. The difficulty is to keep this attention fixed upon the real situation to prevent it from returning surreptitiously to the self. . . . Realism, whether that of the artist or of the agent, is a moral achievement. This explains the central insight of Kantian ethics: 'The more the separateness and differences of other people is realized, and the fact seen that another man has needs and wishes as demanding as one's own, the harder it becomes to treat a person as a thing.' "[108] We can perceive the moral significance of a situation only if we care about accuracy. In the trial context, "treating a person as a thing" involves treating his case as "symbolic" or as an opportunity to achieve some purpose beyond showing fairness and thus respect to the individual person. Such a distorted perspective is, of course, indifferent to any question of factual accuracy and is rather an expression of what Collingwood called the "untruthful consciousness" in the moral sphere, "shrinking from something which its business is to face."[109]

The evidentiary phase of the trial moves its center of gravity from a meaningful story to the inconvenient details of the evidence presented in as little theory-laden a manner as possible. Paradoxically, by giving particularity and empirical truth their due, the trial disciplines and clarifies the meaning of the norms and purposes around which the narratives of opening are spun. "It is only when we are confronted by the demands of action *in context of a particular set of circumstances* that we get a true understanding of what our ends really are, and reassess those ends in relationship to a new understanding of our life as a whole. Action in the

[106] Beiner, *Political Judgment*, 24.
[107] Murdoch, *The Sovereignty of Good*, 89.
[108] Ibid., 66.
[109] R. G. Collingwood, *The Principles of Art* (Oxford: Clarendon Press, 1938), 384–86.

particular circumstances of life is a continuing dialogue between what we think our life is about, and the particularities of moral and practical exigency."[110] It is precisely this experience of their own capacity for moral judgment that lies at the basis of so many jurors' testimony to the personal significance of jury service. It comes as a revelation because the trial's languages and the discipline of adversary presentation challenge and actualize this capacity. By contrast, mass-circulation journalism and sentimental mass-media fiction are designed to anesthetize this capacity by eliminating most of the tensions between general norms and the particulars of the story. Not only are "trials and their stories . . . the embodiment of the law's self-criticism,"[111] but they also serve as the criticism of the inevitably overgeneralized "scripts" within which we hold our moral convictions. This is part of what Bernard Jackson means when he says that the semiotic of the trial is designed to undermine the implicit judgment processes of commonsense evaluation.[112] Jurors experience this actualizing of an often debased *sensus communis* as a revelation, as they are offered a set of linguistic practices that is more demanding of and more adequate to the range of their subjective capacities.

The Justice That Is Strife

The consciously structured hybrid of languages which the trial comprises respects a plurality of social values that are often in conflict. The deepening tensions among the linguistic practices of the trial thus represent serious and sometimes tragic conflicts among those values within a practice that is fair to the important values on all sides. The legal order in the trial reflects in the world of language what the Greeks called the *nomoi*, the concrete morality of practices and institutions. Its languages "preserve the special separateness and the importance of each of the gods and the sphere of human life protected by each. They offer no solution in bewildering tragic situations—except the solution that consists in being faithful to or harmonious with one's sense of worth by acknowledging the tension and disharmony."[113] The trial is a space in which the agonistic or competitive phase of civilization still lives.[114] It confers on the exertions of all the participants "a certain ethical value in so far as it means a testing of the player's prowess: his courage, tenacity, resources, and last but not least,

---

[110] Beiner, *Political Judgment*, 24. Beiner is discussing Gadamer's reading of Aristotle.
[111] Luban, *Legal Modernism*, 381.
[112] Jackson, *Law, Fact, and Narrative Coherence*.
[113] Nussbaum, *The Fragility of Goodness*, 81.
[114] Huizinga, *Homo Ludens*, 75.

his spiritual powers—his 'fairness.' "[115] But the constitutive rules of the trial put those agonistic virtues at the service of a justice that is strife by creating a fair contest between or among real values where the appropriate balance or tension can *only* be fought out. For each situation is unique. A legal system where decisions flow easily from the "sort" of situation it is, because of relatively generalized and abstract features of situations, is a system where there will be relatively little internal strife and correspondingly little justice. Even in physics, where an infinitely more abstract perspective is appropriate, "only by entertaining multiple and mutually limiting points of view, building up a composite picture, can we approach the real richness of the world."[116] What Bakhtin thought of the novel is in some ways even more true of the linguistic conflicts at work in the trial:

> At the heart of everything . . . is a highly distinctive concept of language. The conception has as its enabling *a priori* an almost Manichean sense of opposition and struggle at the heart of existence, a ceaseless battle between centrifugal forces that seek to keep things apart, and centripetal forces that strive to make things cohere. . . . The most complete and complex reflection of these forces is found in human language. . . .[117]

I turn next to discuss how the depth of the tensions represented at trial can lead to a realistic normative understanding of this great practice.

---

[115] Ibid.

[116] Richard Rhodes, review of *Niels Bohr's Times: In Physics, Philosophy, and Polity,* by Abraham Pais, *New York Times Book Review,* January 26, 1992.

[117] Bakhtin, *The Dialogic Imagination,* xviii. The trial reflects the importance of *both* centrifugal and centripetal forces. Recall Hannah Arendt's notion that totalitarian regimes seek to force all men together into a unity so tight that action becomes impossible, and that law seeks to maintain the boundaries that *both* separate men *and* make concerted action possible. Arendt, *The Origins of Totalitarianism,* 465–66.

VII

The Two Sides of the Trial Event

A man cannot see by another's eye, nor hear by
another's ear; no more can a man conclude
or infer the thing to be resolved by another's
understanding or reasoning; and though the
verdict be right the jury give, yet they, not being
assured it is so from their understanding, are
forsworn, at least *foro conscientia* . . . [Juries]
resolve both law and fact complicatively, and not
the fact by itself.
> (Chief Justice Vaughn of the Court of
> Common Pleas in Bushell's Case, 6 How.
> St., Tr. 999, 1011, 1015)

I have never yet been able to perceive how any
thing can be known for truth by consequitive
reasoning.
> (Keats)

Everything is always going on, all of the time.
> (Wynton Marsalis)

A More Adequate Model: The Web of Languages and Meanings

We are beginning to see that trial languages and practices reflect the multiplicity of normative spheres. I suggest throughout the rest of this book that, for precisely this reason, the trial has evolved into an institution peculiarly appropriate for the conditions of modern life: to varying degrees, modern trials "are emblems of the simultaneous creation of justice and of the enabling conventions of justice" and are thus a response to the modernist predicament of our needing our conventions while simultaneously knowing that we have created them and can criticize them.[1] The trial is the "law's self-criticism" specifically because the elements of the consciously structured hybrid of languages and practices that it comprises

---

[1] Luban, *Legal Modernism*, 380.

are in such sharp tension with one another. It is an institution, perhaps the institution, where we moderns can do what we need to do: pass judgment on our practices not from a single authoritative perspective "above" those practices but rather from the resources that exist within the multiplicity of those practices.[2] In our kind of modern society, conflicts among those spheres and their animating principles occur regularly. Often only one determinate resolution of those conflicts is possible. When Chesterton analogized the experience of the trial to that of tragedy, he saw that virtually any resolution of the "tragic conflicts" could succeed only by "acknowledging the tension and disharmony" among the spheres of human life at stake.[3] The participants' experience of "moral elevation" or "substance" or "significance" in the trial process is precisely the experience of identity with and responsibility for this resolution of conflicts among spheres of life that our concrete historical situation mandates.

Throughout, we have been considering the multiplicity of values, modes of social ordering, and forms of life that can come into conflict at trial. This should come as no surprise. Even in the area of individual moral agency, in many ways a simpler forum, "we naturally think, when uncorrupted by theory, of a multiplicity of moral claims, which sometimes come into conflict with each other"[4] such that those conflicts are at the heart of moral life, not at its periphery. In her profound account of individual moral experience, Iris Murdoch argues that we have a way through those conflicts,[5] "an exercise of justice and realism and really *looking*. The difficulty is to keep this attention fixed upon the real situation. . . . Realism, whether that of the artist or of the agent, is a moral achievement."[6] The provocative argument I am making here is that the trial's devices seek to achieve an artificially (in the sense that it is achieved through institutional artifice, not through individual virtue) elevated moral vision of the sort Murdoch describes.

---

[2] David Kolb, *The Critique of Pure Modernity: Hegel, Heidegger and After* (Chicago and London: University of Chicago Press, 1986), 259. ("Our task is less to create constantly new forms of life than to creatively renew actual forms by taking advantage of their internal multiplicity and tensions and their frictions with one another.")

[3] Chesterton, *Tremendous Trifles*, 64–65.

[4] Hampshire, "Public and Private Morality," 42.

[5] She gives the following examples: "Should a retarded child be kept at home or sent to an institution? Should an elderly relation who is a trouble-maker be cared for or asked to go away? Should an unhappy marriage be continued for the sake of the children? Should I neglect them in order to practice my art?" Murdoch, *The Sovereignty of Good*, 66. She argues that the common feeling that "moral choice is something arbitrary, a matter of personal will rather than attentive study," is just wrong, a product of "[i]gnorance, muddle, fear, wishful thinking, lack of tests. . . ." Ibid.

[6] Ibid.

The number and kinds of tensions deepen when one is considering not a personal moral decision but rather a legal judgment. The trial is a place where legal, political, and moral ordering, each internally complex, compete. Figure 2 represents my attempt to provide a more adequate model of the intellectual operations the jury must perform on the trial's linguistic practices.

Some Preliminary Points

First, figure 2 is only a model. The insight of active practical intelligence into the proper resolution of the tensions cannot be objectivized in a model. An ancient metaphor for the human mind describes "a spider sitting in the middle of its web, able to feel and respond to any tug in any part of the complicated structure."[7] To continue the metaphor, the web over which the spider moves and through which it perceives *can* be modeled. As should be clear by now, the web represents the tensions among the components of the trial. It is, however, too homogeneous to represent adequately the ways in which the *differences* among the trial's incommensurable components structure the jury's perceptions, because tensions represented are tensions among values, forms of social ordering, and, ultimately, forms of life. Still it is a useful metaphor, and figure 2 provides a useful model.

The key conflicts in different trials will be in different places. There are cases where there is virtually no conflict over the physical description of the circumstantial evidence or even over the bare narrative of the movements in space or time. All the controversy may surround which evaluative terms[8] are more properly predicated of those actions and actors, and which story is more compelling. In other cases—for example, some criminal cases where the defense is mistaken identity, and where there is close to total convergence of the normative sources of decision (moral, legal, political, instrumental)—the only significant questions may concern who did what to whom, where there is little ambiguity as to how the "what"

---

[7] Nussbaum, *The Fragility of Goodness*, 300.

[8] Julius Kovesi's *Moral Notions* (London: Routledge and Kegan Paul, 1967) has emphasized the ways in which evaluative terms are really developments of descriptive terms. Murdoch has argued persuasively that the center of gravity of the moral life concerns which middle-level descriptive-evaluative terms ought to be applied in a situation, rather than the application of broad terms, like "right" and "good." *The Sovereignty of Good*, 23. Hanna Pitkin has followed Cavell and Wittgenstein in explaining how, in describing human action, terms carefully bereft of all evaluation are not more basic or fundamental than those which do have significant evaluative content. *Wittgenstein and Justice*, 166.

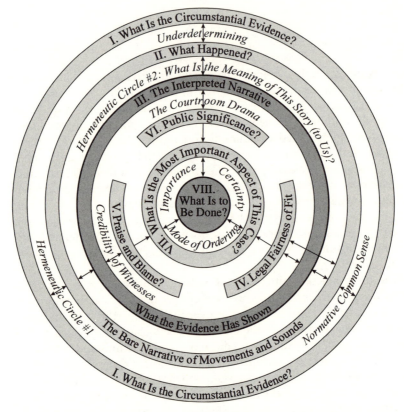

Figure 2

should be described. In these cases the key issues will concern primarily the nature of the circumstantial evidence (Was the defendant "unconcerned" when he was told of his wife's death?), represented by Level I of the model, or the bare narratives of movements in space and time (Did the defendant fire the gunshot that killed his wife?), represented by Level II. The metalevel problem as to which question presents the key issue is always a normative question.

The question at Level III—which interpreted narrative should a jury accept—is at the heart of the trial. This is because of the fundamental character of narrative for the understanding of human action and the corollary that any attempt to understand human actions "in themselves," before, so to speak, the "imposition" of narrative categories, will yield only "the disjointed parts of some possible narrative."[9] Thus Levels I and II are not more fundamental or more basic, as an empiricist philosophy of knowledge might have it. Rather, as a purely descriptive matter, the jury will ask questions at Level I and Level II in order to answer one sort of question generated at Level III, that is, which interpreted narrative "constrains" more of the facts, as Bennett and Feldman put it. The jury will often seek to imagine, literally to visualize, a sequence of past events in order to decide which of the two opening statements is more adequate. It is to that visualized narrative that many of the more evaluative judgments at Level III will attach. By contrast, at Level II, the jury is asking which bare narrative is the more likely: what would you have seen if you had been there? In order to decide what the evidence has shown, one must often determine what physical actions took place and what words were spoken in the past. In order to determine that, one must usually ask what the evidence was. Those questions are not fully independent, but they are sufficiently independent that the jury will often move "out" to another level of questioning in order to determine what the evidence has shown. My only point at this stage is that the jury does not begin temporally, psychologically, or epistemologically with the evidence.

The intellectual operations that the jury must perform are answers to questions. Those are questions that the trial's practices make virtually unavoidable. The implicit metaphysics of the trial is simple: reality is what corresponds to justified answers to the well-formed questions that intelligent and responsible persons would ask under the circumstances.[10] Those questions are represented by the various levels of figure 2.

It is important to note that the account given here is an account of those cases that actually go to trial. Except where there are serious miscalculations or where a party (usually a criminal defendant) is given no alterna-

---

[9] MacIntyre, *After Virtue*, 215.
[10] See generally Lonergan, *Insight*.

tive but to go to trial, those tend to be what lawyers call "triable" cases. They are precisely those cases where some social norm available through the rules and practices of the trial renders some important issue debatable. Cases that are not triable are screened out by pretrial procedural devices and by the strategic judgments of lawyers. Thus to emphasize the apparent indeterminacy of trial decision making, as I do, is not to claim that the likely resolution of all important problematic situations is profoundly debatable. It *is* true that the percentage of problematic situations which yield triable cases is a measure of the multiplicity of incommensurable values and forms of life in a society.

A Model of Trial Decision Making

Having put aside any notion that we are starting at the "foundation," I begin with Level I. Here, the jury must ask, "What is the circumstantial evidence?" This is a question because, even at this level, the jury must make what the philosophical literature sometimes calls perceptual judgments, which always require the predication of some descriptive term of an individual. The individual itself, is, as the medievals would have it, *ineffable*, "unspeakable." We begin to understand it as we predicate universal terms of it, for the nature of most circumstantial evidence and the relevance of all circumstantial evidence is not self-interpreting and is often in dispute. Did the defendant "point" a weapon at the victim in an assault case? Did the victim look at her assailant's face during a purse snatching? Witnesses' recollections of those details are often imperfect and are likely to be reorganized to support an overall impression of the events. Slight variations in the simplest movements and sounds (including words) may have enormous normative significance. Did the victim say, "Oh, no! Oh, no, Joe!" or "Oh, no. Oh, no, no!"? In a case where the difference between probation and a life term for murder is the existence of intent to kill, did the defendant "push" an infant off the bed or "throw" him to the floor after lifting him from the bed? In the latter case, the "lifting" could have occurred in less than a second. In the infamous Lozano[11] case, where a police officer shot and killed a motorcyclist approaching him on a Miami street, and the officer claimed to be in fear for his life, how fast was the cyclist going, how far was he from the officer when the latter fired, was the police car positioned such that the officer could not step easily out of the way? These crucial factual details are often underdetermined by the evidence and fiercely contested. This underdetermination is

[11] *People v. Lozano*, 584 So.2d 19 (Fla. Dist. Ct. App. 1991).

one of the reasons why all the levels of judgment above the first may affect the jury's judgment even as to these very basic factual issues.

The law of evidence distinguishes between circumstantial evidence and direct evidence. From circumstantial evidence the jury must take several inferential steps to warrant the conclusion that some element of a claim or defense has been proven. ("Footprints in the snow . . ."; "Lipstick on your collar . . ."). Direct evidence, typically testimony of an eyewitness, requires only that the jury accept the credibility of witnesses. Since the credibility of a witness always rests in part on circumstantial evidence, the probative value of all evidence always effectively rests on circumstantial evidence. Thus these questions of significant factual detail often devolve into issues of the circumstantial evidence for or against the credibility of witnesses. There are fine gradations of credibility and more than a dozen rhetorical commonplaces[12] that can be used to throw credibility into question.

Even where what we may call, with deliberate naïveté, the "bare" facts are undisputed, the proper characterization of those facts may be deeply problematic. Again, was the utterance at the heart of a defamation case an "accusation" or merely a question ("Miss, have you seen my wife's ring")? Was the defendant in a murder case who was not under arrest at the time (1) walking innocently past the front door of the police station to make a telephone call, (2) walking innocently toward the front door in order to get a breath of fresh air, (3) walking "quickly" toward the front door, (4) walking "furtively" toward the front door, (5) "making a break for it." As alternatives (1) and (2) make clear, even what appears to be an unproblematic perceptual judgment involves at least a "collapsed inference." This inferential character of perception becomes even more obvious as we move up through the alternatives into more heavily characterized descriptions. Again, "more heavily characterized" does not mean "more embellished." In fact, the more characterized descriptions may well convey more of the truth of what occurred. On the other hand, the "inferences" involved are likely to raise more complex issues of credibility.

The notion of a "bare narrative" at Level II is an abstract answer to one set of questions a jury will naturally ask: "What would you have seen and heard had you been there?" Recall that the jury will naturally ask that question to help adjudicate between the competing fully characterized narratives at Level III, presented concretely in opening statement and supported in closing argument. The jury will naturally want literally to picture a series (and perhaps several series) of past events in order to actualize its own normative judgments. It is true, however, that even in the best-prepared cases the bare narratives the jury can construct will be under-

---

[12] See chapter 2, above.

determined by the circumstantial evidence presented. First, it is simply impossible to assign relative probabilities to the conflicting views of the nature of the circumstantial evidence at Level I. Second, there will be potentially significant "episodes" of a visualized reconstruction of events—which could have occurred in many different ways—for which there will simply be *no* circumstantial evidence at all.

This is one reason why the arrows running between Level I and Level II run both ways. As we saw above, one bare narrative can be more plausible simply because it conforms to Louis Nizer's "rule of probability"[13]; it is, as a purely empirical matter, consistent with the usual pattern of events, the way it usually goes, regardless of the "amount" of evidence there is to support that version. The relative indeterminacy of both the existence and proper characterization of evidence at Level I allows the trier of fact to determine what the circumstantial evidence is based on its consistency with the more generally probable factual account. This determination of the nature of the evidence is inevitably circular. Further, even when the identity of the circumstantial evidence is relatively determinate, that evidence is always linked to an episode in the "bare narrative" at Level II by a commonsense generalization which provides its "logical relevance."[14] The jury will necessarily ask implicitly, "How universal is the commonsense generalization that links the circumstantial evidence to the episode (F1) in the bare narrative for which it is offered as proof?" Since the structure of the commonsense generalizations that provide those links is always "Generally and for the most part . . . ,"[15] the next question is always "Are all the particular additional facts in this case (F1 . . . Fn) such as to make the generalization more or less powerful than it would be, other things being equal?" But the existence of these latter facts (F1 . . . Fn) and their proper characterization will themselves be in dispute just as is F1. And the strength of the commonsense generalizations that link those facts to what the proponent seeks to show is also caught in another web of mutually determining probabilities.

The more radical thesis, which I do not advance, is that the circumstantial evidence is so completely plastic to interpretation based on the more plausible bare narrative that the arrows of causality run only outward. This would be consistent with a pure coherence theory of truth at trial—within such a theory individual bits of circumstantial evidence and "brutally elementary" episodes of historical fact could never have any justified effects at all. They would be completely determined by the higher-level generalizations and values. For reasons I explore in the next chapter, I do

---

[13] Nizer, *My Life in Court*, 17.
[14] See chapter 2, above.
[15] Lonergan, *Insight*, 173–81.

not accept a pure coherence theory of the factual truth that emerges at trial. Though the existence and interpretation of the circumstantial evidence are subject to mutual determination, this process is not completely fluid. The evidential field is, as I suggested, "lumpy" in that some bits of circumstantial evidence (including evidence of credibility) are supported by generalizations that possess higher levels of universality, or are understood to apply with particular power in the specific circumstances of the case. The trial's multiplicity of languages and practices provide, in effect, for an internal critique of all higher-level abstractions, a critique that allows for a convergence on the concrete. Of course, if the existence of one such fact were the necessary "consequence" of a generalization that possessed full universality, was infinitely "lumpy," there would be something approaching a fixed anchor from which other facts could be determined. There are very few such anchors in the world. But there are some. One could imagine eyewitness testimony by Mother Theresa offered against the Catholic Church of events that occurred over a long period of time and in which she had a strong reason to be attentive and to check her perceptions continually. It is the function of the rules insisting on orderly presentation of testimony in the language of perception to respect the high probative value of some forms of testimony, and the values underlying their importance.

In a well-tried case, the individual facts will be united in and supportive of a fairly universal factual theory at this level. Thus decisions on the individual facts will tend to "fall into place" along with the acceptance or the rejection of the entire theory. In fact, the representation of the facts by advocates within fairly unified theories of the case simply allows the parties to anticipate the way in which a jury would inevitably reach a decision through a unifying insight that is only secondarily articulated in concepts and arguments.

In "triable cases," cases where something is really debatable, it is only a bit of an exaggeration to say, as trial lawyers do, that "every fact has two faces." Both the nature and the implications of a large range of the most significant facts in a triable case will be indeterminate, dependent upon which of two competing commonsense generalizations the jury accepts. Is the fact that a parent had beaten her child previously and not done great bodily harm probative that she was "consciously aware of the strong probability of great bodily harm" in a similar beating that led to the child's death, or quite the opposite, that she believed her conduct was unlikely to cause such harm? Assume that a wealthy householder had earlier reprimanded a servant for eavesdropping, a servant to whom, unbeknownst to the householder, a subsequent libel is "published"—that is, it is the servant's overhearing the statement that satisfies the "element" that the damaging statement was made public. Should the prior instance have made the householder aware that his servant may have been listening, or would his reprimand have assured him that he could speak frankly without being overheard? Did the fact that the criminal defendant had four beers an hour before an accurate shooting of the victim make it more or less likely that he did the killing? Which is the more powerful inference: that the beers lowered his inhibitions, or that they made it less likely that he could have performed the shooting?

In each case one can ask which inference is the "more universal," but then, more important, which inference is the more compelling *under the particular circumstances of this case*, themselves in dispute in the ways described above. Such a determination cannot be made without the simultaneous determination of an entire range of bare narrative fact through a single insight that grasps the implicit intelligibility of all the evidence. In the context of the trial, this insight is usually, though not always, a matter of accepting one of the bare narratives implicit in one of the theories of the case. That is one reason why trial lawyers say that the trial is a battle for the imagination of the jury. To anticipate somewhat, it is also why it is so important that the jury want to accept one account rather than another. It is one of the reasons why social scientists say that the acceptance of one theory rather than another "causes" the verdict. Trial "facts" are heavily theory-laden.

This notion of a "bare narrative" is an abstract answer to one set of questions the jury will naturally ask: "What would I have seen and heard had I been there?" The legitimacy of that question is institutionalized in the rules that control direct examination, one of the linguistic forms of the trial. But knowing is not taking a look.[16] A sequence of relatively uninterpreted "sense-data" is not truer or realer than a more fully characterized account. The trial takes this into consideration as well by giving prominence of place to the fully characterized storytelling of opening statement. As we have seen, those accounts will be more or less compelling because of their "factual" probability and because of the power of the norms around which they are woven, moral and political. Here again, there is a relation of mutual reciprocal determination, the second hermeneutical circle in the jury's task of interpretation. "What probably happened," the story at Level II, is relatively plastic to the power of the competing meanings of the alternative stories at Level III. Those meanings are mediated and thus shaped by the practices of the trial itself: its performances, its drama, its personal interactions.

The interpreted narrative mutually determines and is determined by yet another level of questioning: which of the parties more deserves to be

---

[16] Ibid., 372.

praised and/or blamed?[17] That such a level even exists in trial decision making might be theoretically disturbing for the Received View. After all, so the argument goes, the trial is to achieve corrective justice; the moral desert of the parties is irrelevant. Nonetheless, individual moral evaluation is an inevitable aspect of almost all trials. It is inevitable that the jury be aware that its task has a practical consequence, and that it is "engaged in the terrible business of singling a human being out for judgment" (though, in the civil context, the judgment need not be all that terrible). The jurors will naturally be disinclined to "hurt good people." Though they are instructed, in effect, only to do corrective justice, and many of the trial's constitutive rules push in the same direction, they will inevitably be drawn into doing distributive justice as well, distributing benefits and burdens according to the perceived characters of the parties.

The instructions are unlikely to stand in the way. Bad things are done by bad people. Once a moral judgment emerges from the evidence, the jury will likely conclude that the person did whatever it is that the instructions make the key legal issue. Perhaps more important, the parties are almost always important witnesses at trial.[18] Truthfulness, in a very broad sense, becomes equivalent to moral character. Any failure of truthfulness by the party as witness is an injury done to the jury itself, here and now, deliberately interfering with the performance of its sworn task. The truthfulness of the witness is a powerful lens on the rest of the case, specifically on the decision as to which interpreted narrative should be accepted, and on the lower-level judgments that both determine and are determined by that narrative. To the extent that some jurors need to check their decision making against the instructions, the jury's estimate of the party-witness's general character will affect the credibility they assign to the party-witness's claims and denials on legally crucial facts.[19]

The question of moral blameworthiness mutually determines and is determined by the interpreted narrative in different sorts of ways. We have already seen that one or the other interpreted narrative will be more

[17] This involves what Aristotle called specifically "forensic" rhetoric. *Rhetoric* 1358b.

[18] The exception is the criminal defendant who may exercise his constitutional right not to incriminate himself. There has been a steady erosion of the traditional prohibitions on "other crimes" evidence, available to the prosecution even if the defendant chooses not to testify. See, e.g., Edward Imwinkelried, "The Need to Amend Federal Rule 404(b): The Threat to the Future of the Federal Rules of Evidence," *Villanova Law Review* 30 (1985): 1465.

[19] Does this mean that the case of a party-witness who has told a single lie in the past is doomed regardless of the justice of his or her cause? Once again, another of the devices of the trial—closing argument, for example—can place the single lie in perspective. See McElhaney, *Trial Notebook*, 497–99, for an engaging example of such a use of closing argument.

or less plausible in part because of the moral norms around which it is woven, its "theme," as trial lawyers put it. The moral significance of a narrative cannot be limited solely to the external conformity of the major actors in the narrative to norms governing external conduct. The trier of fact will inevitably make, and know it is making, judgments of "praise and blame"[20] concerning the personal moral dispositions[21] of the characters in the stories. Furthermore, insofar as parties and other major participants in the real-world drama that brings the case to trial are witnesses (almost always), the jury will bring a vast repertoire of tacit skills of character assessment to bear on the witnesses. Peopling the interpreted narrative with this or that character whom the jury has actually seen will affect the meaning of that narrative. A witness's performance "always means more." The appearance and performance of a witness, whether or not a party, profoundly affects the significance of one or the other of the competing narratives in ways that have little to do with the specific "content" of that witness's testimony. In the case from which the opening presented in chapter 4 was taken, two members of the defendant's household testified. One appeared so crafty and the other so intimidating that the evaluation of the defendant's background was significantly altered. The jury cannot but understand the issues before it in moral terms.

Level IV represents specifically legal decision making, which I have already described in setting out the perspective of the Received View. Recall[22] that the Received View considers this to be an operation of fair categorization of the already-determined more probable version of the bare narrative of movements in space and time. Once this act of categorization has occurred, in that view, there are no more decisions to be made. Rather, a simple act of inspection of the acts of categorization or refusals to categorize is all that remains. Recall too that the Received View properly understands that sometimes the dispositive legal category (e.g., "killed") will appear in the more probable narrative, so that a further act of categorization is unnecessary.

Level IV is one form of decision making that the constitutive rules of the trial seem to privilege. As we have seen, they operate together to draw the jury into "taking law seriously." Even in the model I am offering, there are circumstances under which this form of decision making will be important. Where the norms emerging from the moral or public significance of the issues presented by the trial are weak—that is, where the

---

[20] Aristotle, *Rhetoric* 1359a.

[21] Donagan, *The Theory of Morality*, 52–57 (distinguishing first-level precepts controlling acts and second-level precepts controlling moral dispositions or virtues).

[22] See chapter 1, above.

resolution is morally or politically indifferent[23]—the issue of fair categorization may gain in importance.

Concretely, when the juror performs this act of categorization, she has before her both the patchy and incomplete narratives of direct examination and the more complete and normatively rich narratives of opening. The juror may "cycle"[24] between legal categorization and Level II or Level III narratives (and so, given the mutual determination, Level I judgments). This allows her, even if the case has not been decided at Level III, and even if the instructions turn out to be a factor in deliberation, to adjust the stories to fit defensibly into the legal categories. Thus, even in those cases where the jury instructions or, in bench trials, the judge's knowledge of legal doctrine is a central part of the decision-making process, there exists a "hermeneutical"[25] codetermination of the rule and the meaning of the particular case.

The full or interpreted narrative at Level III has an especially close relationship with the public or political[26] dimension of the case, represented by Level VI. As we saw above, the jurors will inevitably be defining their public identity by deciding the case. Because the jury must determine law and fact "complicatively," as Lord Vaughn put it, they cannot avoid responsibility for the determination they are making. It is only their own active self-determination that holds together the predication of this particular bit of narrative evaluative-descriptive language on the basis of *this* particular bit of incompletely determined evidence.[27] For this reason their judgment can be called a "reflective" judgment.[28] It is their public identity that they are forging by reaching a decision. Most obviously, they are determining the response of a public institution to the problematic situation that has brought the case to trial. Because it is a public determination, and not solely a matter of personal morality, the importance of all the

---

[23] On the relative indifference of many legal norms even within natural law thinking, see Thomas Aquinas, *Summa Theologiae* 2, 2, q. 95, art. 2.

[24] See Kuhn, Weinstock, and Faton, "How Well Do Jurors Reason?"

[25] *Truth and Method*, 36–38, 289–94. Indeed, Gadamer argues that law "application" has "exemplary" significance for hermeneutics as a whole.

[26] I am generally avoiding this term because of the serious danger of misunderstanding. "Political" in this context has little to do with the "interest group politics" that the term almost always connotes in ordinary language. See Abramson, *We, the Jury*, 100–142.

[27] In Kantian language, it is the definition of public identity that provides the principle of the synthetic judgment which combines the partially determinate particular with the evaluation predicated of it. Just as moral education begins with, "We don't do that!" so the jury's determination is something like, "We call this bullying or mean-spirited. . . ." The description says who we are in our public identity as well as what the particular is, and says the one by saying the other.

[28] See chapter 8, below.

processes of public argument and reason giving is elevated.[29] Further, that structure, understood concretely, both insists on and dramatizes the plurality of perspectives on and so of positions within the community from which the events leading to the trial are viewed. The significance of the "enlarged mind" that trial rhetoric invites, and which I describe later in this chapter, is a political or public significance: it allows the jury to imagine the case from a number of differing and often opposed perspectives. Its judgment is a redetermination or, literally, a reconstitution, of the public balance of those perspectives, an implicit recognition that the common project of democracy requires respect for and the tautest tension among those perspectives. In some cases, these conflicts provide the stuff of tragedy, the preeminently public literary form. The jury, then, is called upon to exercise what Wolin called specifically political wisdom:

> Taken as a whole, this composite type of knowledge represents a contrast with the scientific type. Its mode of activity is not so much the style of the search as of reflection. It is mindful of logic, but more so of the incoherence and contradictoriness of experience. And for the same reason, it is distrustful of rigor. Political life does not yield its significance to terse hypotheses but is elusive, and hence meaningful statements about it often have to be allusive and imitative. Context becomes supremely important, for actions and events occur in no other setting. Knowledge of this type tends, therefore, to be suggestive and illuminative rather than explicit and determinate.[30]

It is the sheer multiplicity of factual and normative considerations and the subtle shadings of their force that overwhelm any attempt to assimilate trial decision making to deductive reasoning.

There is another sense in which the centrality of the interpreted narrative at trial invites the jury to consider the trial as a political event. I have emphasized that the freedom afforded lawyers in opening allows them to invoke powerful norms whether or not those norms are embedded in the instructions. Some of those proposed norms are public norms in that they control the way public institutions should treat problematic situations. This role of the trial has gained in importance under specifically modern conditions, as Luban has pointed out. The trial not only does justice but creates the conditions for the doing of justice, where the latter are understood to be within human power and so responsibility.[31] To put it in the language of classical rhetoric, the trial's languages and tasks are both

---

[29] Hampshire, "Public and Private Morality."

[30] Sheldon Wolin, "Political Theory as a Vocation," in *Machiavelli and the Nature of Political Thought*, ed. M. Fleischer (New York: Atheneum, 1972), 44–45.

[31] Luban, *Legal Modernism*, 380.

forensic and deliberative: they resolve the individual controversy and also purposefully affect the perceived public treatment of the kind of conduct that brings the case to trial. In short, trial does "political justice," something always "characterized by both promise and blasphemy."[32]

It is because of the danger of blasphemy that the purposeful use of the trial is so carefully constrained by the rules of the trial, its legal structure, so that the trier of fact cannot avoid conscious responsibility for any "political" determination made. The doctrine of materiality requires that most of the evidence presented have some relation to the legal norms. Advocates must always be concerned about the possibility of a directed verdict. The evidence will thus at least implicitly suggest that the norms embedded in legal doctrine and the instructions themselves are surrounded with rituals which emphasize their authoritativeness. More important, the jury is forced to determine any broader political significance they see in the trial in the context of the highly specific accounts of the key events by witnesses including, almost always, the parties themselves. The almost obsessive concern with the details of past events, together with the aural and dramatic form, is designed to make it extremely difficult for the participants to treat the trial simply as a tool for prospective policy or purely political statement.

On the other hand, the public dimension of trial determinations is intrinsic to trial judgment, not something mechanically added on by willful juries and judges. This is true because of the nature of the commonsense judgments and the web of belief on which they rest. Such judgments determine the probative value of circumstantial evidence. Since they always apply generally and for the most part, and since a determination about whether a generalization applies here is always a matter of judgment, it is a judgment for which the trier of fact is responsible. One element of that responsibility is the risk of error. In a criminal case, the jury is responsible not only for treating the defendant respectfully (morally, if you want) but also for preserving the mode of social ordering that is the criminal justice system—for example, maintaining both general and individual deterrence. The actual consequences of an error favoring the criminal defendant (for example, releasing a serial killer or affording impunity to gang violence or domestic terrorism) cannot but affect the "fact-finding" process, a conclusion I have represented in figure 2 by the arrows moving outward from Level VI, through Levels III, II, and I. By contrast, the jury's legitimate public purposes are limited by the *moral* and *legal* obligations to treat the parties "not solely as means" to those purposes.

---

[32] Otto Kirchheimer, *Political Justice: The Use of Legal Procedure for Political Ends* (Princeton: Princeton University Press, 1961), vii.

There are subtle though important differences between a purely instrumental (or "bureaucratic") use of the trial device and the political dimension of the trial. For now, let me say that a purely instrumental use of the trial will tend to treat the forms of trial communication solely as means by which the participants reach relatively predetermined ends, with relatively less regard for preserving or respecting the meanings implicit in the ordinary language in which the trial is inevitably carried out. That is what is meant when a procedure is called "Orwellian" or "Kafkaesque." For example, despite organized, and partially successful, resistance by administrative law judges in the Social Security Disability system, perceived budget constraints and rejection quotas imposed on the judges led to decisions that could, in ordinary language, be viewed as absurd.[33] In decision making that respects the political or public dimension of adjudication, there exists a deeper tension—"dialectic," if you want—between respect for the individual litigant and for the public meanings of the language employed, on the one hand, and, on the other hand, for maintaining the institutional structure that serves interests beyond the courtroom—between, in other words, the "simultaneous creation of justice and the enabling conventions of justice."[34] Furthermore, in political decision making, the public identity of the decision-maker is in play in a way that it is not in bureaucratic contexts. Bureaucrats can have a Cartesian kind of aloofness from the manipulation of facts and concepts controlling the "objective" world before them. Bureaucratic decision making can too easily become Rule by Nobody.[35]

Level VII makes explicit a decision-point that was implicit in the sheer multiplicity of levels. Judgments of importance among the forms of social ordering and judgment are implicit in the "accurate" characterizations of human situations, especially those that call for action.[36] These are ques-

---

[33] See, e.g., *Morin v. Secretary of Health and Human Services*, 835 F. Supp. 1414 (D.N.H., 1992) (administrative law judge's conclusions "disturbing," "disingenuous," and "preposterous"); *Trent v. Secretary of Health and Human Services*, 788 S. Supp. 939 (E.D. Ken. 1992) (conclusions "ridiculous"); *Martin v. Schweiker*, 562 S. Supp. 912 (D.Kan. 1982) ("ridiculous").

[34] Luban, *Legal Modernism*, 380.

[35] Hannah Arendt, "On Violence," in *Crises of the Republic* (New York: Harcourt Brace Jovanovich, 1972), 103, 137–38. See also Arendt, *The Origins of Totalitarianism*, 398–409, and Arendt, *Eichmann in Jerusalem*. In my experience, bureaucratic decision-makers are highly impatient with opening statements, I suspect because they eschew any form of language that engages them normatively. There is a deep connection, one that Orwell understood, between the use of ordinary language and the engagement of the moral personality.

[36] On the fundamental character of the notion of importance, see Alfred North Whitehead, *Modes of Thought* (New York: Macmillan, 1938), 1–19. Whitehead put it more provocatively in *Adventures of Ideas* (New York: Macmillan, 1933), 243: "It is more im-

tions of political justice in the highest sense: what sorts of norms will govern the different spheres of human cooperation and competition, and which should concretely prevail in cases of conflict.[37] I argue, however, that these issues survive into the trial itself, such that the juror must, again inevitably, decide what is most important about the case. Once again, it is the relative importance of an error in one direction or another that dramatizes the inevitability of these higher-level judgments. The space for political judgment is, it turns out, the truth embedded in the tension between the rules invoked by the Received View and the anomalies already described.

The juror's judgment is, finally, a practical judgment, as Level VIII indicates. In fact, as I have noted, all participants in the trial shape their performances with this practical task in mind.[38] The jury grasps not the accurate objective characterization of a situation in theoretical terms but something far more difficult to describe. The trial can show a truth that cannot be articulated as a simple description of past observations of a "reality" that was just there, "already-out-there-now-real." The trial does not create a single most factually probable screenplay for a past event. It focuses instead on the past for moral-political reasons, but intrinsic to its most "factual" reconstructions are normative and political ideals and determinations. What the juror grasps is a literally indescribable structure of norms, events, and possibilities for action. Philosophically, pragmatism can give some sense to such a structure. The empiricism that has long informed academic and judicial thinking about trial procedure and the law of evidence cannot. A more radical empiricism, one open to the actual processes that prevail at trial, is necessary.

What does it mean to say that the last level of juror decision making is explicitly practical? The jury understands its verdict as a practical resolution of a situation, just as the trial has throughout been implicitly structured to perform that practical task. There are various aspects to this practical task. Only one is explicitly epistemological: the juror continually

---

portant that a proposition be interesting than that it be true. . . . But of course a true proposition is more apt to be interesting than a false one." *Why* is a true proposition more likely to be interesting than a false one? Because truth is more complex and subtle than the lazy abstractions through which we usually understand human reality. And so understanding a dense bit of human reality actualizes more of our (usually anesthetized) cognitive powers. Again, the often-described experience of "elevation" of faculties experienced by jurors has its roots here.

[37] They are questions of the "basic structure of society" in Rawls's sense, "the way in which the major social institutions distribute fundamental rights and duties and determine the division of advantages from social cooperation." Rawls, *A Theory of Justice*, 7.

[38] The fact that the evidence, over which the parties in common law systems have control, has been shaped by this practical task again shows the abstract nature of the Received View's understanding of the factual base of its judgment.

asks, "Do I know enough for these purposes, to make this judgment?[39] A high level of certainty from the perspective of one of the sources of norms (legal, moral, political, instrumental) may draw the jury into elevating the importance of that perspective.[40] The juror may decide that following the legal rules is the most important thing about this case, perhaps where reliance on them was high[41] or competing norms are weak. And so she will scrupulously follow the instructions. Or she may decide that rewarding individual decency or honoring the moral claims of promises dominates the significance of the case. And so the case will be decided before the instructions are read. She may rather see the case as an opportunity to reconstitute the terms of the social contract, overtly or implicitly to "send a message." Then the political dimension of the case will be dominant. My argument is that assigning the authority to make these determinations, which are usually tacit and always inevitable, to the juror is now part of our considered judgments of justice; this assignment is consistent with the kind of society we have become.

The rules of the trial are not neutral among the various levels of mutual determination. For example, they resist the dynamic by which every individual case is understood as a political opportunity to reshape the basic structure of society. They do that in what I call moral interests. They also resist the dynamic by which the trial may become a moral referendum on the character of the parties. They do so in the interest of maintaining a liberal legal order that, somewhat paradoxically, serves real moral aims.[42]

Still, practical truth emerges at trial from the most demanding tension of opposites. We have already seen how there exist tensions among the questions that a juror will put to himself. There are also related tensions among the various linguistic devices that the trial comprises. There are tensions between the fully characterized narratives of opening statement and the bare, stripped-down narratives of direct examination. There are tensions between the narratives of direct examination and the deconstruction of those narratives on cross-examination. There are tensions between what a witness wants to say and what he can defensibly and admissibly say. There are tensions among the roles of the judge, the advocate, and the witness, and in jury trials, between the judge and the jury. There is a tension between the narratives of opening statement and direct examina-

---

[39] Explicit burdens of proof are of limited value here.

[40] See Lonergan, *Insight*, 279–318. Lonergan uses the term "reflective insight" for the second-level insight into the adequacy of the evidence for a given particular judgment. It is dependent upon the adequacy of the first-level insight into a concrete situation (Peirce's "abduction") that proposes the question, "Is it so?" for reflective understanding.

[41] Note that this is implicitly a moral reason.

[42] Riley describes Kant's appreciation of the power of liberal legal formalisms to avoid corruption both of morality and of law. Riley, *Kant's Political Philosophy*, 176.

tion and the argument of closing, often aided by cross. And so the trial is the "crucible of democracy." What it allows is the emergence of a truth beyond storytelling.

American society exists as a tension among different spheres, each relatively autonomous, each operating according to principles that are discontinuous with those of others.[43] The market economy, the political sphere, the legal sphere, the moral sphere, professional life, family life—each has its own constitutive principles. Cases that go to trial often question the relative importance to this concrete case of the principles informing those spheres. *Somewhere* in such a society judgments have to be made about the relevance of the principles of each sphere to a particular problematic situation. It is no surprise that in such a society the constitutive rules and practices of the trial have evolved to allow an incisive choice by the jury of what is most important about a controversy, which of the often conflicting principles ought to control. This is what the trial has become for us.

The Subjective Side: Understanding Judgment as Performance

We have worked our way through the consciously structured hybrid of languages and performances that constitutes the trial. We have thus been focusing on the "objective"[44] side of the trial. If trial decisions can best be understood as a response to the evidence, we have every reason to believe that the subjective side of the equation, the jury's cognitive operations, allows some sort of grasp specifically of those diverse languages and performances.[45] What could such a grasp look like? Even if we think that juries usually get it right, do we have any reason to believe that we

---

[43] Niklas Luhmann's theory of autonomous ("autopoetic") social systems may be the most radical statement of this independence. See Niklas Luhmann, "Operational Closure and Structural Coupling: The Differentiation of the Legal System," *Cardozo Law Review* 13 (1992): 1419, 1424. The trial is of theoretical interest, it seems to me, because it is precisely a forum, a "speech situation" if you will, in which a moral perspective is taken on otherwise relatively autonomous systems, the question of the possibility of which separates Luhmann from his great critic, Jürgen Habermas. See Habermas, *Between Facts and Norms*, 48–52.

[44] The scare quotes indicate my acceptance of the view that the understanding which occurs at trial reaches beyond the subjective-objective dichotomy. It is, in Gadamer's terms, an "event." See generally Bernstein, *Beyond Objectivism and Relativism*, 34–38.

[45] One understands understanding not primarily by introspection but by examining the intellect's operations. See Lonergan, *Insight*, xx. Taking seriously the range of intellectual operations required by an active engagement with the diverse forms of languages and performances implies a correspondingly complex notion of truth. See, e.g., Alasdair MacIntyre, *Whose Justice? Which Rationality?* (Notre Dame, Ind.: University of Notre Dame Press, 1988), 356–58. See chapter 8, below.

can give an account of what they do? In this section I want to suggest that we have good reason to believe that we do possess a power of judgment as intelligent performance[46] which has precisely the characteristics necessary to resolve the issues presented by the deep tensions among the trial's languages and the incommensurable values they represent.

Even sympathetic students of the trial have resorted to explaining the jury's success as flowing from an "emotional" as opposed to a "rational" reaction to the evidence. This has stemmed from the failure of the Received View's concept of judgment to account for what occurs at trial. The notion of judgment underlying the Received View is a form of what Peter Steinberger has identified as the "tripartite model of judgment." That notion runs like this:

> Any judgment—as the bringing together somehow of a universal and particular—would seem to require at least three things: (1) the universal *qua* concept must be identified, and this means being able to specify at least some of the conceptual features that make it what it is; (2) the particular must be identified, and this means being able to specify at least some of the characteristics that individuate it; and (3) there must be a mental faculty that allows us to establish some kind of demonstrable and explicable connection between the universal's features and the particular's characteristics such that we can say with some justification that "X is (or is not) Y."[47]

Judgment, then, "is a matter of subsumption," with our minds "pictured as a series of cubbyholes," and "[p]articular objects are to be placed in the various cubbyholes according to whether their characteristics correspond to the conceptual features of those cubbyholes"[48] subject to rules of valid inference. In the Received View, those cubbyholes are of only two sorts: value-free empirical generalizations that allow the construction of a value-free narrative through inferential processes, on the one hand, and the legal categories embedded in the instructions, on the other.[49]

We can now see how the intellectual operations that must occur at trial cannot conform to this model of rationality. The "particulars" are

---

[46] Peter J. Steinberger, *The Concept of Political Judgment* (Chicago: University of Chicago Press, 1993), 211–80.

[47] Ibid., 91. This notion is "often thought to imply, further, that there are rules and procedures of inference according to which the features of the various concepts and the characteristics of various particular things are juxtaposed to one another so that certain features can be said to correspond to certain characteristics and not to others." Ibid., 92.

[48] Ibid.

[49] Recall that sometimes, in the Received View, we must rely on an additional empirical generalization to move from the value-free narrative of events to the determinative legal categories, and sometimes we need only decide whether that narrative falls within the fair meaning of the legal categories. See chapter 1, above.

indeterminate in different ways and are always already structured by the different levels of human meaning embedded in narrative and its enactment. The determination even of the nature of the circumstantial evidence and the truth of the narrative within which it finds its place is inevitably circular. Many different sorts of normative judgments occur before any confrontation between particulars and the concepts embedded in the jury instructions. Most significant, trial judgments call for determinations of relative importance, including the moral and political significance of different sorts of risks of error, and the appropriateness of competing modes of social ordering. All of those judgments involve different kinds of circular movements between particulars that have different levels of determinacy and different kinds of general concepts and norms, many of them very open-textured. Not just a hermeneutical circle, but circles within circles. What we grasp in this, and what the languages and practices of the trial seem designed to offer our grasp, are precisely the tensions among narratives, languages, and performances, a kind of understanding that does not fit the tripartite model at all. To be adequate to what the trial offers, the mind must dwell[50] within tensions that require new insight into the nature and significance of the poles of each conflict. Finally, there is the practical dimension that runs through the entire enterprise: trial theories are chosen based in part on their likely consequences, and juries find a story acceptable—find it true—based on its consistency with its perception of what ought to be done in response to what is most important about the meaningful situation in which it is engrossed, the trial itself.

We have good reason to believe that these operations yield genuine knowledge. Because my goal is to present a theory of the trial, and not a theory of everything, I want here simply to describe some of the philosophical resources available to provide what will always be a partial account of the subjective side of the trial, the cognitive operations adequate to the trial's languages and performances. A full account here is out of the question, and, in any event, my suspicion is that only so much is possible here, for the kind of understanding that we engage in at trial is, like many forms of knowing how, "mysterious."[51] Having described the trial's languages and practices, I could heed Wittgenstein's advice[52] and say something like, "Well, this is a form of genuine understanding we have. If it does not fit your concept of reason, so much the worse for your concept." We can, I think, do a little better.

---

[50] See Michael Polanyi, *Knowing and Being: Essays by Michael Polanyi*, ed. Marjorie Grene (Chicago: University of Chicago Press, 1969), 147.

[51] Steinberger, *The Concept of Political Judgment*, 222. My account of the basic forms of noninferential intelligence in the next section is heavily indebted to Steinberger's incisive discussion.

[52] "Explanations come to an end." *Philosophical Investigations*, par. 1.

In this section I briefly describe the pervasive operation of noninferential intelligence in ordinary language use and skilled physical and intellectual performance; I show that that kind of intelligence outruns our explicit inferential powers. Both scientific theorizing and moral decision making require modes of thought that are not exclusively inferential, while acute observers of the trial have noticed that these nonformal intellectual operations are precisely those which dominate at trial. Finally, I then provide an account from the philosophical literature of three understandings of noninferential judgment that illuminate the actual operations of juries.

Nonformal Intelligence outside the Trial

Noninferential Intelligence Is Pervasive in Ordinary Language Use and Comprehension

A denial that we can, at least sometimes, make the judgments necessary to engage in effective communication through language use is self-refuting. The forms of intelligence intrinsic to language comprehension and use are thus paradigmatic for human intelligence in general. It turns out that the most common forms of ordinary language use employ forms of noninferential integrative intelligence which go well beyond the tripartite model of judgment lying at the root of the Received View.

Recall that the latter understands human intelligence functioning exclusively through *inferential* or logical processes. With respect to language comprehension, there have been a number of attempts throughout the twentieth century to understand our undeniable ability as a kind of inference. Within these views, words have their meanings by virtue of conventional rules of inference that allow us to subsume these spoken or written symbols under shared conceptual categories. In some versions, the meaning of a statement is exhaustively determined by its truth conditions, the conditions under which a proposition is true. Students of language have come to see, on the contrary, that we consistently understand what others mean in daily conversation through an instantaneous grasp of the contexts within which statements are made and the background conditions against which they are made. That kind of grasp or *integration* cannot be reduced to representation, definition, and inference but requires a tacit grasp of the situation as a whole and the human context of linguistic performances. For example, the full meaning of the utterance "Counsel will call a witness," which could easily be a question, a statement, a wish, or an order, depends on context and performance, not solely on the rules that determine the meanings of its nouns and verbs.[53] That people are able to perform an integration of content and performance is true not only of this contextual grasp of the illocutionary force of utterances but also of our understanding of what theorists have called "conversational implicature," the simple fact that we routinely mean more than, and sometimes something wholly different from, what we literally say. ("Yeah, right!" in response to a statement, or "How 'bout dem Bulls?"[54] in response to an invitation to have a serious conversation.) This wholly unproblematic form of ordinary conversation plays off implicit background assumptions about conversation itself[55] or about the community's commonsense generalizations. Thus "the implicature of an utterance is rooted in ineffable, tacit and communal dispositions irreducible to rational method" and "succeeds only insofar as it emerges out of a complex array of practices, judgments, and implicit stipulations that . . . help to form . . . the intellectual bases of a community."[56]

Further, as Wittgenstein's analysis of rule following suggests, we seem to be able to participate deftly in rule-governed practices, even intellectual practices, without consciously directing our actions by an ongoing interpretation and application of the rule.[57] Our grammatical use of our native language, for example, or our appropriate conduct in social situations reflects an understanding that is a "knowing how" and only rarely adverts to the rules which we have been habituated implicitly to follow.

These considerations have something in common:

Each seeks to account for successful judgment in terms of an ineluctable grounding in social or communal contexts. Illocutionary force operates on the basis of tacit conventions that interlocutors share by virtue of being part of the same linguistic community. Implicature similarly presupposes a world of common assumptions and preunderstandings that make it possible to comprehend nonliteral meanings, often without much evident difficulty. Or again, rule-following in linguistic activity involves reliance not on truth conditions but on assertion

[53] Philosophers and linguists sometimes distinguish "propositional content" from "illocutionary force." If someone "is to *grasp* an utterance, he or she must grasp or *understand* its illocutionary force." Steinberger, *The Concept of Political Judgement*, 160.

[54] The latter example is Steinberger's, though my choice of teams reflects my upper midwestern biases. Ibid., 165–66.

[55] For example Grice's background conditions for intelligible statements in conversation are that they be true, provide an appropriate amount of information, be relevant and unambiguous. H. P. Grice, *Studies in the Way of Words* (Cambridge: Harvard University Press, 1988), 26–29, discussed in Steinberger, *The Concept of Political Judgment*, 166. When a speaker flouts one of those conditions, the hearer will assume that even such a violation was intended to communicate.

[56] Steinberger, *The Concept of Political Judgment*, 167.

[57] Ibid., 172–84.

conditions that are embedded in the community—the form of life—that make
an intelligible speaker intelligible in the first place. All of this suggests that reliable and accurate judgment is often a matter of invoking, however automati-
cally and unconsciously, the range of norms, assumptions, conceptual materials,
and rhetorical tools that constitute the linguistic/intellectual community of
which one is a part.[58]

The power of language to invoke dimensions of situations beyond the
simple referents of its statements is thus a pervasive aspect of ordinary
conversation. Indeed, those unspoken dimensions are the meanings that,
in a strong sense, actually "constitute" the community's identity.

Skillful Performances Outrun Our Analytical and Inferential Powers

The deepest levels of integration represented in figure 2 suggest that the
jury's task involves a practical resolution of incommensurable norms. As
I argued in the previous section, this means that the jury grasps a literally
indescribable structure of norms, events, and possibilities for action and
not a mental representation of a past event. In a broad range of situations
we can act deftly and purposefully without a determinate picture of what
precisely occurred or the state of affairs we want to bring into being.[59]
This is obviously true in sports and music, but also in all areas of skillful
coping, including intellectual coping where "instances of apparently complex problem solving . . . may be best understood as direct responses to
familiar perceptual gestalts."[60] Any normative rule, for example, applies
everything else being equal, and we are never able to spell out the rule's
range of exceptions and exceptions to exceptions; the conditions for the
application of a rule never explicitly capture, but rather tacitly presuppose, our background practices. Since those practices are an aspect of our
ordinary transparent ways of coping, understanding can be said to be less
in our minds than in the skilled ways we comport ourselves.[61] And so even
intellectual work depends on our immediate access to a transparent set
of coping skills that always resist full formalization: "[T]he accumulation,
the pondering and reconsideration of various subject matters in terms of

---

[58] Ibid., 185.

[59] "[I]n a wide range of situations human beings relate to the world in an organized
purposeful manner without the constant accompaniment of representational states that
specify what the action is aimed at accomplishing." Dreyfus, *Being-in-the-World*, 93–94.

[60] Ibid.

[61] For the later Wittgenstein, too, "understanding is not a mental process." *Philosophical
Investigations*, par. 154.

the symbols designating them—is . . . a tacit, a-critical process. *It is a performance.* . . . Our whole articulate equipment turns out to be merely a tool-box, a supremely effective instrument for deploying our inarticulate faculties."[62] We have seen that we impose extremely modest burdens of explicit reason giving on decision-makers at the trial level. This recognizes the prominence of the dimensions of decision making that cannot be assimilated to the construction of mental representations.

Even Scientific Theory Choice Requires Modes of Thought That Are Not Exclusively Inferential

Scientists, too, engage in theory choice.[63] The postempiricist philosophy of science has come to understand that scientists make intelligent choices among theories even though it is impossible "for an individual to hold both theories in mind together and compare them point by point and with nature."[64] The particulars that the empiricist philosophy of science (and the Received View) require are always already theory-laden. I have no intention to pronounce here on the most adequate philosophical account of all the complex elements of the scientific enterprise. That issue is deeply controversial and the literature is enormous. I am certainly aware that any short comparison of the world of the laboratory and that of the trial court cannot but be facile. In fact, I have made that very point in chapter 5. With all those caveats and disclaimers, there still seems to be *one* comparison that is worth making. We have reason to think that the scientific community routinely reaches convergence on the superiority of one theory over another long before anything that can be described as a decisive experiment has been performed.[65] What occurs is *"not a deduction but an integration."*[66] This integration is analogous, and just analogous, to the grasp of those competing norms which are most relevant or appropriate to a concrete context that is pervasive at trial. In scientific investigation, one integration is recognized[67] as superior to another based on a set

---

[62] Michael Polanyi, *The Study of Man* (Chicago: University of Chicago Press, 1959), 25. Brian Leiter argues persuasively that even appellate decision making, a much simpler operation than trial decision making, is not something about which one can have a normative theory, understood as a web of general rules and exceptions to rules that would reliably determine what outcomes will be. Leiter, "Heidegger and the Theory of Adjudication," 253.

[63] See Bernstein, *Beyond Objectivism and Relativism*, 52–61. Bernstein refers to the *"practical* rationality of theory choice" in discussing Kuhn and his critics. Ibid., 52.

[64] Kuhn, "Objectivity, Value Judgment, and Theory Choice," 320, 338.

[65] Ibid., 327.

[66] Polanyi, *Knowing and Being*, 212 (emphasis added).

[67] On the centrality of the notion of "recognition" in hermeneutical theory, see Gadamer, *Truth and Method*, 102. ("In recognition what we know emerges, as if through an illumina-

of somewhat independent criteria, of which predictive accuracy is only the most important, that "function not as rules, which determine choice, but as values, which influence it."[68] On the reasons why such a holistic value-based enterprise succeeds so regularly, Kuhn, for one, can only express wonder and ignorance: "Even those who have followed me thus far will want to know how a value based enterprise of the sort I have described can develop as a science does, repeatedly producing powerful new techniques for prediction and control. To that question, unfortunately, I have no answer at all, but that is only another way of saying that I make no claim to have solved the problem of induction."[69] Analogously, a jury's limited ability to give an account of its judgment, and our limited ability to provide a theory that would serve as a justification of those same judgments, do not mean that a reliable and pervasive form of truly intelligent theory choice is not at work.

Tacit Powers Are Central to Moral
Decision Making

In the context of individual moral decision, we are often unable fully to articulate the considerations that underlie our judgments. Even in cases where a final commitment among diverging paths has resulted from long reflection on a situation in light of our most basic philosophical or religious beliefs, our ultimate intuitions of the right way may be very partially explained. This limitation on an agent's ability to provide reasons for his decisions does not suggest that the decision was irrational. As Stuart Hampshire put it, "[I]t does not follow from the fact that man does not know what his reasons were for a decision just taken that there were no good reasons, and that he acted under the influence of causes that do not count as reasons."[70] The likelihood of correct but incompletely explicable decisions stems from features of our cognitive powers: "Any situation which confronts me, and which is not a situation in a game, has an inexhaustible set of discriminable features over and above those which I ex-

---

tion, from all the chance and variable circumstances that condition it and is grasped in its essence. It is known as something.")

[68] Kuhn, "Objectivity, Value Judgment, and Theory Choice," 331. Kuhn explicitly invokes the analogy of judicial soul searching seeking to reconcile countervailing considerations.

[69] Ibid., 332. Peirce speculated weakly that our "abductive" ability to hit on the correct hypothesis with statistically startling regularity must have provided some advantage in the process of natural selection.

[70] Hampshire, "Public and Private Morality," 30. As I noted above, the jury studies suggest that such nonmoral "causes" have proven hard to come by.

plicitly notice at the time because they are of immediate interest to me. Second, the situation has features over and above those which are mentionable within the vocabulary that I possess and use. I 'take in' the situation, notice the features that are particularly relevant to my interests at the time, and I respond to it in accordance with my prevailing desires and purposes. . . ."[71] Notice that there are two aspects of moral decision making, both relevant in the trial context, that Hampshire emphasizes here. First, a situation may be described in inexhaustibly numerous ways. Second, we can perceive aspects of a situation that we could never describe within our inherited words and concepts at all. Thus personal moral decisions contain features similar to those of decisions made during other performances that are guided by tacit knowledge:

> The analogy between decisions in translating from language to language, and the intuitions of rightness involved, and on the other side decisions about the right conduct in a situation requiring judgment is, first, analogy in respect of multiplicity of unaccountable background features normally involved in the deciding mind; secondly, in respect of the mind's ability, in sophisticated actions as in routine movements, to draw upon a vast store of memories which are preconscious; thirdly, in respect of the thinking that is in both cases highly condensed, and that is not for this reason to be reconstructed easily, as amounting to arguments which could be used in conclusive support of the decisions.[72]

We exercise noninferential "integrative" intellectual powers in different ways in many spheres, some basic and ordinary, some specialized, some theoretical, some practical. All evince an ability of the mind to perform operations that bear a family resemblance to those that a realistic understanding of the trial's languages and performances require. It should come as no surprise, then, that careful students of the world of the trial court have described trial decision making in similar terms.

Nonformal Intelligence at Trial

These applications of our capacities for practices directed by tacit knowing have, in fact, been recognized by acute observers to be the very processes by which judges and juries actually decide. As Holmes put it in *Chicago, B. & O. Ry. v. Babsock*, "many honest and sensible judgments . . . express an intuition of experience which outruns analysis and sums up many unnamed and tangled impressions—impressions which may

---

[71] Ibid., 30.
[72] Ibid., 33.

be beneath consciousness without losing their worth."[73] Judge Jack Weinstein, perhaps the foremost trial judge and evidence scholar in the United States, put it this way: "The jury's evaluation of the evidence relevant to a material proposition requires a gestalt or synthesis of evidence which seldom needs to be analyzed precisely. Any item of evidence must be interpreted in the context of all the evidence, introduced. . . . In giving appropriate, if sometimes unreflective, weight to a specific piece of evidence the trier will fit it into a shifting mosaic . . . [C]onfirming evidence of that other line of proof may require a reevaluation of the witness's credibility and a complex readjustment of the assessment of all the interlocking evidence."[74] Or, as Louis Nizer explains: "Although jurors are extraordinarily right in their conclusions, it is usually based on common sense 'instincts' about right and wrong, and not on sophisticated evaluations of complicated testimony. On the other hand, a Judge, trying the case without a jury, may believe that his decision is based on refined weighing of the evidence; but . . . he, too, has an overall, almost compulsive 'feeling' about who is right and who is wrong and then supports this conclusion with legal technology."[75]

Finally, I must include Judge Joseph C. Hutcheson's florid, classic (and tongue-in-cheek) description of his own "hunching" his way to decision at trial, which scandalized the formalists of his day: "I, after canvassing all the available material at my command, and duly cogitating upon it, give my imagination play, and brooding over the cause, wait for the feeling, the hunch—that intuitive flash of understanding which makes the jumpspark connection between question and decision, and at the point where the path is darkest, for the judicial feet, sheds its light along the way."[76]

The capacity which leads courts so consistently to get it right is, I suggest, a specialization of a general cognitive ability that functions in somewhat different ways in both factual and normative investigations, and somewhat differently still in the combined normative-factual inquiry that is the trial. It is holistic and interpretive. It can grasp "the cumulations of probabilities . . . too fine to avail separately, too subtle and circuitous to be convertible into syllogisms."[77] It is likely to "to trust rather in the multitude and variety of its arguments than to the conclusiveness of any one. Its reasoning should not form a chain which is no stronger than its weak-

---

[73] 204 U.S. 585, 598 (1907).

[74] *United States v. Chipani*, 289 F.Supp. 43 (E.D. N.Y.) *aff'd* 414 F.2d 1296 (2d Cir. 1969).

[75] Nizer, *My Life in Court*, 359.

[76] Hutcheson, "The Judgment Intuitive," 279.

[77] Newman, *An Essay in Aid of a Grammar of Assent*, 288.

est link, but a cable whose fibers may be ever so slender, provided they are sufficiently numerous and intimately connected."[78] The devices of the trial both supply innumerable such fibers and dramatize their possible connections in ways directly relevant to court's tasks.

Some Philosophical Resources: Reflective Judgment, Practical Wisdom, and Interpretive Understanding

So far, then, we seem possessed of a mode of understanding that is not reducible to formal inference, that functions in analogous ways in very different sorts of activities,[79] and that seems to provide an integrative grasp of the mutually determining and incommensurable issues the trial presents. It is inconsistent with the Received View's understanding of the trial yet does not spell nihilism or a relegation of jury decision making to "emotional" reaction. But can anything more positive be said about these intellectual powers?

Three notions from the philosophical literature cast considerable light on the "subjective" side of jury decision making. One is the notion of "reflective judgment," a concept originally identified by Kant as germane to judgments of what we may call artistic coherence, and extended by Hannah Arendt to the kind of judgments appropriate to public issues. The second notion is Aristotle's concept of *phronesis*, variously translated "prudence" or "practical wisdom." The third notion is "hermeneutic judgment," which attempts to describe a fundamental "circular" form of human understanding by which we can interpret texts and "text-ana-logues" such as the trial. I believe these to be the fairest descriptions of the intellectual operations that juries actually exercise, and that the trial's hybrid of languages and performances *requires* that they exercise, in order to reach their decisions.

---

[78] Charles Saunders Peirce, *Collected Papers of Charles Saunders Peirce*, vols. 1–6, ed. Charles Hartshorne amd Paul Weiss (Cambridge: Harvard Univesity Press, Belknap Press, 1958), 5:264. It is interesting to note that John Henry Wigmore, the greatest represen-tative of the "rationalist tradition" in the law of evidence, thought of circumstantial evidence as linked with the elements of a claim or defense in "chains." He called the infer-ences from circumstantial evidence to elements "catenate inferences," from the Latin *catena*, chain.

[79] I want to stress that the activities are only analogous. For example, there exists a spir-ited controversy concerning the degree to which the admittedly "holistic" forms of under-standing that prevail in natural science are analogous to the holistic and "fully hermeneuti-cal" forms of understanding that prevail in the human sciences. The trial is not a scientific investigation or even a case study in the interpretive human sciences. My account of the objective side of the trial reflects those important differences.

Reflective Judgment

Reflective judgment is the form of judgment we employ when we proceed without predetermined categories or concepts.[80] It is focused on the particularity of the particular, and its task is to find and apply the appropriate universal. It says, "This was wrong!" not "Murder is wrong."[81] Arendt insists that in the judging of particulars a "community of judgment" is an intrinsic moment in a way that is not true for determinative or inferential judgments.

> I form an opinion by considering a given issue from different viewpoints, by making present to my mind the standpoints of those who are absent; that is, I represent them. This process of representation does not blindly adopt the actual views of those who stand somewhere else, and hence look upon the world from a different perspective; this is a question neither of empathy, as though I tried to be or to feel like somebody else, nor of counting noses and joining a majority but of being and thinking in my own identity where actually I am not. The more people's standpoints I have present in my mind while I am pondering a given issue, and the better I can imagine how I would feel and think if I were in their place, the stronger will be my capacity for representative thinking and the more valid my final conclusions, my opinion.[82]

Thus reflective judgment achieves its impartiality not by achieving a Platonic point of view above the contending views nor by an empathic intuition of the feelings of others, but by "enlarging" its understanding in a distinctive manner: "The greater the reach—the larger the realm in which the enlightened individual is able to move from standpoint to standpoint—the more 'general' will be his thinking. This generality, however, is not the generality of the concept. . . . It is, on the contrary, closely connected with particulars, with the particular conditions of the standpoints

---

[80] The weight of my argument above, of course, is that this is precisely the situation in which the jury finds itself at trial. Kant calls a judgment that applies a pregiven universal a "determinate" judgment. Kant himself thought that moral judgments were "determinate" judgments because the rule under which the individual was to be subsumed was always pregiven by the categorical imperative. This "rule-orientation" is a major source of dissatisfaction with Kant's moral, legal, and political philosophy. At least in his later writings, there is every reason to think that Kant himself was aware of how little about particular situations could be derived deductively from a general rule. See generally Robert B. Louden, *Morality and Moral Theory: A Reappraisal and Reaffirmation* (Oxford: Oxford University Press, 1992), 99–124.

[81] Ronald Beiner argues that Kant's notion emphasizes more the spectator's respect for the meaning and so human dignity of the particular while Aristotle's focus is the wise purposefulness of the judge-in-action. Beiner, *Political Judgment*, 83–101.

[82] Arendt, "Truth and Politics," 241.

one has to go through in order to arrive at one's own general stand-point."[83] Judgment operates, then, within the sphere of common sense, the faculty that reveals to us the nature of the world insofar as it is a common world. Making judgments is one of the ways in which we come to share a world with others.[84] Commonsense reflective judgment relies on the give-and-take of opinion about the desired shape of the public world and dominates decisions about the kind of action consistent with human purposes.[85] The multiplication of perspectives on which it relies succeeds when "a particular issue is forced into the open that it may show itself from all sides, in every possible perspective, until it is flooded and made transparent by the full light of human comprehension."[86] The multiplicity of trial languages and performances is designed to achieve that kind of illumination.

Practical Wisdom

For Aristotle the core of moral judgment is a kind of perception, or, more strictly, perceptual identification. Once again, a person may not be able to say what features of the object led him to identify it as what it is. No one aspect of the object is decisive, and the judging subject is relying on a broad range of largely tacit knowledge. Ethical perception can exhibit a nuance, flexibility, and sense of the concrete that greatly outrun the capacity of the principles likely to be established ahead of time.[87] The Aristotelian notion of ethical perception, Nussbaum argues, is a philosophical statement of a tragic moral sensibility, characterized by a sort of tacit grasp of considerations in deep tension with each other. Because it comes so close to a description of the kind of judgment that the trial is designed to engender, I quote at length:

---

[83] Hannah Arendt, *Lectures on Kant's Political Philosophy* (Chicago: University of Chicago Press, 1989), 44.

[84] Hannah Arendt, "The Crisis in Culture, Its Social and Its Political Significance," in *Between Past and Future: Eight Exercises in Political Thought* (New York: Penguin Books, 1977), 218. As Steinberger puts it, this kind of judgment relies on insight that "is *common* but not *plebiscitary.* . . . Rather common sense refers to a faculty that is widely shared by the members of a community, but that is not always cultivated, and not always employed with appropriate care and attention. . . ." *The Concept of Political Judgment*, 226 ff.

[85] Arendt, "The Crisis in Culture," 223. Arendt sharply distinguishes those issues from those of "knowledge and truth." Her notion that common sense's sphere of judgment has little to do with "truth" is a function of her very specific, and inadequate, concept of truth. See Bernstein, *Beyond Objectivity and Relativism*, 215.

[86] Arendt, "Truth and Politics," 242.

[87] Nussbaum, *The Fragility of Goodness*, 300.

We reflect on an incident not by subsuming it under a general rule, not by assimilating its features to the terms of an elegant scientific procedure, but by burrowing down into the depths of the particular, finding images and connections that will permit us to see it more truly, describe it more richly; by combining this burrowing with a horizontal drawing of connections, so that every horizontal link contributes to the depth of our view of the particular, and every new depth creates new horizontal links. . . . The Sophoclean soul is more like Heraclitus's image of *psuche*: a spider sitting in the middle of its web, able to feel and respond to any tug in any part of the complicated structure. It advances understanding of life and of itself not by Platonic movement from the particular to the universal, from the perceived world to a simpler, clearer world, but by hovering in thought and imagination around the enigmatic complexities of the seen particular . . . seated in the middle of its web of connections, responsive to the pull of each separate thread. . . . The image of learning expressed in this style . . . stresses responsiveness and attention to the complexity; it discourages the search for the simple, and, above all, for the reductive. . . . [C]orrect choice (or: good interpretation) is, first and foremost, a matter of keenness and flexibility of perception, rather than of conformity to a set of simplifying principles.[88]

Thus while Arendt stresses the multiplication of perspectives on a common problem and the enlightenment that it brings, Aristotle focuses on our ability to perceive the significant details in the particular.[89] His notion of practical judgment relies, once again, on our capacity for genuine insight—for an immediate grasp of morally relevant features in human situations, without the mediation of inferential processes. This is a capacity the existence of which itself cannot be rigorously demonstrated by inferential means but can only be presupposed in an account that saves the appearances of actual human moral judgment.[90] Once again, the practices, rules, and basic aspects of the trial are crafted to keep the jury's imagination hovering around "enigmatic complexities of the seen particular."

---

[88] Ibid., 69. All the apparatus of the trial on the "objective" side is designed to cultivate this kind of decision making. For example, lawyers attempt to supply the "images and connections" in opening statement and, in closing, explicitly point out the "horizontal links" they have forged.

[89] Aristotle uses the word *nous* for this intuitive capacity, the same capacity he argues we have to intuit first principles in the theoretical domain, such as the principle of noncontradiction.

[90] Steinberger, *The Concept of Political Judgment*, 226.

Interpretive Understanding

Hermeneutics stresses our capacity to understand through processes of circular codetermination of particulars and universals, on the one hand, and the circular comprehension of particulars and our projects or purposes, on the other. I will use the term "interpretive understanding" for hermeneutical understanding. The literature is, of course, immense, and I want only to say enough about certain aspects of the hermeneutical tradition to show its relevance to an understanding of the actual structure of the understanding deployed at trial.

Interpretive understanding envisions "a continuous dialectical tacking between the most local of local detail and the most global of global structures in such a way as to bring both into view simultaneously."[91] The elements of interpretive understanding can, for example, be a particular action and a universal norm, each of which illuminates the other. Gadamer takes as paradigmatic for hermeneutics the situation of a judge who "does not simply 'apply' fixed, determinate laws to particular situations [but] must interpret and appropriate precedents and law to each new, particular situation. It is by virtue of such considered judgment that the meaning of the law and the meaning of the particular case are codetermined."[92] This is simply a special case of the circular nature of all normative judgment. Since there is no "ethical mass production," even where our commonsense morality, our public identity, and our legal rules are sound, they cannot be mechanically applied. After all, "[t]he choice that is right cannot be determined in advance or apart from the particular situation, for the situation itself partly determines what is right.[93] As Gadamer himself recognized, this mutual codetermination of universals and particulars characteristic of ethical know-how is a form of interpretive understanding that distinguishes ethics from technical (and, as I have suggested, bureaucratic) decision making: "[W]hile technical activity does not require that the means that allow it to arrive at an end be weighed anew on each occasion, this is precisely what is required in ethical know-how. In ethical know-how there can be no prior knowledge of the right

[91] Clifford Geertz, "From the Native's Point of View: On the Nature of Anthropological Understanding," in *Interpretive Social Science: A Reader*, ed. Paul Rabinow and William M. Sullivan (Berkeley and Los Angeles: University of California Press, 1979), 239.

[92] Bernstein, *Beyond Objectivity and Relativism*, 147–48. I have, of course, argued throughout that at trial "the law," taken in a positivist sense, is only one of the sources of norms.

[93] Joel Weinsheimer, *Gadamer's Hermeneutics: A Reading of Truth and Method* (New Haven: Yale University Press, 1985), 190. Of course, the very multiplicity of norms at trial would make mechanical application all but impossible.

means by which we realize the end in a particular situation. For the end itself is only concretely specified in deliberating about the means appropriate to a particular situation."[94]

Interpretive understanding is dependent on our prejudgments: the web of belief that constitutes our common sense and defines who we are. As Gadamer puts it provocatively, "it is our prejudices that constitute our being."[95] These prejudgments are, however, fluid enough that we can "fuse horizons" with alien perspectives. We can understand an opening statement that challenges our prejudgments and specific testimony that is inconsistent with our prejudices. We cannot understand at all, however, except through these prejudgments, by situating events within a system of beliefs.[96] But even to call this background of prejudgments "beliefs" is likely to be misleading, a point that becomes important when we consider the deeper levels of explicitly practical integration in our model of trial decision making. The meaning of this background is contained in ways of acting, of coping with people and institutions. The know-how that makes possible skillful coping is more basic than the distinction between thought and action. It is, rather, the condition of all sorts of both practical and intellectual orientation. It is not only that we possess an enormous range of tacit knowledge, understood as a sort of implicit theory, which we bring to bear on everyday problems. It is a "learned way of *acting*— or coping with things and situations—that renders the world meaningful" and this because "the way human beings exist or dwell in the world is fundamentally in a state of practical absorption in tasks and skills in which theoretical knowledge . . . is only a secondary and parasitic phenomenon."[97] Our practical skill always outruns the power of any theory to address new situations and involves a shared capacity, learned through participation, to take one's place and move around in an existing social world.

Powerful strands in twentieth-century philosophy, then, agree: "the source of the intelligibility of the world is the average public practices through which alone there can be any understanding at all. What is shared is not a conceptual scheme, i.e., not a belief system that can be made explicit and justified. . . . What we share is simply our average comportment. Once a practice has been explained by appealing to what one does, no more basic explanation is possible. As Wittgenstein puts it in *On Cer-*

---

[94] Bernstein, *Beyond Objectivity and Relativism*, 147.

[95] Hans-Georg Gadamer, "The Universality of the Hermeneutical Problem," in *Philosophical Hermeneutics*, trans. David E. Linge (Berkeley and Los Angeles: University of California Press, 1976), 9.

[96] Hans Georg Gadamer, "The Problem of Historical Consciousness," *Graduate Philosophy Journal* 5 (1975): 8.

[97] Leiter, "Heidegger and the Theory of Adjudication," 270.

tainty: 'Giving grounds [must] come to an end sometime. But the end is not an ungrounded presupposition: it is an ungrounded way of acting.' "[98] That the understanding embedded in this way of "comporting" oneself can be shared, often indirectly, "is a consequence of the fact that its intelligibility depends on *shared* practices."[99]

There are, then, two interrelated circles of the understanding. The first is the circle by which the whole is understood in light of the parts and the parts in light of the whole, the universal in light of the particular and the particular in light of the universal. As the notions of reflective judgment and practical wisdom emphasize, there is an element of freedom in these integrations, though always constrained by the perspectives of other judging individuals. The second, and more basic, circle[100] moves between the situation and the purposes of the interpreter: the meaning of the situation, what the interpreter takes it *as*,[101] "occurs only as an element within a system of practically oriented activity."[102]

To return to figure 2, the theoretical holism implied by the first sort of hermeneutical circle tends to dominate at the outer levels of "proof." The defendant's drinking just before the killing will be evidence of his lack of inhibitions, on the one hand, or his lack of the necessary dexterity to fire the fatal shot, on the other, depending on the jury's interpretation of all of the remaining evidence. The holism implied by the mutual determinations of factors becomes more and more a practical holism as we move toward the center of the structure. The defendant's behavior will be "knowing" or not depending on the dangers implicit in releasing this particular person back into the community. The representational aspects of the juror's grasp that seem to dominate, though never completely, at the outer levels are redetermined insofar as they remain within the juror's cognitive horizons as we move into the deeper levels. Ultimately, the representational forms of knowledge recede as the jury becomes more and more certain of what is to be done in this particular case.

Reflective judgment, practical wisdom, and interpretive understanding all claim first a "communal validity," a validity within the public horizon of the community with which the judging subject identifies. In the case of reflective judgment, the "claim to validity can never extend further than the others in whose place the judging person has put himself or herself in

[98] Dreyfus, *Being-in-the-World*, 155.

[99] Ibid., 165.

[100] See Mark Okrent, *Heidegger's Pragmatism: Understanding, Being, and the Critique of Metaphysics* (Ithaca: Cornell University Press, 1988), 165.

[101] Recall that this is precisely the task of opening statement, to propose "what this case is about."

[102] Okrent, *Heidegger's Pragmatism*, 165.

the process of making a judgment."[103] When Kant says that such a judgment claims validity "for every single judging person," the "emphasis is on '*judging*' . . . not for those who do not judge or those who are not members of the public realm where the objects of judgment appear."[104] Similarly, what Arendt sought to discriminate in reflective judgment was "[a] mode of thinking that is neither to be identified with the expression of private feelings nor to be confused with the type of thinking that is characteristic of 'cognitive reason.' It is a mode of thinking that is capable of dealing with the particular in its particularity but which nevertheless makes the claim to communal validity. When one judges one judges as a member of a human community."[105] Likewise, Aristotelian practical wisdom was a disciplined immediate understanding of a particular situation in light of the rich web of public norms. Interpretive understanding as a noninferential faculty of insight or intuition is, as we have seen, also dependent on shared meanings, themselves dependent on shared modes of acting.

Does all this mean that the judgment available at trial is limited by the perspectives, norms, and practices of the community from which judge and jury are drawn? The short answer is "Yes." Trial judgments are intrinsically limited by the common sense of the community within which they occur. "A man cannot see by another's eye, nor hear by another's ear; no more can a man conclude or infer the thing to be resolved by another's understanding."[106] Thus juries whose common sense is enmeshed in systematic injustice can do injustice. On the other hand, the faculty of interpretive insight that is called upon at trial is "common but it is not *plebiscitary.*"[107] We all have this common sense, but it exists only as a potentiality that must be actualized.[108] My contention is, of course, that the trial's consciously structured hybrid of languages is designed precisely to actualize our reflective judgment, practical wisdom, and interpretive understanding in ways that can at least sometimes lift the common sense of a given community above the least common denominator of the institutions and practices of that community. That accounts for the experienced "ele-

---

[103] Bernstein, *Beyond Objectivity and Relativism*, 217.

[104] Ibid.

[105] Ibid. Steinberger puts it this way in the explicitly legal context: "Similarly, the jurist who decrees that an act was lawful is telling us that in light of our shared insight into certain acts and certain laws—in light of our common sense—*we* judge the act lawful; the jurist is merely the self-conscious and duly appointed vehicle for rendering a communal judgment." *The Concept of Political Judgment*, 257.

[106] Chief Justice Vaughn of the Court of Common Pleas in *Bushell's Case*, 6 How. St., Tr. 999, 1011, 1015.

[107] Steinberger, *The Concept of Political Judgment*, 230.

[108] Ibid., 231.

vation" of the faculties which is so regularly reported by jurors. The trial places before the common sense of the jury the trained and motivated presentations of lawyers, each designed to invoke the perspectives, norms, and practices that most powerfully support each position and which count against their opponents. To invoke Heraclitus's image, they build the "web" over which the common sense of the jury can range. The performances of the trial, however well executed, remain in service to common sense. The finest trial lawyers are engaged in a practice whose deepest goal is to actualize these powerful sources of human judgment.

Conclusion

The ultimate question for the jury is "What is to be done?" The "meaning" of the trial event appears to the trier of fact at the same moment and in the same act of understanding in which he grasps what is to be done. Judgment is, in Steinberger's happy phrase, an "intelligent performance," based on insight and interpretation, relying on a skillful response to a carefully structured situation with which we can cope often better than we can explain.

VIII

The Truth of Verdicts

[M]an is in his actions and practice, as well as in
his fictions, essentially a story-telling animal. He
is not essentially, but becomes through his history, a teller of stories that aspire to truth.
> *(MacIntyre)*

[I]n being ourselves we are more than ourselves;
to know that our experience, dim and fragmen-
tary as it is, yet sounds the utmost depths of
reality.
> *(Whitehead)*

Catch only what you've thrown yourself, all is
mere skill and little gain. . . .
> *(Rilke)*

Five Theses Supporting the Truth of Verdicts

The sense in which a verdict can be said to be correct under the Received
View seems relatively straightforward:[1] a verdict will be correct if it is
based on accurate fact-finding followed by legal categorization that respects the meanings of the key terms in the instructions. From that perspective, it is difficult even to think of a verdict as "true."[2] "Justified"
or perhaps "correct," but never quite "true." I have proposed another
understanding of what, concretely, the trial has become for us that I argue
is fair to the different sources of evidence, and have invoked "the mutual
support of many considerations, of everything fitting together into one
coherent view."[3] I have suggested that we humans have the sorts of intellectual capacities consistent with that model.

---

[1] As it turns out, trying to provide a fairly rigorous account of the nature of trial decision
making in terms of the abstractions of the Received View produces unsolvable paradoxes.
See Ronald J. Allen, "The Nature of Juridical Proof," *Cardozo Law Review* 13 (1991): 373.

[2] Marianne Constable (*The Law of the Other*) has written perceptively of the impoverished sense of the truth of verdicts within the dominant legal positivist perspective. My
argument suggests that there is much more afoot in the trial than the positivist view suggests,
and thus reason for Constable to be more optimistic than she is.

[3] Rawls, *A Theory of Justice*, 579.

The next question that naturally arises is the sense in which verdicts in this understanding of the trial can be said to be "true." I am more than aware that contemporaries are especially reticent in the use of that term, and so a decent regard for those sensibilities requires caution. My approach thus is to ask: What are the conditions of the possibility that the trial's practices and languages can reveal, or at least converge on, the truth of a human action? I identify five such conditions.

The first is that narrative forms, if constrained and criticized, are in some way congruent with and so reveal the intelligibility of human action. The second is that common sense contains resources for the discernment of the truth of highly particular situations, not merely overgeneralized determinations of the probable. The third is that the harsh tension of opposites created by the trial actually reveals something that could not be stated more directly. The fourth is that interpretive methods can converge on the essence of a human situation. The last is that the trial's constellation of languages and practices best deploy the epistemological and normative resources necessary for practical judgment. It will turn out that those conditions are defensible philosophical positions which strengthen and, conversely, are themselves supported by the accounts already provided. A global defense of those positions is well beyond my scope. But, to invoke once again Peirce's image of philosophical argumentation, they provide a number of shorter strands of argument, which when added to the many others that have gone before, create a strong cable. And, of course, one of the strands may stretch very thin without the cable's failing to do its job.

Narrative Is Embedded in the Nature of Human Action, Always the Subject of the Trial

If it were the case that narrative structure was utterly alien to the reality upon which it was "imposed,"[4] the trial's central form would tend to distort rather than to reveal. This would be so whether "narrativization" occurred in the interest of a consoling coherence or of moralism's will to power.[5] A theorist might well agree with me on the descriptive level concerning the narrative character of the trial but argue that it is precisely this which demonstrates the purely instrumental function of the trial, at

[4] See, e.g., Louis O. Mink, "History and Fiction as Modes of Comprehension," *New Literary History* 1 (1970): 541–58. Hayden White, *Metahistory* (Baltimore: Johns Hopkins University Press, 1973).

[5] Roland Barthes, "Historical Discourse," in *Introduction to Structuralism*, ed. Michael Lane (New York: Basic Books 1970), 145–55.

the expense of any real power to reveal the truth of events that occurred in the past. For example, storytelling at trial might serve to strengthen the identity of a community threatened by deviance of one sort or other, or to strengthen the power of a ruling minority.[6] After all, the criminal trial allows the threatened community to condemn, discipline, and punish, then send the scapegoat into the desert.

Investigators in many different fields, however, have concluded that narrative forms the deep structure of human action.[7] In other words, the bedrock of human events is not a mere sequence upon which narrative is imposed but a configured sequence[8] that has a narrative character all the way down. To act at all is to hold an immediate past in memory, to anticipate a goal, and to organize means to achieve that goal—analogously the "beginning, middle, and end" of a well-constructed story.[9] Both action and storytelling are intrinsically chronological and logical: narrative structures that have a "logical" character "are to be found . . . in the midst of experience and action, not in some higher level linguistic construction or reconstruction of the experiences and actions involved."[10] The very experience of acting meaningfully, which is ubiquitous, includes a sense of direction and purpose that we grasp in narrative form regardless of whether we actually tell the story of those actions to other people. Stories "are told in being lived and lived in being told."[11] Or, as Barbara Hardy put it, "We dream in narrative, day-dream in narrative, remember, anticipate, hope, despair, believe, doubt, plan, revise, criticize, construct, gossip, learn, hate and love by narrative."[12]

The questions "What really occurred?" and "To what storytelling genre does the account of what occurred belong?" are the same question. This is as true at trial as it is in historiography. Opening statements often include this kind of assignment: for example, "We have here a tragic sequence of events" by a lawyer seeking to avoid moral (and so legal) responsibility. Or, "We have here a real comedy of errors" by a lawyer

---

[6] Kai Erikson, *Wayward Puritans* (New York: Wiley, 1966).

[7] Among the theorists in different fields who have agreed that narrative forms the deep structure of human action are critic Barbara Hardy ("Toward a Poetics of Fiction: An Approach through Narrative," *Novel* 2 [1968]); historian Peter Munz (*The Shapes of Time* [Middletown, Conn.: Wesleyan University Press, 1977]); philosophers Wilhelm Schapp (*In Geschichten Verstrickt*, 2d ed. [Wiesbden: B. Heymann, 1976]), Alasdair MacIntyre (*After Virtue*), and Frederick Olafson (*The Dialectic of Action* [Chicago: University of Chicago Press, 1979]). See David Carr, *Time, Narrative, and History* (Bloomington: Indiana University Press, 1986), 16–17.

[8] Carr, *Time, Narrative, and History*, 44.

[9] Ibid., 48.

[10] Ibid., 50.

[11] Ibid., 61.

[12] Hardy, "Toward a Poetics of Fiction," quoted in MacIntyre, *After Virtue*, 211.

seeking to assign responsibility for negligent behavior while telling the jury that it does not have to find that the defendant was morally depraved in order to rule for the plaintiff. Morality play, political foundational story, legal statement of facts are all such genres.

The hinge or connection between the event and the story of the event is the notion of intelligibility. For the event is intelligible only through its narrative structure, which explains the significance of the centrality of Level III in our model. There certainly is a metaphysical question of the relationship between the intelligibility of past events and their "reality," a question that I touch on below, but their reality, at least for us, is their intelligibility, first grasped, then reasonably affirmed. MacIntyre uses a historical example to make the point:

> Consider the question of to what genre the life of Thomas Becket belongs, a question which has to be asked and answered before we can decide how it is to be written. . . . In some of the medieval versions, Thomas' career is presented in terms of the canons of medieval hagiography. In the Iceland *Thomas Saga* he is presented as a saga hero. In Dom David Knowles' modern biography the story is a tragedy, the tragic relationship of Thomas and Henry II, each of whom satisfies Aristotle's demand that the hero be a great man with a fatal flaw. Now it clearly makes sense to ask who is right, if anyone: the monk William of Canterbury, the author of the saga, or the Cambridge Regius Professor Emeritus? The answer appears to be the last. The true genre of the life is neither hagiography nor saga, but tragedy. . . . To what genre does this history belong . . . is the same question as: What type of account of their history will be both true and intelligible?[13]

Thus any attempt to understand human experiences and actions "in themselves," before, so to speak, the employment of narrative categories, will yield only "the disjointed parts of some possible narrative" and will almost inevitably ignore the teleological character of even the simplest of human actions. In our model, the jury asks and answers the outer-level, purely "factual" questions only to answer questions that are generated by the need to interpret what occurred in fully characterized narrative terms. Before that integration, the lower-level material forms only "the disjointed parts of some possible narrative."

Any real-world action considered at trial is always social. The trial is a story about a story that, in a strong sense, publicly determines what occurred. It has "a double practical function, that of constituting actions themselves" and that of "[d]iscovering or rediscovering the story, picking up the thread, reminding ourselves where we stand, where we have been and where we are going—these are typical narrative-practical modes of

---

[13] MacIntyre, *After Virtue*, 212–13.

discourse which are as prevalent and as important for groups as they are for individuals."[14] Concretely, there is no discontinuity between the task of the proper characterization of the past act and the implicit story the jury is telling about itself and its society in the present. The event that brings the case to trial is an event in the society's history. What it was that occurred, what story we accept about it, defines us insofar as *that* was something which happened to us, and we further define ourselves in the judgment we enter about it. There is only one story including both the past event and the action we take today. (Recall how stories of justice inevitably draw the jury into their structure.) To an extent that far eclipses the real extent to which a historian is always already a participant in the history he or she writes, the jury already is a participant with a preunderstanding of the event that arrives at trial. And so the narrative character of the human action(s) that constituted the event which led to the trial is prestructured narratively to be truly grasped in stories told by the lawyers and witnesses and by the jury when it tells the kind of story that all the devices of the trial allow it to tell—whether that focuses in the given case on the details of "what happened" or on the jury's deciding what kind of community they have.

I want to avoid sophistry here. There are "brutally elementary data." An important part of our moral universe requires that we respect them. This is most obvious at Level I of our model. Indeed, part of the self-definition that occurs at Levels III and IV is that decent societies respect such data. "Conceptually, we may call truth what we cannot change; metaphorically, it is the ground on which we stand and the sky that stretches above us."[15] And so the lines of justification in the model do run inward. As we move toward the center, however, the judgments we make, that we must make, are intertwined with our practical self-definitions in ways that make the moral and public identity of the judging subject more central. There is a sense in which the question of whether an arm moved through space at a certain time or certain sounds were made is more independent[16] of the forms of life of a community than is the question of whether such movements or sounds were "threatening." Sometimes—most times—that self-definition amounts to a reaffirmation of a relatively settled conviction, though, given the uniqueness of each case, there will always be some redefinition. The reach of settled convictions is always indeterminate, and, in law, extension *is* definition. In other situations, as we move inward

---

[14] Ibid.

[15] Arendt, "Truth and Politics," 264.

[16] This is true of the ultimate fact. But whether we should accept a particular witness's testimony, given the significance of the risk of error, inevitably injects moral-political issues even into those determinations, as we have seen.

in figure 2, there will be an almost total identity among the judgments of "what this is," "who we are," and "what is to be done." The truth of the first of those inquiries will be dependent almost exclusively on the truth of which the latter two judgments are capable. And, it should be clear by now, I do not regard this conclusion as at all suggesting that the determinations made at trial are arbitrary. The trial's consciously structured hybrid of languages usually succeeds in revealing who we really are and what is really to be done.

There remain the metaphysical questions. Educated contemporaries find it hard to resist the notion that narrative structures are a kind of epiphenomenon overlaying the "real" causes of human behavior. Though this seems wrong,[17] the contention raises fundamental questions well beyond my purposes here. At the very least, "there is nothing below this narrative structure, at least nothing that is experienceable by us or comprehensible in experiential terms," so that "[n]o elements enter our experience . . . unstoried or unnarrativized."[18] Insofar as there exists a self at all, and, therefore, insofar as the entire repertoire of categories on which the civil and criminal law rests has any foundation in reality, narrative categories provide "the structure not only of experiences and actions but also of the self."[19]

Failure to understand how fundamental narrative is to the comprehension of human action and human selves has led to similar elevation of

---

[17] The radical view is the so-called replacement hypothesis, under which *all* of the usually moral categories that define the life world can be "replaced" by scientific causal categories without loss. Such a "replacement" has not, in my judgment, ever been successful and usually remains a "program," not an accomplishment. Among other difficulties, the program suffers from severe reflexive problems in accounting for science itself as a normative enterprise that is teleologically structured to converge on the truth, and not a sequence of "behaviors" "caused" by antecedent independent variables. See generally Richard Bernstein, *The Restructuring of Social and Political Theory* (Philadelphia: University of Pennsylvania Press, 1976).

[18] Carr, *Time, Narrative, and History*, 66. The grudging admission of the categories of "incompetent to stand trial" and "not guilty by reason of insanity" are the exceptions that prove the rule. See *Federal Rules of Evidence* 704(b) (restrictions on psychiatrists' ability to testify as to the mental states of defendants). In establishing either, narrative structure is crucial in several ways. Usually there exists a story that provides the grounds for the genesis of the condition and of its growing manifestation. Then there is a story of the defendant's behavior at crucial times that cannot be assimilated to the story-model, where reasons and motives are causes. See William Dray, "The Historical Explanation of Actions Reconsidered," in *Philosophy and History*, ed. Sidney Hook (New York: New York University Press, 1963, and Donald Davidson, "Action, Reasons, and Causes," in *Essays on Action and Events* (Oxford: Oxford University Press, 1980). The defendant's opening statement presented above tries to do just that. See chapter 4, above.

[19] Carr, *Time, Narrative, and History*, 73. On the mutual implication of selfhood and "moral space," see Taylor, *Sources of the Self*, 3–52.

what we may call analytic-logical categories in the philosophy of history
and in the understanding of the trial. Some analytical philosophers have
argued that "narrative is merely the literary surface, the manner in which
historians write up the result of the research, which is really incidental to
the scientific work of discovery or reconstruction."[20] Similarly, Wigmore
seemed to believe that what he called the "Narrative Method" of organizing trial evidence was casual and primitive compared to his own "Chart
Method," which attempted to map out and criticize the logical relationships among all the propositions offered for the jury's belief.[21] Carr's reply
to the philosophers of history applies to attempts to turn the trial into a
purely logical enterprise: "For what are historians discovering or reconstructing? *Insofar* as the actions and experiences of individuals and communities constitute the objects of their inquiry . . . historians are dealing
with and evaluating narratives from start to finish. Narrative, on our view,
lies in the *objects* of historical research, not merely in its own manner of
writing about those objects."[22] Yet, as we have seen, the opponents of
narrative do have a point, as well. Narratives can be the tools of self-
satisfied moralism or raw power. The case against narrative history, as
White recognizes,[23] is a moral case. And, I hope I have shown, the trial's
languages and procedures are deeply sensitive to that danger. The competition between narratives, the different *kinds* of narrative, and the deconstruction of narrative all recognize those dangers. The implicit premise of
the trial seems to be that constructive and representational knowledge of
human action takes a narrative form. Those constructions will suffer from
all the limitations that infect the common sense of the community in
which they are told. We can use the trial's critical devices to challenge the

---

[20] Carr, *Time, Narrative, and History*, 176–77.

[21] William Twining, "Lawyers' Stories," in *Rethinking Evidence*, 239. Twining criticizes
Wigmore for giving "the impression that his 'Chart method' involves an almost mechanical
application of ordinary principles of inductive logic. Any one who tries to apply the method
to a mass of evidence soon learns that Wigmore's theory provides almost no guidance in
making *strategic* choices in constructing or criticizing a complex argument." He offers the
converse criticism of Bennett and Feldman: that they overestimate the importance of the
inner coherence of stories "by ignoring almost entirely such lawyers' notions as facts in
issue, materiality, relevance, burdens of proof, presumptions and, most surprising of all, the
advocate's notion of 'the theory of the case[.]' " Ibid., 241–42. The theory I am presenting
moves into the middle ground defined by those criticisms.

[22] Carr, *Time, Narrative, and History*, 177. Carr qualifies his contention by adding: "It
may indeed be true that historical research will often penetrate to causal connections among
events and actions (particularly psychological or economic connections) which were hidden
from the historical agents themselves. But this is not to deny that these agents lived in a
narrative fashion: it is just to say that *their* story of what they were doing must be revised
or indeed replaced by a better one." Ibid. That qualification is consistent with the qualifications on the power of narrative described in the text.

[23] White, "The Value of Narrativity in the Representation of Reality," 1–23.

easy complacency of that common sense, to elevate it, if you will. But these critical moments are not likely, in the end, to produce a better story. In the same way that a "critical natural law" can point out the shortcomings of legal rules without laying out a utopian blueprint, the critical devices of the trial can take the jury to a moral plane somewhat beyond the narrative resources their own society alone would allow. The trial's languages and practices, taken together, can encourage the emergence of a truth beyond storytelling. Plato would smile.

Common Sense Contains Resources for the Discernment of the True, Not Just the Generally Probable

In the *Phaedrus*, Plato's Socrates muses about the problem of the probable and the true in the context of trial rhetoric. The world of human action, for the Plato of the middle dialogues, is inevitably one of very limited intelligibility: since we can *know* only what is intelligible and to the extent it is intelligible,[24] our beliefs about human affairs are unlikely in any robust sense to be true. We will "know" human affairs through opinion, the web of belief flawed both epistemologically and morally. Socrates tells his conversation partners that trial lawyers have even said that one should present evidence which is probable, based on commonsense generalizations, rather than evidence which is true. For the improbable truth is likely to be disbelieved. Plato understood what Bruner called the discontinuity between the meaningfulness of a story and its truth.

But then Socrates has second thoughts. In a suggestion that is just tentative, Socrates says that the notions of probability held by the people are founded on "a likeness to the truth."[25] And so, Socrates suggests, a speaker who knows both the truth about human nature and what we may call a "truthful" way of classifying (and so describing) things may actually prove the most persuasive.[26] The suggestion, which Aristotle develops, is

---

[24] This is the point of the cave allegory and the divided line metaphor in the *Republic*. In a late dialogue, the *Statesman*, Plato suggests that the best state will be governed by a philosopher-statesman who does not need the constraining overgenerality of law, who is, in effect, possessed of an intellectual intuition of the concrete particular in the world of human action. Plato is quick to remind us that we will be fortunate to live even in the second-best state governed by law.

[25] Plato, *Phaedrus*, at 273d: *to eikos tois pollois di' omoioteta tou alethous tugkanei eggignonmenon.* Literally: "the probable for the many has happened to come to be through a likeness of the truth."

[26] Of course, Socrates goes on to say that persuading other men ("other slaves") is a matter of small import compared to speaking uprightly before the gods. Ibid. The addition is necessary, I suggest, because the power of unconstrained rhetoric before the large Athenian juries is never far from Plato's mind. Once again, the rules of trial can be under-

that common sense may not be quite so divorced from the truth about the dark world of human action as Plato's middle dialogues generally argued.[27]

Aristotle's development of Socrates' second thoughts occurs largely in the *Rhetoric* and forms the basis of an "epistemological optimism"[28] about the results of disciplined public debate in law and politics he there defends. In sharp contrast to Socrates' arguments in the middle dialogues, Aristotle concludes that the dependence of rhetoric on commonsense premises is a strength, not a weakness.[29] Common sense has a powerful intellectual core.[30] Thus a rhetoric rooted in common sense is "useful because what is true and what is just are naturally stronger than their opposites, so that if legal judgments do not turn out correctly, truth and justice are necessarily defeated by their opposites, and this deserves censure."[31] Thus ordinary citizens (if they are not operating as a mob)[32] who have no pretense of theoretical sophistication "both intrinsically and as a consequence of their situation in an arena of public debate might nevertheless naturally incline toward correct verdicts, naturally attain a state of true (if unjustified and perhaps unarticulated) belief." As Aristotle argues throughout the *Rhetoric*, "to speak without qualification, what is true and what is better are always naturally easier to argue for and more persuasive."[33] Not that the truth will always prevail. Two dangers, both *ethi-*

---

stood as a set of "Platonic" constraints on willful speech. But even without such constraints, the roots of commonsense "opinion" in truth may impose some limitations on pure manipulation.

[27] On the *Phaedrus* as a dialogue that throws into question some of the deepest commitments of the middle dialogues, see Nussbaum, *The Fragility of Goodness*, 200–233.

[28] Robert Wardy, "Mighty Is the Truth and It Shall Prevail?" in *Essays on Aristotle's Rhetoric*, ed. Amelie Oksenberg Rorty (Berkeley and Los Angeles: University of California Press, 1996), 56, 60.

[29] This links up with many central Aristotelian themes that, in different ways, elevate the importance, indeed the ultimacy, of concrete judgment and action. See, e.g., Nussbaum, *The Fragility of Goodness*, 240–63.

[30] Bernard Lonergan presents a contemporary Aristotelian restatement of "common sense as intellectual" in *Insight*, 173–80. The ways in which closing argument can be used to solve the problems posed by the most obvious implications of commonsense reasoning may be the best single exhibition of the subtlety of common sense itself. See chapter 2, above. Of course, closing argument is dependent on all the other trial devices: for example, young lawyers are taught to think of cross-examination as laying the foundations for closing.

[31] *Rhetoric* 1355a24 (Wardy's translation in "Mighty Is the Truth," 59).

[32] *Ochlos*. For a suggestion, much disputed, that Athenian juries were so large and orderly evidentiary procedures so undeveloped that they could easily degenerate into "mobs," see Allen, *Socrates*, 24 ("Gorgias defines rhetoric, at one point, as power of persuasion 'in courts and other mobs'. . . , and the technique of the popular orator involved much of applied mob psychology").

[33] *Rhetoric* 1355a37–38.

cal failures, may defeat the truth: "Disputes in which truth is worsted suggest themselves: our just cause may be defeated because we are ourselves 'unnaturally' puny in disputation, so that our audience falls prey to malicious rhetoric despite the persuasive edge truth lends us; or our political arrangements may themselves go against nature, in that they lessen the advantage those in the right ought to enjoy, and usually do."[34] The strengths of common sense can appear only when supported by vigorous advocacy and institutional arrangements consistent with our complex nature.

This natural superiority of the true story would provide a condition of the possibility of the truth of verdicts. Under the right institutional arrangements, we may be able to distinguish what Arendt calls "stories" from "fictions." The latter have the form of a humanly meaningful narrative but are really a series of partial descriptions spun around artful abstractions. In the trial lawyer's language, they present thin or artificial theories of the case. Common sense, here taken as a reservoir of beliefs, is an enormously complex and subtle instrument. Even at the "purely factual" level, its prejudgments about what is concretely probable are deep and flexible, and common sense itself is capable of generating genuine insight into genuinely novel situations. The outlines of a particular story may in general be implausible, but common sense is capable of comprehending which additional details and descriptions bring the narrative within the realm of what we may call concrete plausibility. Recall again that the principles of common sense always have the structure "Generally and for the most part. . . ." In the hands of the right speaker, someone who understands his or her culture and who can describe "truly" (in the sense that a performance or an action within a craft is "true"), an initially implausible but true event may be brought within the realm of plausibility.

Consider once again how the practices of the trial aid this process. The opening statement is a promise as well as a story: without supporting admissible evidence, it is a broken promise. Lawyers are prohibited from mentioning anything in opening that will not be supported by such evidence. They are constrained in the process of trial preparation both of their own clients and of nonclient witnesses by ethical rules against the creation and presentation of false evidence and by the criminal law against the suborning of perjury. Lawyers are prohibited from suggesting anything in cross-examination that they do not have a good-faith basis to believe is true or (sometimes) admissible evidence to support. Testimony is given under oath. It is subject to cross-examination. Lawyers are permitted to introduce evidence to support their own cases and also to undermine their opponents'. The law of evidence, at least in the hands "of a

[34] Wardy, "Mighty Is the Truth," 60.

strong and wise trial judge," serves to exclude both utterly unreliable evidence and the sorts of evidence that serve to dissipate the fruitful tensions of the trial with irrelevancy.[35] So a lawyer cannot just tell the most plausible story, regardless of its truth. To the extent that a theory of the case is rendered initially plausible by a description which relies on the omission of details that ought fairly to be included, the correction will not be long in coming. To the extent that the jury was initially "taken in," then immediately disillusioned, to that extent will the general plausibility of the position be undermined, not only because of the performative offense, but also because of the implicit admission that such a distortion was the only way the position could be defended. In short, the ethics of the bar aim at dissuading "puny" disputation, and the devices of the trial are designed to create the likelihood that the better argument and stronger evidence will prevail.

There Is a Human Capacity to Grasp a Truth Manifest in the Tensions Created by the Trial's Consciously Structured Hybrid of Languages

Recall Heraclitus's image of psyche on the spider's web. The notion was that the mind grasps the web not as an object but as a tool ("ready-to-hand," in Heideggerian language) through which it understands what comes into it. Further, the tensions in the web, the ways in which the strands pull against one another and establish fields of force, create the conditions for perception of the nature and location in the moral world of what has come into it.

Bakhtin's notion of literary truth in the novel relies on a similar metaphor. The novel, too, is a consciously structured hybrid of languages. Language, like reality itself, is constituted by an "almost Manichean sense of opposition and struggle at the heart of existence, a ceaseless battle between centrifugal forces that seek to keep things apart, and centripetal forces that strive to make things cohere."[36] It is precisely the tensions of

---

[35] The combined effect of these conditions means that conclusions drawn from experimental subjects' inability to discern a simple true story from a simple false one have almost no applicability to the trial. See Bennett and Feldman, *Reconstructing Reality in the Courtroom*, 69–90.

[36] Bakhtin, *The Dialogic Imagination*, xviii. Once again, *both* centrifugal and centripetal forces are necessary, the latter to counter social atomism and destructive conflict, the former to counter the totalitarian instinct, with which Bakhtin was all too familiar, to "substitute for the boundaries and channels of communication between individual men a band of iron which holds them so tightly together that it is as though their plurality had disappeared into One Man of gigantic dimensions." Arendt, *The Origins of Totalitarianism*, 465–66. For

opposites created linguistically that give us an insight into the conflictual nature of reality, the backward-bending bow. Analogously, in the course of the trial, the jury will feel the moral force of factual plausibility, legal stability, moral decency, social identity, and political purpose in ways that dramatize and sharpen tensions which those perspectives create in individual cases.

This notion of a kind of truth that can emerge only through a tension of opposites is invoked by other modernist writers as well. Tensed language "makes something appear by juxtaposing images or, even harder to explain, by juxtaposing words. The epiphany comes from between the words or images, as it were, from the force field they set up between them, and not through a central reference which they describe. . . ."[37] In the trial context, such language achieves a kind of correspondence with the structure of social reality, which itself is a tension of opposites. One thing that *appears* is the way in which that structure must be reconfigured in this particular case. That the trial seeks a practical interpretive understanding of a past event, itself necessarily multivalent, rather than "poetic truth" is an added complexity[38] to which I have tried to be fair, but it does not affect the essential point.

We see through the tensions created by the trial to a reality that cannot be "pictured" or otherwise "represented." Though representations of one sort or another are necessary elements in practical understanding, the multiplicity of trial languages and the incommensurability of the perspectives they embody *force* us to look through them. It is at a point beyond those representations that understanding occurs.

The notion of complementarity in physics, which influenced modernist writers to focus on the tension among languages, has this important feature: "only by entertaining multiple and mutually limiting points of view . . . can we approach the real richness of the world."[39] And so we have the familiar notion that a subatomic entity may be both a particle and a wave, an analogy that does not seem so facile in light of the moral origins of Bohr's insight: "Let me say now what Niels Bohr told *me*. The idea of complementarity in quantum theory, he said, came to him as he thought of the impossibility of considering his son simultaneously in the light of love and in the light of justice, the son just having voluntarily confessed that he had stolen a pipe from a local shop. His brooding set him to

---

Arendt it is positive law that maintains these benign centrifugal forces: "To abolish the fences of laws between men—as tyranny does—means to take away men's liberties and destroy freedom as a living political reality; for the space between men as it is hedged in by laws, is the living space of freedom." Ibid.

[37] Taylor, *Sources of the Self*, 465–66.

[38] See chapter 6, above.

[39] Rhodes, review of *Niels Bohr's Times*.

thinking about the vases and the faces in the trick figure-ground pictures: you can see only one at a time. And then the impossibility of thinking simultaneously about the position and the velocity of a particle occurred to him."[40] What the jury must understand, and does understand, is "a juxtaposed rather than integrated cluster of changing elements that resist reduction to a common denominator, essential core, or generative first principle."[41] The elements are irreducible, incommensurable, and in some ways opposed, yet can be grasped and held together in a way that yields real understanding.

This all may seem quite mysterious until we recall that this ability to steer between incommensurable and potentially conflicting values is an aspect of our ordinary moral experience. "When uncorrupted by theory," we usually judge that we are in the grip of incommensurable values, and, where the conflicts are most severe, those values are reflections of different ways of life that are mutually incompatible.[42] Nonetheless, we harbor a notion of "good judgment" even in those cases. It is the theoretical intellect that seeks unity. As Plato, one of the very greatest theoreticians, warned us, we should not go from the many to the One too quickly.

So, then, trial languages do not simply play off one another. Their interplay *reveals* something and recovers contact with a moral source. Modernists believed that the languages of literature had the power to reveal something that "has great moral and spiritual significance; that in it lies the key to a certain depth, or fullness, or seriousness, or intensity. . . ."[43] The various testaments to the meaningfulness of participation in the trial all stem from a conviction that the trial's languages have a similar power. The experience of the trial can be described only as "recovering contact with a moral source."[44] The experience is one of submersion in "ethical substance,"[45] the moral quality embedded in concrete institutions and practices expressed primarily in the trial's free narratives. The contrasting hyperconcrete language of direct examination and the acid of cross and argument provide jurors with the special craft to see things the way they are. When opening statements have relied on "false consoling modes of representation,"[46] direct examination and cross-examination can force us

[40] Bruner, *Actual Minds, Possible Worlds,* 51.

[41] Richard J. Bernstein, *The New Constellation: The Ethical-Political Horizons of Modernity/Postmodernity* (Cambridge: MIT Press, 1991), 201.

[42] Hampshire, "Public and Private Morality," 42.

[43] Taylor, *Sources of the Self,* 422 (discussing the modernist view of art). He notes that this conviction was often accompanied in early modern times by a hostility to the instrumental or bureaucratic style of the growing capitalist economy.

[44] Ibid., 428.

[45] Taylor, *Hegel,* 365–88.

[46] Taylor, *Sources of the Self,* 431.

to see what we would not. Sometimes "[i]t takes new, fiercely veridical portrayal to break through the veil."[47]

Thus the constellation of languages and practices of the trial can "actually put us in contact with the sources it taps. It can *realize* the contact."[48] It "brings us into the presence of something which is otherwise inaccessible, and which is of the highest moral or spiritual significance; a manifestation, moreover, which also defines or completes something, even as it reveals."[49] And that is why the experience of a well-tried case is so powerful.

Fundamentally Interpretive Methods Can Converge on the Truth of a Human Situation

Genuine interpretation is "intrinsically linguistic . . . not as the tool of a manipulating consciousness but as the medium through which a world comes to stand before us and in us." Interpretation discloses "both the being of an object" and "our own being" so that "it is truth that happens, emerges from concealment, and yet eludes every effort to reduce it to concepts and objectivity." The exercise of our relatively tradition-bound common sense is capable of an encounter that confirms some of our traditional horizon and negates other portions of it. There occurs not a "conformity of statement to fact" but the emergence of being "into the light of manifestness," a movement in which we are seized. Genuine interpretation does not involve a "gaining of conceptual knowledge through observation or reflection." It is an experience that involves a breaking down of some of one's old way of seeing in light of the decisional needs of the present. It is "dynamic, temporal, personal," and "we perceive the events not through the clean clear world of scientific concepts but through our "historical self-understanding of the world of conflict, ambiguity, and suffering."[50]

---

[47] Ibid. Iris Murdoch, who avows her Platonic roots, has perhaps most powerfully drawn this relationship between the vision of the artist and that of the moral agent. According to Murdoch, our minds are "continually active, fabricating an anxious, usually self-preoccupied, often falsifying veil" over moral reality. Murdoch, *The Sovereignty of the Good*, 83. The realism of the agent, like the realism of the artist, is a moral achievement. Ibid., 66.

[48] Taylor, *Sources of the Self*, 512.

[49] Ibid., 419.

[50] Richard E. Palmer, *Hermeneutics: Interpretation Theory in Schleiermacher, Dilthey, Heidegger, Gadamer* (Evanston, Ill.: Northwestern University Press, 1969), 242–53. The quoted language in the text is from Palmer's "Theses on Interpretation."

The truth that emerges at trial is, then, analogous to that which is implicit in a traditional mimetic theory of drama.[51] Drama does not produce a copy of reality; rather, it manifests an aspect of reality that is not visible outside the artistic representation:

> Works of art are not reproductions of a reality that can be identified independently of the work of art and used to judge the adequacy of its representation; rather, the features of the objects works of art represent . . . are illuminated only by means of the representation itself; certain events or features are exaggerated, the importance of others minimized and the like. Hence the representation does not provide a mirror of reality that exactly reflects it; rather, on Gadamer's view, artistic presentation shows the "truth" of "reality," as he puts it. "Reality" is defined as what is untransformed and art as the raising up of this reality into its truth. . . .[52]

The linguistic medium provides genuine knowledge insofar as it "shows us something familiar, as something we knew or should have known. . . . something we could not see without it; yet having seen it, we recognize it as a crucial aspect of what we always saw."[53]

This notion of "truth" is roughly equivalent to the aspects of the original reality that are most significant or important, Level VII in our model of the trial. Insofar as the trial provides a fully hermeneutical experience, it illuminates a problematic situation by allowing the jury to see what is essential about it. And so, insofar as very traditional philosophical doctrines—transformed and "recovered," as those in the hermeneutical tradition say—are themselves true, it is likely that the trial can yield the truth of a human situation. Those doctrines preserve a sense in which human intelligence and disciplined language provide the place where the "being" or truth of the world is realized and, at the same time, illuminated. What is "there" before human attention is brought to bear is in complex ways still only potentiality.[54] Things, especially human things, become what they are in modes of knowing, like those deployed at trial, whose aim is not exclusively prediction and control. To the extent that all this is true, to that extent will the judgments reached at trial be true.

Without the trial's languages and performances we would not see the significance of the situation at all; yet once we have experienced the trial, we cannot see the situation other than in the light the trial has shed. We cannot in many important circumstances ask whether the trial has accu-

---

[51] Warnke, *Gadamer: Hermeneutics, Tradition and Reason*, 56–64. Gadamer extends that theory to all forms of art, including nonrepresentational art.

[52] Ibid., 57.

[53] Ibid., 59.

[54] Once again, one of the characteristics of the human knowledge deployed is a "disinterested" desire for the truth.

rately portrayed reality, since the truth about the reality it portrays is invisible save in its light. Thus the truth of the event being tried and the moral and political identity of the jury are realized only in the jury's participation in the trial itself.

The Contemporary Trial Comprises the Practices Best Designed to Achieve Truth-for-Practical-Judgment

What transpires at trial is the most important determinant of jury judgments. The trial, as we have seen at length, comprises a complex set of rules, practices, and languages. It is hardly a value-free presentation of "the facts," whatever that would be. Trial judgments will be true if (1) there exist no institutions—and, more robustly, no possible inquiry will identify institutions—that are better designed to achieve the practical purposes of the trial, and (2) those purposes are rooted in the most important human interests. The concrete examination of the trial's practices that we have undertaken suggests that those practices are designed to achieve not social scientific truth[55] or historical truth or religious truth, but a specific kind of truth-for-practical-judgment. Thus the truth of trial judgments rests on the primacy (or ultimacy) of "the practical." To say something useful about truth in the context of the trial is thus "to explore practice rather than theory . . . action rather than contemplation."[56] The kinds of issues presented by the trial "are not to be judged by limiting oneself to [or by ignoring!] questions like, 'Does that assertion get it right?' " Put another way, trial judgments will be practically true if it is important that the moral sources which the trial elicits be brought to bear on and help "steer" the course of public events in ways that their own momentum could not carry them. Those sources are, once again, multiple and incommensurable. Bringing them to bear on a problematic situation disrupts the smooth functioning of our other, more "automatic" forms of social ordering, in particular, those of public and private bureaucracy and the more or less self-regulating market.

Philosophically, there are two main versions of the conviction that practical truth, the form of truth that serves as the premise for action, is primary. The Kantian version claims only that for us finite beings the practical is primary because moral action is the activity which brings us into the intelligible world, the world of the "things-in-themselves."[57] *We can*

---

[55] On the contrast between social scientific truth and the traditional understanding of the truth of jury verdicts, see Constable's fine book *The Law of the Other.*

[56] Bruner, *Acts of Meaning*, 26, quoting Richard Rorty.

[57] See Richard Kroner, *Kant's Weltanschauung* (Chicago: University of Chicago Press, 1956).

never achieve a theoretical or scientific knowledge of the whole and are limited, in the theoretical uses of our reason, to the world of phenomena.[58] Though there are many transmutations historically, the pragmatic tradition draws much of its inspiration from Kant's understanding of the primacy of the practical.

The other possible version is more robust and more willing to tell "likely stories"[59] about ultimate reality. In some of those stories we are participants in a drama or an action that defines the nature of things.[60] For those philosophers for whom dramatic categories are ultimate, for whom reality is "an action," for whom, usually, knowledge comes from participation, it is relatively easy to understand why practical judgment is primary. In either version, being is an action that we know by participating. What this means is that, finally, what Dreyfus calls "practical holism"[61] is true: human background practices can never be objectified as beliefs, assumptions, norms, rules, stereotypes, or anything else. At the central levels described by our model of the trial, we are engaged in a practice, dispersed in often bureaucratic legal institutions, that preserves inherited noninstrumental understandings and modes of judgment. Put more prosaically, it means that we are learning to engage in a cultural practice, which has deep roots in the jury's place in our constitutional order, which can never be completely thematized theoretically, and in which the correct tension among moral judgment, legal structuring, and public purpose is achieved. There is no theory or set of rules that provides a single language in which, or scale on which, this is achieved. "[O]nly by entertaining multiple and mutually limiting points of view, building up a composite picture, can we approach the real richness of the world."[62] Because, however, the task of the jury is practical, because it must *do* something, its grasp must stretch into the future in a way that can never be pictured.

---

[58] Thus MacIntyre tweaks the more ambitious of social scientific attempts to eliminate unpredictability from the social world as an attempt to "be like God." *After Virtue*, 96–97.

[59] Plato, *Timaeus* 29d. The degree of claimed "likelihood" varies quite a bit by philosopher, from a claim to "absolute knowledge" by Hegel to a more playful appreciation of the "mythical" and fallibilist nature of the story by Plato, Whitehead, and others. At a certain level of fallibilism and self-consciousness about mythic categories, the latter philosophers start to edge toward the Kantian position.

[60] John MacMurray, *Persons in Relation* (Atlantic Highlands, N.J.: Humanities Press, 1979), 222.

[61] Theoretical holism holds sway at the outer levels of the model: the part is understood in relation to the whole and the whole in relation to the part. As we move toward the center, the hermeneutic circle becomes less that between part and whole, and more that between representation and practical project.

[62] Rhodes, review of *Niels Bohr's Times*.

Moreover, for us Americans, practical truth involves the right adjustment of the tensions (1) among the distinct principles that animate important spheres of social life, and (2) among the available means of social ordering. Conflicts among those spheres are likely to be close to the core of many of the cases that become "triable cases." They are likely to be "triable" because the incommensurability of underlying values allows for the telling of different plausible narratives. So for us, practical judgment, itself ultimate, has a moral and a public dimension—practically speaking.

There is an important corollary to the thesis that the trial constitutes its object in the manner most consistent with the practical tasks that it serves. The conclusions of research into the trial that abstracts from those normative issues and studies the trial "scientifically" must be carefully critiqued before policy (and so normative) conclusions are drawn from them. Marianne Constable has shown how the most prominent attempts to evaluate the work of the jury, including the social science research summarized above, almost inevitably make assumptions that the account I have given disputes.[63] In effect, it assumes the vision of the trial embodied in the Received View and renders impossible comprehension of how a jury might have "established *in a deep sense*, the guilt or innocence of a defendant."[64] In one way or another, the studies assume that the law is what Hart has called "the law of the officials"[65] and not the "law of the community," which is usually reduced to the "beliefs," "sentiments," and "attitudes" expressed in jury verdicts.[66] Such studies "preclude the possibility of asking the more radical question: "How is it that judges and legislators have come to lay claim to what is called 'law' "? [67] And by focusing on the legitimizing function of the jury, they assume a patronizing scientific vantage point above its work, and assume away the very conception of truth that the languages and practices of the trial are designed to achieve: "Affirmations that people *believe in* the justice of the jury system or that the jury is just *according to the officials* come to the same thing when one understands law and justice as the law and justice of the officials; both claims privilege the belief in justice, or the appearance of justice, or justice from a point of view, over justice itself; they point to the emergence of 'legitimacy' as a value, a value that takes on meaning only in the absence of justice 'itself.' "[68] There is no objection to social scientists' "bracketing" the question of justice and studying "proxies" like legitimacy. The danger is when the methodologically dictated "prox-

---

[63] Constable, *The Law of the Other*, 55–66.
[64] Ibid., 47.
[65] Hart, *The Concept of Law*, 20–21.
[66] Constable, *The Law of the Other*, 55.
[67] Ibid., 56.
[68] Ibid., 58.

ies . . . take over the meaning of the word to such an extent that appearance and reality become interchangeable—as has become the case with justice."[69] Then "the official order, its justice and law, provides . . . the standards" for judgment of the justice that emerges from the trial, something, I have argued, which is often immeasurably richer.[70] "Such justice, such power, and such law—that of social science, that of the officials—risk becoming the only law."[71]

Constable is resigned to the fact that an alternative vision of the trial has passed away forever: "Gone is the juror as member of a community of persons who share the same law. . . . Gone are the communities of early jury history, for whom law is knowledge of how to act and who one is."[72] My hopeful suspicion is that this counsel of despair comes from a focus on what "the officials" say about the legal structure of the trial within the rhetoric of the Received View, and from methodologically driven social science which, as Kalven and Zeisel were happy to admit,[73] assumed the vision of the trial's success or failure from within the Received View. I suspect that she would be among the first to be surprised by the survival in the trial's practices and languages of a vision of justice that may serve to qualify other modes of social organization.

Some Concluding Notes on the Contemporary Importance of the Trial

Thus far, I have stayed resolutely within the languages and practices of the trial. When I asked about the truthfulness of what those practices and languages reveal, I avoided an Archimedean perspective outside the trial

---

[69] Ibid.

[70] And so the proposals for reform of the jury that presuppose a jury informed by the truths of social science are preferable to those presupposing a jury informed by "common sense." They presuppose a jury whose verdict is the product of information processing that is very like the sort of processing believed to occur in the social sciences. Their ultimate goal becomes "a jury whose 'perception, memory, information and decision processes' best approximate the processes of social science, a science that serves to correct the mistaken assumptions of (an official) law." Ibid., 64.

[71] Ibid., 58. Constable suggests that the early history of the jury points to a possibility (a "pretechnological understanding scattered in this background practice") of a "jury of neighbors, whose verdict of 'speaking of truth' was law—and whose law, irrespective of distinctions between fact and law, was justice."

[72] Ibid., 65.

[73] "It is the special advantage of empirical studies of legal institutions that the law supplies a pre-existing framework of significance and expectation to which the quantitative dimension can be added; it permits, that is, measurement with meaning." Kalven and Zeisel, *The American Jury*, 492.

from which one could pretend to assess the correspondence of trial languages to their objects. There is no such perspective. Nor is there often a perspective sufficiently provident as to distribute problematic situations among modes of social ordering before an individual mode of social ordering is brought to bear on that situation. This poses a real problem, since the modes of social ordering are not neutral in how they illuminate each situation. Once you begin negotiating, or mediating, or seriously preparing for trial (and you must begin doing *something*), you have begun to shape the situation through the methods that mode of social ordering provides.[74]

I have argued that a great advantage of the contemporary trial is its internal complexity, comprising empirical, moral, political, and strictly "legal" languages and values. It is sufficiently flexible to allow, indeed to require, that the jury determine what the most important aspect of the case is. And so the trial has evolved into a general-purpose remedy. Consider, for example, the vast differences among the sorts of disputes that find their way to trial: violent crimes where only the identity of the perpetrator is at issue; child custody disputes where highly contextual assessments of "best interests of the child" are made; patent infringement cases where the novelty of an invention in a highly technical field is disputed; classwide determinations of the disparate racial impact of general policies; individual civil rights or criminal cases where the key issue is the intent of the defendant, and only circumstantial evidence exists; personal injury actions where there is little dispute about what the defendant did, and the sole issue is the "reasonableness" of the defendant's actions—all are decided through the same practices and under the same rules. Consider, too, that in a particular case within any one of the disputes, the crucial issue may turn out to be one of the reliability of circumstantial evidence, the accurate determination of past events, the fair interpretation of the meaning of those events, the moral character and so credibility of party-witnesses, the definition of public identity, and so on. Any forum capable of resolving the issues that arise in those kinds of cases would have to allow the jury to make subtle determinations of normatively charged fact and then equally subtle determinations of relative importance, in just the way I have argued the trial does. Further, the internal complexity of the trial allows for a determination of how a concrete dis-

---

[74] I have argued elsewhere, for example, both that mediation is in a very specific sense moral conversation and that, since moral conversation may turn out not to be the appropriate response to a problematic situation, the path to other forms of ordering must be preserved. Robert P. Burns, "The Appropriateness of Mediation: A Case Study and Reflection on Fuller and Fiss," *Ohio State Journal on Dispute Resolution* 4 (1989): 129, and "The Enforceability of Mediated Agreements: An Essay on Legitimation and Process Integrity," *Ohio State Journal on Dispute Resolution* 2 (1987): 93.

pute should be treated without reliance on a necessarily overgeneralized precategorization based inevitably on a small number of abstract features of a situation. Even with the availability of pretrial procedures, it is often true that exactly what is at issue emerges only during the trial.[75]

In closing, I want very briefly to place the account I have given in a somewhat broader historical and theoretical structure. Understanding the trial in this context, I believe, enhances the appreciation of its importance for us, though it raises questions that must be postponed to another day. Initially, it is useful for us to consider, again very broadly, the recent history of influential theoretical attempts to specify the norms that should apply to the "basic structure" of society, prominently the legal rules at play in all trials. It is when we understand the failure of such attempts that we understand more deeply how important the trial is for us.

Let me tell an extremely compressed story about where we stand culturally on determining the justice of the legal order. (It is at least sometimes true, as Holmes put it, that an ounce of history is worth a pound of logic.) Adam Smith, a distinctively modern theorist who both reflected and crucially shaped legal institutions, is the key figure.[76] Smith developed what he took to be a scientific theory of the structure and evolution of social institutions, including legal institutions.[77] When we know that theory, we know the design that a benevolent God has placed in those institutions, usually through the mediating mechanism of a created human psychology. Since God is benevolent, we should not be surprised to see developing a "system of natural liberty" that will produce roughly the greatest happiness for the greatest number. However, the last thing that human beings should do is to attempt to hurry along God's plan, especially in the legal context. For a judge directly to aim at forging a rule that would produce the greatest happiness for the greatest number would be Promethean nonsense. Instead, human beings, as lawyers and judges, should make their legal determinations relying on their ordinary "moral sentiments,"

---

[75] The only situation, then, where trial should be avoided is where we make a considered judgment that one aspect of a situation (including, of course, the agreement of both potential parties that a trial is inappropriate), about which no reasonable dispute can be had, is of such overriding normative significance that the situation should not be considered in light of the rich range of normative considerations available at trial. Where such situations exist is a big question beyond my present scope. On both bureaucracy and legal formalism as devices for divorcing public decision making from "substantive justice in concrete cases for concrete individuals," see Max Weber, *Wirtschaft und Gesellschaft*, 660–665, reprinted in *Max Weber: On Law in Economy and Society*, ed. Max Rheinstein, trans. Edward Shils and Max Rheinstein (New York: Simon & Schuster, 1967), 349–56.

[76] Karl Polanyi, *The Great Transformation* (New York: Farrar & Renehart, 1944); Theodore Lowi, *The End of Liberalism*, 2d ed. (New York: Norton, 1979).

[77] See generally T. D. Campbell, *Adam Smith's Science of Morals* (London: Allen & Unwin, 1971); Joseph Cropsey, *Polity and Economy* (The Hague: Martinus Nijhoff, 1957).

consoled by the expectation that those created sentiments will, given the providential design, lead in the direction of the greatest happiness. For example, the shape and protection of property rights emerge from the operation of the moral sentiment of resentment in litigants and judges, which should be allowed to guide the framing and application of the rules of property law.

The next steps are fateful. Strip away the Deistic faith, and Smith's humility before the actual (albeit implicit) direction of institutional development drops away. This occurred among the economists of the next generation, from whom Marx inherited it,[78] and certainly with Bentham.[79] Large-scale institutional developments are now in human hands.[80] But the thinkers of the next generation also inherited from Smith the notion that moral judgment operates "within" a framework to which those ordinary moral norms do not apply. So classical Marxism purports to provide a scientific account, not a normative theory, of legal institutions,[81] and a grim battle rages within Marxism as to whether moral judgments[82] apply either to the tactics of the vanguard or to the shape of social institutions generally. A conviction that normative judgments are irrelevant to the shape of the basic structure of society in large part defines the dark side of modernity. Bentham tries to avoid the problem by transvaluing ordinary morality into the principle of utility, which applies both to individual action and to public rules and policies. (Insofar as ordinary morality does not conform to that principle, it is "nonsense on stilts.") Bentham's attempt fails, though in less concretely disastrous ways than does a Marxism that is beyond good and evil.

It is in response to utilitarianism and classical Marxism, respectively, that our two most important contemporary theorists of justice, John Rawls and Jürgen Habermas, write. Rawls accepts Smith's problematic and tries to identify normative principles that apply to a "basic structure" within which ordinary morality functions, and which ordinary morality

---

[78] Leszek Kolakowski, *Main Currents of Marxism: The Founders* (Oxford: Clarendon Press, 1978).

[79] Daniel Boorstin, *The Mysterious Science of the Law* (Chicago: University of Chicago Press, 1996).

[80] The French Revolution was the event that convinced European thinkers of the end of either a providential or traditional justification of inherited institutions. Arendt, *On Revolution*, 185. Ackerman argues that the full human responsibility for the basic structure did not enter popular American consciousness until the New Deal. Bruce A. Ackerman, *Reconstructing American Law* (Cambridge: Harvard University Press, 1984).

[81] Kolakowski, *Main Currents of Marxism*, 1:376–96.

[82] Leszek Kolakowski, *Main Currents of Marxism: The Golden Age* (Oxford: Clarendon Press, 1978), 240–54. Arthur Koestler's novel, *Darkness at Noon*, the story of a committed communist caught up in Stalin's show trials, is a sustained meditation on what a trial would look like under a consistent classical Marxism. See 99–101, 153, 246–49.

cannot control.[83] This initial attempt fails,[84] and Rawls returns to a
"Hegelian" vision of moral philosophy, whose task is to provide a kind
of rationalized version of the implicit values of the regime.[85] Habermas
continues to assert the viability of his "discourse ethics," which promise
a critical perspective on existing institutions, but increasingly invokes a
principle of "appropriateness" in specific individual moral-political questions, a norm that seems inevitably to draw more directly on the concrete
moral resources of a community.[86]

Significant difficulties in the thought of important thinkers always reflect real tensions in the practices and norms of their cultures. A central
contemporary challenge is to develop and refine the norms that ought to
apply to the basic structure of society, often expressed in the legal order.
This challenge provides the broader context for an understanding of the
function of the contemporary trial. The trial supplies a functioning concrete set of practices and languages that enable us to connect up moral
resources which are more developed in other spheres of practice with the
normative problems posed by the "newly" discovered fact that we are
responsible for the basic structure of society. Rawls and Habermas fail to
produce plausibly principled answers to concrete public normative questions because those questions cannot be resolved on the level of generality
on which they move, a conclusion implicitly conceded by both thinkers'
later work—at least not until our moral resources for addressing these
questions are far more developed than they are presently. The trial, especially the jury trial, is, as Tocqueville recognized, now a key forum for the
concrete development of our resources for evaluating and incrementally
reconfiguring the basic structure of society.

The trial does so without trying to get up over that structure, a position
no one can achieve. It does so by placing different sorts of languages in
the tautest tension with each other within sets of rules that guard specially
against the traditional disease of sophism and against the yet more viru-
lent and peculiarly modern disease of ideologically driven amoral instru-
mentalism. It thus fulfills a peculiarly modern function, "less to create
constantly new forms of life than to creatively renew actual forms by
taking advantage of their internal multiplicity and tensions and their fric-
tion with one another."[87] There is no place, it seems to me, where those
tensions and frictions are played out more intensely and more consistently
with the best of the "characteristically modern understandings of freedom

---

[83] Rawls, *A Theory of Justice*, 303–10.

[84] I have tried to show why it *must* fail in "Rawls and the Principles of Welfare Law,"
265–74.

[85] John Rawls, *Political Liberalism* (New York: Columbia University Press, 1993).

[86] Habermas, *Between Facts and Norms*.

[87] Kolb, *The Critique of Pure Modernity*, 259.

and dignity and rights, the ideals of self-fulfillment and expression, and in the demands of universal benevolence and justice"[88] than in the modern trial. That is an important part of what David Luban means when he writes that a modern trial is law's self-criticism: it does justice and creates the condition of possibility of justice's accomplishment.

It is true that the norms which find their natural homes in different forms of social practice can have only an analogous relationship to each other. The most balanced social theories recognize both the existence and the legitimacy of a separation of spheres in social life: family, friendship, neighborhood, business enterprise, life in mediating institutions such as church, school, and political life. Authors suspicious of liberalism are often critical of what they take to be a rigid delineation of spheres in contemporary societies—for example, the limitations of the norms of mutuality and fraternity to the family and small consensual communities.[89] Other authors, themselves from divergent traditions, argue that a delineation of spheres of human action, each with its own distinctive principle of action, is not merely a pathology of liberal societies. Arendt's linguistic phenomenology reveals a multiplicity of principles in different realms of human practice that must be kept distinct if they are to "redeem" each other.[90] Pitkin, writing within the linguistic turn in philosophy, finds relatively distinct "language regions" or "language strata" such as the moral and the political.[91] Kantians distinguish perfect from imperfect duties and, derivitively, the moral world of virtue from the legal world of external conformity.[92] Aristotelian thinkers, including Thomists, likewise find social realms differentiated by distinctions that have a foundation in the nature of things.[93] Luhmann and Habermas agree on a descriptive divide between life world and system but disagree about the degree of autonomy modern social "systems" do and ought to have from the rich ethical substance of the "life world."[94] For purposes of institutional design, the important differences among these thinkers have to do with the depth of the trenches, if you will, between the various spheres, and the extent to which an analogous application of principles that arose in one sphere to prob-

---

[88] Taylor, *Sources of the Self*, 503.

[89] See, e.g., Roberto Unger, *False Necessity: Anti-Necessitarian Social Theory in the Service of Radical Democracy* (Cambridge: Cambridge University Press, 1987).

[90] Arendt, *The Human Condition*. It has often been remarked that Arendt "loved distinctions." In this regard, she remained a "critical" thinker in the Kantian sense, convinced that one of the marks of human finitude is the inevitability of multiple spheres with irreducible principles. See Burns, "Hannah Arendt's Constitutional Thought," 178–79.

[91] Pitkin, *Wittgenstein and Justice*.

[92] Riley, *Kant's Political Philosophy*.

[93] Bernard J. F. Lonergan, *A Third Collection* (New York: Paulist Press, 1985), 179.

[94] Luhmann, "Operational Closure and Structural Coupling." Habermas, *Between Facts and Norms*, 48–52 (criticizing Luhmann's "autopoetic" theory of law).

lems arising in another is tolerable or necessary.[95] The modern trial respects the differences among these realms without sealing them off from one another; it acknowledges that most problematic situations have moral, legal, and political dimensions; and it creates a forum within which a judgment can be made about the relative importance of those dimensions to the concrete case that must be resolved; and, in particular, it provides a full range of normative resources for a practical reshaping of the basic structure in a careful case-by-case process.

But there is more. The trial's constitutive rules and practices allow for delicate choices about the inevitable metalevel questions woven into the trial's different linguistic practices. If these incommensurable spheres exhaust our social perspectives, if there is no Platonic perspective from which one might determine which sphere is ultimately dominant, from which (partial) perspective ought the jury to decide which perspective is the right one? The answer seems to me clear. The jury decides the metalevel questions from the perspective of commonsense morality, rigorously applied, criticized, and sometimes challenged by the devices of the trial. The existence of such a forum is a challenge to any form of social ordering that cannot justify its distinctive principles in the language of ordinary morality. The trial's importance cannot be overemphasized. It is the condition of a decent society. For it is, perhaps ironically, a deeply conservative institution, one of the last bulwarks against the bureaucratized cruelties that have accompanied the "onslaught of modernity."[96]

---

[95] Perhaps the most important theoretical differences, which do have practical consequences, have to do with the source of the unity of the various spheres. For example, Kant conceived of all the spheres as grounded in different operations of reason, theoretical, practical, reflective, but that common root had relatively limited consequences (beauty serving as an "image" for morality; understanding's knowledge of a Newtonian cosmos providing the model for a moral "kingdom of ends"). Habermas conceives of his "discourse principle" as the root of both personal morality and democratic law, such that rational freedom and equality radiate in different ways through both spheres. Thomists conceive the same fundamental moral principle as analogously controlling both personal moral and legal determinations, a distinction that tends to be more pragmatic than rooted in deep principle, as with Kant. Theoretical statements such as these are inseparable from a certain vision of concrete institutions, either already in place or sought after. On the intimacy of the connection between political philosophies and concrete social and political development, see MacIntyre, *After Virtue*, 23.

[96] Arendt, *On Revolution*, 196.

Index